Multilateral Counter-Terrorism

Contemporary terrorism is a global phenomenon requiring a globalized response. In this book Peter Romaniuk aims to assess to what extent states seek multilateral responses to the threats they face from terrorists. Providing a concise history and a clear discussion of current patterns of counter-terrorism cooperation, this book:

- analyzes a wide spectrum of institutions from the United Nations and its various bodies to military, intelligence and law enforcement agencies;
- explains the full range of cooperative counter-terrorism activities and the patterns across them, from the use of intelligence and military force to criminal law measures, financial controls and diplomacy;
- examines under what conditions states cooperate to suppress terrorism;
- evaluates how existing international institutions have been affected by the US-led "global war on terror," launched after the 9/11 terrorist attacks.

The book argues that whilst there are several notable examples of successful counter-terrorism cooperation, past and present, the broader trend can only be understood if we accept that across the domains of counter-terrorism policy, cooperation often resembles a competition for influence over outcomes.

Multilateral Counter-Terrorism is an essential resource for all students and scholars of international politics, criminology, and terrorism studies.

Peter Romaniuk is Assistant Professor of Political Science, John Jay College of Criminal Justice, City University of New York, where he is Research Fellow at the Center on Terrorism.

Routledge Global Institutions

Edited by Thomas G. Weiss

The CUNY Graduate Center, New York, USA

and Rorden Wilkinson

University of Manchester, UK

About the Series

The "Global Institutions Series" is designed to provide readers with comprehensive, accessible, and informative guides to the history, structure, and activities of key international organizations as well as books that deal with topics of key importance in contemporary global governance. Every volume stands on its own as a thorough and insightful treatment of a particular topic, but the series as a whole contributes to a coherent and complementary portrait of the phenomenon of global institutions at the dawn of the millennium.

Books are written by recognized experts, conform to a similar structure, and cover a range of themes and debates common to the series. These areas of shared concern include the general purpose and rationale for organizations, developments over time, membership, structure, decision-making procedures, and key functions. Moreover, current debates are placed in historical perspective alongside informed analysis and critique. Each book also contains an annotated bibliography and guide to electronic information as well as any annexes appropriate to the subject matter at hand.

The volumes currently published include:

42 **Multilateral Counter-Terrorism (2010)**
   The global politics of cooperation and contestation
   by Peter Romaniuk (John Jay College of Criminal Justice, CUNY)

41 **Governing Climate Change (2010)**
   by Harriet Bulkeley (Durham University) and Peter Newell (University of East Anglia)

40 **The UN Secretary-General and Secretariat (2010)**
   Second edition
   by Leon Gordenker (Princeton University)

39 **Preventive Human Rights Strategies (2010)**
   by Bertrand G. Ramcharan (Geneva Graduate Institute of International and Development Studies)

2 The UN Secretary-General and Secretariat (2005)
by Leon Gordenker *(Princeton University)*

1 The United Nations and Human Rights (2005)
A guide for a new era
by Julie A. Mertus *(American University)*

Books currently under contract include:

Global Governance, Poverty and Inequality
Edited by Jennifer Clapp *(University of Waterloo) and Rorden Wilkinson (University of Manchester)*

The International Labour Organization
by Steve Hughes *(University of Newcastle) and Nigel Haworth (University of Auckland Business School)*

Global Poverty
by David Hulme *(University of Manchester)*

The Regional Development Banks
Lending with a regional flavor
by Jonathan R. Strand *(University of Nevada)*

Peacebuilding
From concept to commission
by Robert Jenkins *(The CUNY Graduate Center)*

Non-Governmental Organizations in Global Politics
by Peter Willetts *(City University, London)*

Human Security
by Don Hubert *(University of Ottawa)*

UNESCO
by J. P. Singh *(Georgetown University)*

Millennium Development Goals (MDGs)
For a people-centered development agenda?
by Sakiko Fukada-Parr *(The New School)*

UNICEF
by Richard Jolly *(University of Sussex)*

The Organization of American States (OAS)
by Mônica Herz *(Instituto de Relações Internacionais)*

FIFA
by Alan Tomlinson (University of Brighton)

International Law, International Relations, and Global Governance
by Charlotte Ku (University of Illinois, College of Law)

Humanitarianism Contested
by Michael Barnett (University of Minnesota) and Thomas G. Weiss
(The CUNY Graduate Center)

Forum on China-Africa Cooperation (FOCAC)
by Ian Taylor (University of St. Andrews)

The Bank for International Settlements
The politics of global financial supervision in the age of high finance
by Kevin Ozgercin (SUNY College at Old Westbury)

International Migration
by Khalid Koser (Geneva Centre for Security Policy)

Global Health Governance
by Sophie Harman (City University, London)

Think Tanks
by James McGann (University of Pennsylvania) and Mary Johnstone Louis
(University of Oxford)

The Council of Europe
by Martyn Bond (University of London)

The United Nations Development Programme (UNDP)
by Stephen Browne (The International Trade Centre, Geneva)

For further information regarding the series, please contact:

Craig Fowlie, Senior Publisher, Politics & International Studies
Taylor & Francis
2 Park Square, Milton Park, Abingdon
Oxon OX14 4RN, UK

+44 (0)207 842 2057 Tel
+44 (0)207 842 2302 Fax

Craig.Fowlie@tandf.co.uk
www.routledge.com

Multilateral Counter-Terrorism

The global politics of cooperation and contestation

Peter Romaniuk

Routledge
Taylor & Francis Group

LONDON AND NEW YORK

First published 2010
by Routledge
2 Park Square, Milton Park, Abingdon, Oxon OX14 4RN

Simultaneously published in the USA and Canada
by Routledge
270 Madison Avenue, New York, NY 10016

Routledge is an imprint of the Taylor & Francis Group, an informa business

Typeset in Times New Roman by
Taylor & Francis Books
Printed and bound in Great Britain by
TJ International Ltd, Padstow, Cornwall

British Library Cataloguing in Publication Data
A catalogue record for this book is available from the British Library

Library of Congress Cataloging in Publication Data
Romaniuk, Peter.
 Multilateral counter-terrorism : the global politics of cooperation and
 contestation / Peter Romaniuk.
   p. cm.—(Routledge global institutions)
 Includes bibliographical references and index.
 1. Terrorism—Prevention—International cooperation. 2. Terrorism—
 Prevention—International cooperation—History—20th century.
 3. Security, International. 4. Security, International—History—20th
 century. 5. United Nations. 6. League of Nations. I. Title.
 Hv6431.R6495 2010
 363.325′17—dc22   2009034220

ISBN 978-0-415-77647-9 (hbk)
ISBN 978-0-415-77648-6 (pbk)
ISBN 978-0-203-85741-0 (ebk)

Contents

Tables

Foreword

The current volume is the forty-second title—several having already gone into second editions—in a dynamic series on "global institutions." The series strives (and, based on the volumes published to date, succeeds) to provide readers with definitive guides to the most visible aspects of what many of us know as "global governance." Remarkable as it may seem, there exist relatively few books that offer in-depth treatments of prominent global bodies, processes, and associated issues, much less an entire series of concise and complementary volumes. Those that do exist are either out of date, inaccessible to the non-specialist reader, or seek to develop a specialized understanding of particular aspects of an institution or process rather than offer an overall account of its functioning. Similarly, existing books have often been written in highly technical language or have been crafted "in-house" and are notoriously self-serving and narrow.

The advent of electronic media has undoubtedly helped research and teaching by making data and primary documents of international organizations more widely available, but it has also complicated matters. The growing reliance on the internet and other electronic methods of finding information about key international organizations and processes has served, ironically, to limit the educational and analytical materials to which most readers have ready access—namely, books. Public relations documents, raw data, and loosely refereed web sites do not make for intelligent analysis. Official publications compete with a vast amount of electronically available information, much of which is suspect because of its ideological or self-promoting slant. Paradoxically, a growing range of purportedly independent web sites offering analyses of the activities of particular organizations has emerged, but one inadvertent consequence has been to frustrate access to basic, authoritative, readable, critical, and well-researched texts. The market for such has actually been reduced by the ready availability of varying-quality electronic materials.

For those of us who teach, research, and practice in the area, such limited access to information has been frustrating. We were delighted when Routledge saw the value of a series that bucks this trend and provides key reference points to the most significant global institutions and issues. They are betting that serious students and professionals will want serious analyses. We have assembled a first-rate line-up of authors to address that market. Our intention, then, is to provide one-stop shopping for all readers—students (both undergraduate and postgraduate), negotiators, diplomats, practitioners from nongovernmental and intergovernmental organizations, and interested parties alike—seeking information about the most prominent institutional aspects of global governance.

Multilateral counter-terrorism

The early twenty-first century has seen the emergence of an agreement among states that terrorism represents one of the greatest threats to international peace and security. In international relations and elsewhere, however, the devil is in the details. After decades of UN discussions, there is still no agreement on how to define "terrorism," a necessary precondition for effective action to combat the problem. Pirates, nationalist groups, revolutionaries, insurgents, religious zealots, and even ruling governments have all been labeled "terrorists." Terrorism is inherently political, and—as the absence of a multilateral treaty on terrorism demonstrates—all too often so too have been states' responses.

Following the events of 11 September 2001, efforts to combat terrorism were largely framed in terms of the "Global War on Terror" (GWOT). Yet international relations scholars and military officials alike have criticized the use of the term, arguing that terrorism is a means to an end, a method of combat, rather than a physical enemy, and thus a "war on terror" cannot be won, let alone the GWOT. In March 2009, the point was rendered somewhat moot when, two months after taking office, the Barack Obama administration requested that US Pentagon officials stop using the term "Global War on Terror," instead replacing it with "Overseas Contingency Operation." Rather than signaling an end to the problem, however, the change in terminology further highlights the political nature of states' efforts to combat terrorism and the difficulties involved in coordinating states' interests to achieve effective multilateral cooperation.

Many books in the Global Institutions Series—most especially the two on organized crime and international criminal pursuit[1]—deal with topics related to terrorism and the connections between terrorism and transnational organized crime, state fragility, and armed conflict. We were keen, however, to have a book with a specific concentration on the complex and unusual challenges in multilateral actions to fight terrorism. We are fortunate that Peter Romaniuk agreed to our challenge to author a volume on this topic.

Peter has produced a meticulously researched, elegantly structured and insightful assessment. He is a colleague at John Jay College of Criminal Justice and at the CUNY Graduate Center: this book, like his teaching, brings to bear his expert knowledge in both international relations and public international law to analyze efforts by states and other international actors to take meaningful action against global terrorism—a subject about which he has written extensively.[2]

As always, we look forward to comments from first-time or veteran readers of the Global Institutions Series.

Thomas G. Weiss, the CUNY Graduate Center, New York, USA
Rorden Wilkinson, University of Manchester, UK
December 2009

Acknowledgements

I'm grateful to Tom Weiss for reaching out to me to contribute to the Global Institutions Series. Tom and Rorden Wilkinson provided welcome feedback in completing the manuscript. They, along with the staff at Routledge, exhibited much patience throughout the process. The ideas in this book began life as a "Friday Seminar" at the Center on Terrorism at John Jay College. My colleagues at the Center and in John Jay's Department of Political Science—especially Chuck Strozier and Harold Sullivan—have made New York a happy intellectual home. My interest in counter-terrorism cooperation precedes my arrival at John Jay. While in graduate school at Brown University I was fortunate to work with Tom Biersteker and Sue Eckert on the Targeted Financial Sanctions and Targeting Terrorist Finances projects at the Watson Institute for International Studies. Tom B. also chaired my dissertation committee, which included Peter Andreas and Nina Tannenwald. They provided a first-rate environment to develop my thinking about the politics of international cooperation. In New York, I have enjoyed my many interactions with Eric Rosand and Alistair Millar, from the Center on Global Counter-terrorism Cooperation. Their contributions to the study and analysis of multilateral counter-terrorism have come to define the field. In the course of researching this book, as well as in earlier work, I have been fortunate enough to speak with many practitioners of multilateral counter-terrorism, in governments and international organizations, around the world. They remain unnamed herein, but I appreciate their willingness to meet and their interest in the scholarly study of their work.

In writing this book, I have benefited from course release time by virtue of a grant from the United States Department of Homeland Security. A PSC-CUNY Research Award from the Research Foundation, CUNY, and a Research Assistance Fund Award from the Office for the Advancement of Research, John Jay College, facilitated research travel and able assistance from Brian Langdon. All opinions and errors are my own.

I'm most thankful for the love and support of friends and family, near and far. Mum and Dad have been a constant source of encouragement. While I have been working on this manuscript, Melissa, Theo, and Smuckers have provided life's happiest moments and it is to them that I dedicate this book.

Peter Romaniuk
New York City
July 2009

Abbreviations and acronyms

ACSRT	African Center for Study and Research on Terrorism
AFRICOM	United States African Command
APEC	Asia-Pacific Economic Cooperation forum
ARF	ASEAN Regional Forum
ASEAN	Association of Southeast Asian Nations
ASEANAPOL	ASEAN Chiefs of Police forum
AU	African Union
BCBS	Basel Committee on Banking Supervision
BIMSTEC	Bay of Bengal Initiative for Multisectoral Technical and Economic Cooperation
CARICOM	Caribbean Community
CBP	Customs and Border Protection (USA)
CIA	Central Intelligence Agency (USA)
CICTE	Comité Interamericano Contra el Terrorismo (Inter-American Committee Against Terrorism) (OAS)
CIRT	Committee for the International Repression of Terrorism (League of Nations)
CODEXTER	Committee of Experts on Terrorism (Council of Europe)
CSI	Container Security Initiative
CTAG	Counter-Terrorism Action Group (G8)
CTC	Counter-Terrorism Committee (United Nations Security Council)
CTED	Counter-Terrorism Committee Executive Directorate (United Nations Security Council)
CTITF	Counter-Terrorism Implementation Task Force (UN)
EAC	East African Community
EAPCCO	East African Police Chiefs' Cooperation Organization
EC	European Community
ECOSOC	United Nations Economic and Social Council

ECOWAS	Economic Community of West African States
EU	European Union
FARC	Revolutionary Armed Forces of Colombia
FATF	Financial Action Task Force
FIU	Financial Intelligence Unit
FSRB	FATF-style regional body
GCC	Gulf Cooperation Council
GTD	Global Terrorism Database (University of Maryland)
IAEA	International Atomic Energy Agency
IAIS	International Association of Insurance Supervisors
ICAO	International Civil Aviation Organization
ICPAT	IGAD Capacity-building Programme Against Terrorism
IGAD	Inter-governmental Authority on Development
ILC	International Law Commission
ILEA	International Law Enforcement Academy
ILO	International Labour Organization
IMF	International Monetary Fund
IMO	International Maritime Organization
Interpol	International Criminal Police Organization
IOSCO	International Organization of Securities Commissions
IR	international relations
ISAF	International Security Assistance Force (NATO)
ISPS Code	International Ship and Port Facility Security Code
ISWG	inter-sessional working group
JCLEC	Jakarta Centre for Law Enforcement Cooperation
JHA	Justice and Home Affairs
MANPADS	Man-portable Air Defense Systems
MERCOSUR	Mercado Comun del Sur (Common Market of the South)
MSC	Maritime Safety Committee (IMO)
MTSA	Maritime Transport Security Act 2002 (USA)
NAM	Non-Aligned Movement
NATO	North Atlantic Treaty Organization
NCCT	Non-Cooperative Countries and Territories
NGO	nongovernmental organization
NII	non-intrusive inspectional equipment
NYPD	New York City Police Department
OAS	Organization of American States
OAU	Organization of African Unity
OIC	Organization of the Islamic Conference
OPCW	Organization for the Prohibition of Chemical Weapons
OSCE	Organization for Security and Cooperation in Europe

PIA	Preliminary Implementation Assessment
PIF	Pacific Islands Forum
PKK	Kurdistan Workers' Party
PLO	Palestinian Liberation Organization
PNR	passenger name record
PSI	Proliferation Security Initiative
RATS	Regional Anti-terrorism Structure (SCO)
SAARC	South Asian Association for Regional Cooperation
SADC	Southern African Development Community
SAFE Framework	Framework of Standards to Secure and Facilitate Global Trade (WCO)
SAFTI	Secure and Facilitated International Travel Initiative (G8)
SARPs	Standards and Recommended Practices (ICAO)
SCO	Shanghai Cooperation Organization
SEARCCT	Southeast Asian Regional Centre for Counter-terrorism (Kuala Lumpur)
SICA	Sistema de la Integración Centroamericano (Central American Integration System)
SOLAS	Convention for the Safety of Life at Sea (1974)
SPITS	Stockholm Process on Implementing Targeted Sanctions
SR	Special Recommendation (on Terrorist Financing) (FATF)
STAR	Secure Trade in the APEC Region initiative
SUA	Convention for the Suppression of Unlawful Acts against the Safety of Maritime Navigation (1988) and Protocol (2005)
TPB	Terrorism Prevention Branch (UNODC)
TSCTI	Trans-Saharan Counter-terrorism Initiative
TWA	Trans World Airlines
UN	United Nations
UNDP	United Nations Development Programme
UNESCO	United Nations Educational, Scientific and Cultural Organization
UNODC	United Nations Office on Drugs and Crime
UTA	Union de Transports Aériens
WCO	World Customs Organization
WMD	weapons of mass destruction

Introduction
Defining, describing, and analyzing multilateral counter-terrorism

For more than a century, a defining characteristic of terrorist violence has been its international orientation. In his account of the "four waves of modern terrorism," David Rapoport underscores that successive generations of terrorists have sought, and often achieved, the ability to conceive strategies and execute tactics across national borders.[1] For example, the Russian anarchists of the 1880s took advantage of new communications and transportation technologies (telegraphs and railroads) to articulate and disseminate a doctrine of revolution, yielding the "Golden Age of Assassination" in the 1890s. Subsequent anti-colonial terrorists (who emerged in the 1920s and were active for some four decades) had nationalist objectives, but were thoroughly international in taking advantage of sympathetic diaspora populations to fund their activities: in turn, they prompted a response from the League of Nations. According to Bruce Hoffman, the internationalization of terrorism reached new levels in the late 1960s.[2] New tactics evolved, such as hijacking and hostage-taking, and were applied to new targets, especially foreign nationals. In addition, as exemplified by the seizure of Israeli athletes by the Palestinian Liberation Organization's (PLO) Black September group at the Munich Olympic Games in 1972, terrorist incidents received increasing attention in the international media.

Towards the end of the twentieth century, the "religious wave" gave rise to further examples of the transnational reach of terrorists, who again targeted foreign citizens and states, sought support from fellow believers abroad and articulated global or universal programs to justify their use of violence.[3] The attacks of 11 September 2001 ("9/11") provide the most striking example here. They were undertaken in the service of an ideology with global pretensions. In the 1980s, Osama bin Laden had played a coordinating role, helping foreign volunteers join the "jihad" against the Soviets in Afghanistan. In the 1990s, he sought to maintain and extend the militancy of these international "mujahideen" cadres in Bosnia-Herzegovina, Chechnya, and elsewhere. In 1996, he issued a call for violence by Muslims against the "Zionist-Crusader alliance and their collaborators," signaling his intention to target the "far enemy" (especially the United States) over the "near enemy" (perceived apostate regimes in the Muslim world).[4] In 1998, he joined with Ayman al-Zawahiri (leader of the Egyptian Islamic Jihad) and others to found the "World Islamic Front for Jihad Against Jews and Crusaders," stating that, "The ruling to kill the Americans and their allies—civilians and military—is an individual duty for every Muslim who can do it in any country in which it is possible to do it."[5] Later in that year, in pursuit of those broad objectives, the US embassies in Nairobi and Dar es Salaam were attacked. Subsequently, the 9/11 plot took advantage of the conveniences of globalization in a devastating way. A multinational group of hijackers were resident in, or transited through several countries, and received funds from still other jurisdictions while preparing for the attack.[6] In this regard, Robert Keohane suggests that a lesson of 9/11 is that, "The agents of globalization are not simply the high-tech creators of the Internet, or multinational corporations, but also small bands of fanatics, traveling on jet aircraft, and inspired by fundamentalist religion."[7]

In the post-9/11 era, the globalization of terrorism has continued apace. Although states face a variety of terrorist threats, radical Islamist or "jihadi" terrorism again illustrates these developments. Marc Sageman effectively disaggregates Rapoport's "religious wave" into three waves of his own. The first comprises the "old guard ... who fought against the Soviets in the 1980s ... and still form the core of al Qaeda Central": that is, the remnants of the pre-9/11 al Qaeda organization, now resident along the Afghanistan-Pakistan border.[8] Sageman's second wave refers to the multinational cohort of volunteers and recruits that turned to terrorism in the 1990s, many of whom received training in al Qaeda camps in Afghanistan. However, the response to 9/11 denied subsequent terrorists the opportunity to shelter there, and the ensuing "worldwide open season on global Islamist terrorism" brought the second wave to an end.[9] The third wave emerged after the US-led invasion of Iraq in 2003. For this group, the process of radicalization is different, and Sageman coins the term "leaderless jihad" to capture their experience. Largely unable to link up with al Qaeda Central, but motivated by the desire to become a martyr, members of the third wave self-radicalize, often in small, disaggregated groups built upon existing social networks, and preferring the internet as the source for ideas about jihad.[10] Sageman uses this model to explain why most of the post-9/11 attacks apparently inspired by al Qaeda had no operational links to al Qaeda Central.[11] Rather than understanding "al Qaeda" to be an organization, Sageman argues, we should think of it as a social movement with global reach. As a consequence, "The threat to the West has evolved from infiltration by outside trained terrorists ... to inside homegrown, self-financed, self-trained terrorists."[12] In other words, today's would-be jihadis appear to have taken to heart the maxim "think globally, act locally."[13]

To be sure, Sageman's analysis is disputed in some quarters and there is a debate about the nature of al Qaeda and the threat it poses: should we be principally concerned with homegrown terrorists or is al Qaeda Central really "on the march, not on the run"?[14] What is not at issue in this debate, however, is the global scope of terrorism today. To borrow from the United States' 2007 *National Intelligence Estimate*: "Globalization trends and recent technological advances will continue to enable even small numbers of alienated people to find and connect with one another, justify and intensify their anger, and mobilize resources to attack—all without requiring a centralized terrorist organization, training camp, or leader."[15] To be clear, almost all terrorist groups—not just Islamists and those that threaten the West—have internationalized their cause or operations to some extent. For example, the Liberation Tigers of Tamil Eelam (Tamil Tigers) established the ability to raise funds among diaspora populations and to procure weapons and communications equipment in the international black market. Similarly, the Kurdistan Workers' Party (PKK) has sought support from Kurds in Europe and elsewhere. The Shining Path in Peru and the Revolutionary Armed Forces of Colombia (FARC) have at times espoused revolutionary ideologies, operated across national borders and participated in narcotics trafficking. In pursuing its radical leftist agenda, the Revolutionary Organization 17 November in Greece has targeted US officials and embassy employees, Turkish diplomats, European Union (EU) facilities and foreign firms. Other examples abound.[16] As a consequence, the concept of "domestic terrorism" is increasingly called into question as "It is exceedingly difficult to locate cases of terrorist activity—however defined or identified—that are not internationally supported, targeted abroad, fomented by prevailing global circumstances, global in their repercussions, or addressed to the global community in some manner."[17]

In a book about counter-terrorism, it is apt to begin by reflecting on the nature of terrorist violence itself. Intuitively, the effort to suppress terrorism should be crafted to meet the threat that terrorists present. If the threat is globalized, it seems reasonable to posit that an effective response must also be global. Without knowing more, we might expect that more than a century of internationalized terrorism would be reflected in high levels of international cooperation against terrorism. More specifically, being faced with a threat that is international, we might anticipate that states would pursue the various tasks of counter-terrorism policy—including law enforcement actions, the use of military force, intelligence and covert operations, financial controls, and preventive measures (such as in the aviation, maritime and customs sectors)—in a cooperative, multilateral way.

In this book, I assess the extent to which this expectation is borne out in practice. The book has two main objectives: to describe patterns of multilateral cooperation against terrorism and to offer a critical analysis of them. In describing patterns of cooperation, I take a straightforward approach. I address counter-terrorism cooperation chronologically and with a focus on particular institutions, especially the United Nations—the site for much debate and action against terrorism. I also disaggregate the concept of "counter-terrorism" into component parts, identifying patterns of cooperation on the discrete tools that comprise counter-terrorism policy. Overall, I find that patterns of counter-terrorism cooperation among states are decidedly mixed and that three broad empirical trends can be discerned.

First, multilateral action varies across the different elements of counter-terrorism policy. Some counter-terrorism tools yield consistently low levels of multilateralism, as many of the key actors involved—especially national-level intelligence and law enforcement agencies—prefer working on an ad hoc basis with select foreign partners rather than larger, institutionalized groupings of states. Here, counter-terrorism cooperation, where it occurs, is more likely to be bilateral than multilateral. Multilateralism is more likely to proceed where existing institutions and organizations in related domains can be adapted to tasks targeted at terrorists. This has been particularly evident in the post-9/11 period, where multilateralism has been utilized to advance new security measures in the financial, maritime, aviation, migration, and customs sectors, among others. There is now a wide recognition that, in building defenses against terrorists in this way, the "global war on terror" has led to the institutionalization of counter-terrorism, broadly defined, in unprecedented ways.[18]

Second, I describe variation in multilateral cooperation against terrorism over time. As noted above, states attempted to act through the League of Nations to suppress terrorism in the pre-World War II period. However, that effort went the way of the League itself in the contentious politics of the era. The founding of the UN provided new fora for counter-terrorism cooperation, but the result was often

Balkanization. In the General Assembly, states initiated a debate on the definition of terrorism, but split over whether political violence might be justified in some circumstances (and conforming to the cliché, "one man's terrorist is another man's freedom fighter"). For its part, the Security Council was divided by the onset of the Cold War. While both bodies eventually developed a record of action on terrorism-related issues, those measures were necessarily limited by the lack of consensus about what terrorism is and what should be done to stop it. These constraints at the international level led some states to engage regional organizations and such bodies in the Americas and Europe became active on terrorism in the 1970s and 1980s. After the Cold War, multilateral responses to terrorism began to increase, with new treaties concluded, resolutions passed and mechanisms deployed. But, in retrospect, these developments were incremental by comparison to the uptick in multilateral cooperation after 9/11, as the United States pressed the case for action against terrorism at every opportunity. These efforts have waxed and waned somewhat in the post-9/11 period, but the volume of multilateral counter-terrorism in the contemporary era remains historically unique.

A third noticeable trend is that, when states do cooperate against terrorism, there is variation in the forms that cooperation takes and the fora that states utilize. Over time states have sought cooperation through a wide variety of mechanisms, from formal international organizations to informal networks of experts and technical specialists. Less formal arrangements (including at the bilateral level) have often been preferred to advance cooperation on the core, operational tasks of counter-terrorism. But alongside this, a diverse range of organizations—at the international and regional levels, as well as specialized, affinity-based and limited-membership groups—have also been mobilized against terrorism. Different organizations tend to be used in different ways by states, whether to build international law, to articulate norms and principles, to elaborate "best practices," to enable technical assistance, or to facilitate joint counter-terrorism action. Indeed, the volume and diversity of cooperation against terrorism today suggests that states are willing to use multilateralism creatively to advance (or defend) their interests in this area.

In sum, international cooperation against terrorism varies across the different tools of counter-terrorism, as well as over time; when it occurs, cooperation takes diverse forms, in multiple fora. In analyzing these developments, I am guided by theories of international relations (IR) in general, and debates about international cooperation and multilateralism in particular.[19] Given the scope of the topic, my approach is "analytically eclectic,"[20] in that I draw on realist, liberal and constructivist theories. Working within these traditions, scholars have identified different paths to cooperation and multilateralism. Realists are skeptical about the prospects for international cooperation. States are assumed to act pursuant to narrowly defined national interests and, as such, are concerned that others may benefit from multilateralism more than they do. On this view, cooperation emerges when more powerful states seek to impose their will on weaker states; where the latter resist, multilateralism is the outcome of processes of contestation. Liberals are more upbeat about the prospects for cooperation. They also see states as self-interested actors, but argue that, through negotiation and repeated interaction, they are capable of realizing mutual benefits from joint action. As such, liberals expect to see cooperation where multilateralism represents an efficient solution to a common dilemma. Constructivists tend to see cooperation as the outcome of shared principles or understandings. In contrast to the opinion of realists and liberals, states are not viewed simply as self-interested actors. Rather, they are members of an international society of states that has its own norms. These norms are often internalized by states, forming a critical part of their identities. As such, multilateralism reflects a shared set of principles about what constitutes an appropriate response to an issue.

Each of these three approaches provides insight into different parts of the record of international action against terrorism. With that said, not all approaches apply equally well. Rather, what strikes me most about state interactions on counter-terrorism is that they are fundamentally *political*. In other words, despite the history of international terrorism, and despite the frequently heard claims from politicians and pundits about the gravity and urgency of the terrorist threat, counter-terrorism cooperation is often "politics as usual." As a consequence, I am most sympathetic to the realist approach and my analysis of multilateral counter-terrorism emphasizes the competitive nature of cooperation. Different states are affected by terrorism differently and they have varying interests at stake in cooperative action to suppress it. While there are past and present examples of successful counter-terrorism cooperation, reflecting shared interests and/or principles, the broader trend can only be understood if we accept that the pursuit of national interests by states is a persistent constraint on multilateral action. For this reason, we should have modest expectations about what can be achieved through multilateral counter-terrorism, today and into the future.

In the remainder of this introduction, I elaborate these descriptive and analytical claims, and lay the groundwork for the subsequent chapters.

I do this by discussing the concepts of multilateralism and counter-terrorism in turn, and defining the term "multilateral counter-terrorism." I then place the book in context, by briefly reviewing existing studies of multilateral counter-terrorism. These studies, and this book, will appeal to readers interested in international institutions, as well as research in the emerging field of "terrorism studies."[21]

What is "multilateralism"?

A central argument of this book is that the pattern of multilateral counter-terrorism reflects processes of contestation among states. In order to make this claim, I must first give an overview of the dynamics of multilateralism. That is, how should we interpret cases of successful cooperation while accounting for the failure of states to act multi-laterally? What should we look for in state interactions on counter-terrorism issues that would suggest one outcome (multilateralism) and not another? Here, theories of IR can help. Among scholars, as in public debates, "multilateralism" is itself a contested concept. Definitions and understandings of multilateralism tend to correlate with the broader theoretical orientation of the analyst, whether realist, liberal or constructivist.

In this regard, the scene was set by John Ruggie's definition of mul-tilateralism as "an institutional form that coordinates relations among three or more states on the basis of generalized principles of conduct: that is, principles which specify appropriate conduct for a class of actions, without regard to the particularistic interests or the strategic exigencies that may exist in any specific occurrence."[22] Ruggie acknowl-edges that the emphasis on "generalized principles of conduct" in his definition sets the bar for multilateralism rather high, rendering it a "demanding institutional form." In effect, defining multilateralism in this way privileges constructivist explanations, as we would only expect cooperation to emerge where such principles exist, are shared among states, and exert such a pull as to draw them away from their "parti-cularistic interests." It is these shared principles that drive cooperation, rather than any sense of self-interest or any rational calculation about how to maximize the benefits of joint action. It is difficult to make the case that these dynamics are a feature of state interactions against ter-rorism per se. Although the volume of pronouncements against terror-ism issued by international and regional organizations suggests that a broadly stated norm against terrorist violence is emerging, the ongoing failure of states to define terrorism surely constrains that process (i.e. a broadly stated norm against what, exactly?).

Still, if consensual "principles of conduct" cannot be specified at a general level, constructivist arguments might pertain in more specific domains of counter-terrorism policy. In other words, although norms related to counter-terrorism may not be shared among all states, more specific understandings about the kinds of appropriate responses to terrorism might be shared among particular kinds of officials involved in counter-terrorism. Here, it is apt to recall Peter Haas' account of the role of "epistemic communities" in international relations. These are, "network[s] of professionals with recognized expertise and competence in a particular domain and an authoritative claim to policy-relevant knowledge within that domain or issue-area."[23] Rather than addressing the problem of terrorism in its entirety, members of such communities, across different countries, may be called upon to apply their expertise to specific tasks in suppressing terrorism. In situations where decision-makers are seeking responses to an apparent threat, this expertise is likely to be especially valued. Therefore, short of broad multilateral consensus on counter-terrorism under-girded by Ruggie's "generalized principles," another route to multilateralism, also informed by constructivism, involves coordination among issue-area experts, who precipitate cooperation on the basis of their shared professional knowledge. These examples are more prevalent in highly specialized domains such as intelligence, law enforcement, counter-terrorist financing, and maritime security, among others.

A more pragmatic, less demanding definition of multilateralism is offered by Keohane: "Multilateralism ... [is] the practice of coordinating national policies in groups of three or more states, through *ad hoc* arrangements or by means of institutions."[24] Keohane's scholarship is synonymous with the liberal-institutionalist explanation of international cooperation. The contemporary version of this argument emerged out of a debate among scholars in the 1980s, as a new generation of liberals endeavored to show, on analytical grounds, that the prognosis of realist theory (i.e. that the condition of international anarchy means that states are primarily concerned for their security, and therefore unlikely to cooperate), was erroneously bleak. That debate focused mostly on the emergence of "regimes"—a form of multilateral cooperation that came to prominence in the preceding decade amid fears of the decline of American hegemony.[25] Through the use of game theory—especially an iterated prisoner's dilemma—Keohane and others showed that regimes can emerge and persist even among self-interested actors (who are assumed to be rational; an assumption shared with realism).[26] For this to occur, rational actors must benefit from cooperation, for example, through the reduction of transaction costs and uncertainty, and the provision of information. In turn, these benefits make it easier for states to strike agreements. On the whole, Keohane stresses that regimes are useful to states, in the sense of being a functional solution to a common problem.

One upshot of this argument is that cooperation may be more difficult to establish than to maintain, as existing arrangements reduce uncertainty and have proven utility, whereas untested mechanisms do not. However, this logic also suggests that regimes may persist beyond their founding mandate, as the costs of establishing new regimes mean that states are less willing to do so. Writing soon after 9/11, Keohane was struck by the extent to which the Bush administration had turned to multilateral institutions, especially the UN Security Council, as part of its response. This would "provide a fruitful test for institutionalist theory," especially in light of the apparent unilateralist proclivities of administration members.[27] For Keohane, this move rather underscored the value of liberal approaches, as it provided evidence for a key institutionalist claim, that institutions work by "altering the costs of state strategies."[28] In other words, as states contemplate action on any issue, prevailing multilateral arrangements are likely to figure in their calculations and, subsequently, in their negotiations. Where states anticipate that multilateralism will be mutually beneficial, those negotiations ought to yield cooperation.

Keohane's interpretation of the United States' engagement of international organizations after 9/11 would be viewed more skeptically by realists. By itself, the starting assumption of realist theory—that states face an unrelenting "security dilemma" as a result of the anarchic nature of the international system—suggests that cooperation will be the exception rather than the rule. It is unsurprising, then, that realists discuss multilateralism less than liberals and constructivists. Still, two realist arguments can be discerned.[29] The first of these, generally associated with neo-realism, takes the skeptical claim to the extreme. This approach suggests that instances of cooperation are either imposed by powerful states, or worse, are empirically inconsequential.[30] The analytical foundation of the former claim is compelling and addresses a shortcoming in the liberal position. Namely, liberals suggest that states are able to achieve mutual benefits through cooperation, i.e. that the gains from cooperation are "absolute" (all parties gain something). But if we take the security dilemma seriously, surely states would be concerned that their partners would gain more from cooperation relative to themselves. After all, under conditions of anarchy, today's partner may be tomorrow's adversary. In negotiating the terms of cooperation, then, states should be concerned about "relative gains" more than "absolute gains" and that, in turn, is a fundamental constraint upon achieving consensus.[31] This is especially so if we accept that, in cooperating on any particular issue, there may be multiple different agreements that could be negotiated and achieving consensus on the terms of a deal (that benefits everyone, equally) is more problematic than liberals admit.[32] Again, the barriers to multilateralism are likely to be high where cooperation has distributive consequences: that is, where the terms of cooperation benefit some states more than, or relative to, others.

Subsequent realists have built on these claims in a more pragmatic way, acknowledging the volume of international cooperation in world politics today. Beyond simply explaining the failure to cooperate, they analyze patterns of international cooperation. Again, their emphasis is on relative power and they see cooperation as a tool or tactic that states can use to advance their interests.[33] This approach offers an account of why states seek cooperation (to advance interests), how they do it (by acting through fora amenable to their influence) and how others respond. Regarding the latter, if cooperation has distributive consequences, we should expect less powerful states to resist attempts at cajoling them into joint action. That resistance might itself trigger forms of cooperation and, consequently, "forum shopping," where states utilize different cooperative mechanisms to preserve their interests or ameliorate the consequences of being bound by others.[34] Overall, the dynamics of cooperation tend here to resemble a form of "positional conflict," as states compete for influence.[35] Where cooperation can advance or defend states' interests, we ought to observe them pursuing "tactical multilateralism" in this way.[36]

As this brief overview confirms, scholars disagree about the paths to multilateralism. This difference of opinion extends to explanations of the form that cooperation takes. In this regard, as an empirical matter, several observers have noted a trend towards increasing diversity in the way that states cooperate, beyond formal international organizations alone: "Over the past several decades, a range of innovative modalities has emerged in the form of hybrid institutional arrangements ... inter-agency coordinating mechanisms ... new inter-governmental coalitions ... public-private partnerships ... and private sector initiatives."[37] Moreover, as Kal Raustiala and David G. Victor point out, multiple cooperative mechanisms may arise within a single issue domain, giving rise to what they call "regime complexes," i.e. "an array of partially overlapping and nonhierarchical institutions governing a particular issue area ... [and] marked by the existence of several legal agreements that are created and maintained in distinct fora with participation of different sets of actors."[38] Among this diversity, it is useful to note recent evolutions in the concept of "epistemic communities." For example, Anne-Marie Slaughter defines "transgovernmental networks" as "pattern[s] of regular and purposive relations among like government units working across borders that divide countries from one another and that demarcate the 'domestic' from the 'international' sphere."[39] She argues that such networks may emerge from several sources, including within traditional international organizations, through agreement among the executive branches of governments, and as a result of regular contacts between bureaucrats. In turn, these networks tend to perform three sets of tasks: providing information, facilitating enforcement and overseeing the harmonization of policies.

These developments underscore that there is more than one way for states to be "multilateral" and, as such, a variety of cooperative forms is contemplated in any definition of the concept. So, why would states arrive at one form of multilateralism and not another? Here, it is useful to recall Oran Young's argument about the formation of regimes.[40] For Young, regimes may emerge spontaneously (i.e. as a result of the convergence of expectations, without conscious coordination), through negotiation (reflecting a conscious effort to agree upon the terms of a bargain) or as a result of imposition (pursuant to the will of dominant actors). Of course, this categorization reflects the three approaches to multilateralism surveyed above. To elaborate: for constructivists, the form of multilateralism emerges spontaneously, as a product of the shared principles that underlie state action; for liberals, the form of multilateralism is negotiated as part of the bargain that establishes cooperation; and for realists, the form of multilateralism is imposed by great powers, either directly or indirectly (as a result of resistance and subsequent processes of contestation). In analyzing multilateral counterterrorism, then, we should be mindful that our answer to the question "do states cooperate multilaterally?" might inform a response to the question "*how* do states cooperate multilaterally?" This is of particular importance in light of the variation in forms of cooperation against terrorism that we observe, especially since 9/11.

My discussion to date is summarized in Table I.1. To be clear, my purpose in introducing this theoretical discussion here is to provide a touchstone for the main chapters of the book, which draw attention to the many points of contestation that characterize counter-terrorism cooperation. The book does not engage in theory-testing but, more modestly, suggests that, over time, we are best served by approaching the analysis of multilateral counter-terrorism from a realist perspective.

Throughout the book, I use the more modest, pragmatic definition of multilateralism set out by Keohane, i.e. "Multilateralism ... [is] the

Table I.1 Paths to multilateralism

Theoretical approach	Multilateralism emerges when ...	The form of multilateralism is ...
Liberal	• Cooperation is an efficient solution to a common problem	• Negotiated, wherein there are advantages to acting through existing institutions
Realist	• Powerful states compel cooperation from others • "Positional conflict" among states yields cooperation	• Imposed and contested, often preceded by "forum shopping"
Constructivist	• States share "generalized principles" about appropriate responses to a problem • "Epistemic communities" (or transgovernmental networks) share a professional understanding about appropriate responses to a problem	• Spontaneous, reflecting shared understandings among states or among experts

practice of coordinating national policies in groups of three or more states, through *ad hoc* arrangements or by means of institutions."[41] This definition is broad enough to cover both the different paths to multilateralism set out above, and the diverse forms that multilateralism may take. Indeed, the uptick in international counter-terrorism cooperation after 9/11 is a notable example of the trend to diversification in forms of cooperation.[42] One consequence of this definition is that this book does not attempt to cover bilateral cooperation against terrorism (which would be a difficult task in any case, in light of the volume and scope of that activity).

What is "counter-terrorism"?

In his recent survey of terrorism research, Magnus Ranstorp laments that, "In contrast to the efforts to understand terrorism as a complex social and human phenomenon, the critique of the counter-terrorism research landscape is relatively limited or even muted."[43] Part of the reason for this, he suggests, is that many studies of counter-terrorism are context-specific and focus on particular counter-terrorist campaigns. In order to advance knowledge beyond particular cases, and to deal with multilateral counter-terrorism specifically, a first step is to specify what exactly we mean by "counter-terrorism policy." There are several ways of doing so, and a useful starting point is provided by Paul Pillar.

Pillar's approach is to disaggregate the strategic objectives of counter-terrorism from the tactical tools that are implemented to suppress terrorist activity. Regarding the former, he identifies four "elements" of counter-terrorism policy that correlate with different stages in the "life-cycle of terrorism."[44] First, counter-terrorism policy should be targeted towards the "roots" of terrorism, i.e. the background political or socio-economic conditions that give rise to terrorists' grievances. Second, counter-terrorism should reduce the capabilities of terrorists to execute attacks and otherwise further their objectives. Third, counter-terrorism policy should seek to influence the intentions of terrorists, addressing their belief that their cause can be advanced through the use of violence. Finally, a large part of counter-terrorism comprises those defensive measures—including the physical security of buildings as well as other preventive actions—designed to make it more difficult for terrorists to execute attacks. In describing this last category, Pillar introduces the distinction between "counter-terrorism" per se and "anti-terrorist defenses."

Across these four strategic elements of counter-terrorism, states utilize five "instruments" of counter-terrorism policy.[45] These are:

- Diplomacy, comprising the efforts of national foreign policy and specialist agencies in engaging other states on counter-terrorism, including in multilateral fora. Interestingly, writing initially in mid-2001, Pillar was clear that counter-terrorism is better pursued in smaller groupings of states and that, "Much multilateral diplomacy is essentially mood music, but even mood music can be helpful in reaching more specific goals."[46] Still, he notes that diplomatic efforts necessarily cut across the other instruments of counter-terrorism policy, where they are pursued beyond the borders of a state.
- Criminal law, that is, the use of investigation, detention, arrest, extradition, prosecution and incarceration for crimes related to terrorism.
- Financial controls, including the freezing of assets linked to terrorism, as well as the prohibition on material support for terrorism.
- The use of military force against terrorist targets.
- Intelligence and covert action, comprising the collection and analysis of strategic and tactical intelligence from human and technical sources (such as signals intelligence), as well as intelligence operations that target terrorists.

In describing both the elements and instruments, Pillar is clear that there are benefits and potential costs that attach to each aspect of counter-terrorism policy. No single element or instrument can be effective against terrorism in isolation and a pragmatic, coordinated approach is needed to formulate strategies and tactics to suppress terrorist threats. Moreover, counter-terrorism policy is but one part of foreign policy more generally, requiring that it be balanced with other priorities.

Similar typologies of counter-terrorism policy are offered by others. Audrey Kurth Cronin posits that counter-terrorism comprises diplomacy, intelligence, psycho-political instruments, international law, criminal law enforcement, military force, foreign aid and homeland security.[47] Within her specific focus on international cooperation against terrorism, Nora Bensahel suggests that counter-terrorism consists of military, financial, law enforcement, intelligence and "reconstruction" measures (i.e. to address problems emanating from failed states and ungoverned spaces).[48] More generally, Robert Art and Louise Richardson delineate three categories of counter-terrorism tools: political measures (including negotiations with terrorists, socio-economic and political reforms and international cooperation on terrorist financing, border control and extradition, etc.), legislative and judicial measures (to mobilize the criminal justice system against terrorists) and security measures (including military and intelligence operations, as well as preventive or defensive actions).[49] David Cortright and George Lopez distinguish protective measures (including military, police and intelligence operations, and homeland security) from preventive measures (such as addressing political grievances and expanding economic and social opportunity).[50] Similarly, Alexander Lennon draws on Joseph Nye's distinction between "hard power" and "soft power," identifying a range of counter-terrorism tools with the latter (e.g. building international norms, support for moderate governments, addressing underlying conditions that may lead to terrorism and using public diplomacy).[51] In his wide-ranging treatment of the topic, Boaz Ganor, like Pillar, distinguishes "offensive" and "defensive" aspects of counter-terrorism.[52] Most comprehensively, Alex Schmid's "toolbox of counter-terrorism measures" lists a far-reaching set of mechanisms that states may deploy in suppressing terrorism (see Table I.2).

The purpose of surveying definitions of "counter-terrorism" here is to illustrate the breadth of the concept. Indeed, the reach of "counter-terrorism" seems to be expanding in the post-9/11 period. This point invites a normative response from critical scholars, who are wary of the "securitizing" effects of the "global war on terror,"[53] as well as human rights advocates concerned about the expansion of state power in the

Table 1.2 Schmid's "Toolbox of counter-terrorism measures"**

1. Politics and governance	2. Economic and social	3. Psychological-communicational-educational	4. Military	5. Judicial and legal	6. Police and prison system	7. Intelligence and secret services	8. Other
1.1 Address specific political grievances of terrorists	2.1 Address specific socio-economic grievances	3.1 Attempts to establish a common value base with political opponents	4.1 Use of strikes/operations	5.1 International efforts	6.1 Target hardening	7.1 Use of technological and human intelligence	8.1 Concessions and deals
1.2 Engage in conflict resolution	2.2 Engage in socio-economic policies that reduce inclination to engage in political violence	3.2 Providing a forum for freedom of expression	4.2 Use of armed forces for protecting potential victims and objects	5.2 Domestic legislation	6.2 Enhance international police cooperation	7.2 Engage in exchange of intelligence	8.2 Immigration control measures
1.3 Offer political concessions	2.3 Address financial/monetary aspects of terrorism	3.3 Use of media	4.3 Recruitment, training and maintenance of personnel	5.3 Use and protection of witnesses	6.3 Enhance capacity of law enforcement officials	7.3 Use of intelligence to infiltrate terrorist groups	8.3 Victim support
1.4 Participate in broader political process		3.4 Counter-terrorism public relations campaign	4.4. Operating procedures and policies	5.4 Court proceedings	6.4 Use of infiltrators and informants	7.4 Use of secret negotiations	8.4 Governmental strategy
1.5 Amnesty		3.5. Facilitate exit of individuals from terrorist organizations			6.5 Regulating police behavior	7.5 Develop an early warning system based on indicators of public violence	
1.6 Diplomatic pressure on state sponsors to decrease their support					6.6 Police powers		
					6.7 Measures to inhibit the formation and perpetuation of terrorist networks violence in prison		

Note: * Adapted from Alex Schmid, "Towards Joint Political Strategies for Delegitimising the Use of Terrorism," in *Countering Terrorism Through International Cooperation*, ed. Alex Schmid, Proceedings of the International Conference on Countering Terrorism Through Enhanced International Cooperation, Cormayeur, Mont Blanc, Italy, 22–24 September 2000.

name of "counter-terrorism."[54] The point is also made by analysts who note that the scope of counter-terrorism policy has increased, for example, to cover new approaches to "disengagement" or "deradicalization," with the aim of dissuading vulnerable individuals away from the pursuit of violence.[55] Indeed, recent counter-terrorism strategies released by states and international organizations reflect a broad understanding of counter-terrorism, and share an emphasis on addressing the background conditions that are perceived to lead to terrorism. The 2003 *National Strategy for Combating Terrorism* released by the United States undertook to: defeat terrorists and their organizations; deny sponsorship, support and sanctuary to terrorists; diminish the underlying conditions that terrorists seek to exploit; and defend US citizens and interests at home and abroad.[56] The 2006 revision emphasized that:[57]

> The paradigm for combating terrorism now involves the application of all elements of our national power and influence. Not only do we employ military power, we use diplomatic, financial, intelligence, and law enforcement activities to protect the Homeland and extend our defenses, disrupt terrorist operations, and deprive our enemies of what they need to operate and survive. We have broken old orthodoxies that once confined our counterterrorism efforts primarily to the criminal justice domain.

Across the Atlantic, the 2005 *European Union Counter-terrorism Strategy* set out four pillars: prevent, protect, pursue and respond. The first of these entails an explicit focus on "conditions in society which may create an environment in which individuals can become more easily radicalized."[58] In 2006 the then UN Secretary-General, Kofi Annan, recommended that UN member states adopt a counter-terrorism strategy with five pillars: dissuading people from resorting to terrorism or supporting it; denying terrorists the means to carry out an attack; deterring states from supporting terrorism; developing state capacity to defeat terrorism; and defending human rights.[59] With the subsequent *United Nations Global Counter-Terrorism Strategy* (2006), UN member states pledged to address "conditions conducive to the spread of terrorism," while supporting capacity-building initiatives to ensure that all states have the capability to suppress terrorism.[60]

In sum, there is an apparent consensus—among scholars as well as in practice—that "counter-terrorism" should be understood to cover an increasingly broad range of state actions. In part, no doubt, this reflects the changing nature of terrorist threats over time. However, past research has shown that the formation of counter-terrorism policy is affected by many factors, including domestic and bureaucratic politics, and is not a straightforward response to external threats.[61] Therefore, the changing definition of "counter-terrorism" raises important questions. Why has counter-terrorism come to be conceived so broadly? How do states select among the different tools available to them? How do the different tools impact terrorist behavior and which are most effective? What are the normative and empirical consequences of defining terrorism so broadly, and how, in turn, does that affect outcomes in related domains (social and economic policies, foreign policy, human rights implications, etc.)? Research on these questions is ongoing or remains to be done,[62] and I do not address them directly in this book. Rather, for present purposes, the broad understanding of counter-terrorism is necessarily reflected in the empirical scope of the book and in my definition of "multilateral counter-terrorism." I define the latter as coordinated action among three or more states, whether through ad hoc arrangements or institutions, where a stated objective is to suppress terrorism. In several places, I also find it useful to distinguish between, on the one hand, "offensive" counter-terrorism tools and, on the other, "preventive" or "defensive" measures. To clarify, the former comprise actions targeting terrorists and their operations directly and most often entail the use of intelligence and covert action, along with law enforcement and perhaps military power. As noted at the beginning of the chapter, multilateralism makes a modest contribution here. "Preventive" or "defensive" measures are those undertaken in related policy spheres or physical spaces (passport security, border control, cargo inspections, etc.) designed to make it more difficult for terrorists to act. The uptick in multilateral cooperation since 9/11 has been most evident here. Of course, this distinction is not perfect (e.g. action against terrorist financing has both offensive and preventive aspects) and I use it as a guide only. Overall, this is a book about diplomacy as a tool of counter-terrorism where, as Pillar specifies, diplomacy cuts across the totality of counter-terrorism action. Multilateralism, as an outcome of diplomacy, varies across tools of counter-terrorism policy and over time, as well as in the forms it takes.

Studying multilateral counter-terrorism

Ranstorp's critical reflection on the state of research on counter-terrorism, cited above, should perhaps be qualified in light of the ongoing efforts of researchers to understand the relationship between terrorism and counter-terrorism. A fruitful debate on "how terrorism ends" has endeavored to trace the effects of counter-terrorism policies on their targets,[63] while the broader conceptualization of counter-terrorism has triggered research on the effects of specific counter-terrorism tools.[64] Moreover, cross-national comparisons of counter-terrorism policies have aided our understanding of how different states identify threats and formulate responses.[65] Beyond such domestic-level analyses of counter-terrorism, the post-9/11 period has given rise to several studies of the role of international organizations in the broader "war on terror," as well as analyses of counter-terrorism diplomacy in specific sectors (such as terrorist financing, maritime security, etc.).[66] A sign of the vitality of this field is the emergence of an independent research institute, the Center for Global Counter-terrorism Cooperation (www. globalct.org), with offices in Washington, D.C., and New York City. The articles and reports published by the Center focus on the UN but also cover a wide range of topics, including functional and regional cooperation. Reflecting its motto—"Building stronger partnerships to prevent terrorism"—as well as the objectives of the governments that sponsor research, the central analytical contribution of the Center's work has been to identify ways in which counter-terrorism cooperation can be advanced.

In spite of the growth of interest in international cooperation against terrorism, there is still a sense in which the field is under-researched.[67] Indeed, the goals of this book (description and critical analysis, across the broad sweep of multilateral counter-terrorism) have not been pursued in a single-authored monograph since Martha Crenshaw's *Terrorism and International Cooperation* in 1989.[68] This book aims to fill that gap. The next chapter looks back in time to identify the historical precedents for multilateral counter-terrorism. I find that the experience of responding to the threat of anarchism, beginning in the 1890s, bears some resemblance to the present, at least in so far as political constraints impeded the establishment and maintenance of broad-based cooperation.

Chapter 2 surveys multilateral counter-terrorism at the UN in the pre-9/11 period. Here, we can again observe the evolution of certain patterns of cooperation that inform later developments. In particular, in the absence of a consensus definition of terrorism, states settled on a "piecemeal approach," criminalizing certain terroristic acts (such as hijacking, hostage-taking, bombing, etc.). Importantly, the limitations of this approach led some states to seek cooperation in fora other than the UN. Nonetheless, the trend over this period was for increasing levels of cooperation, albeit at an incremental pace. Chapter 3 takes in UN action in the post-9/11 period. The effect of those attacks was to induce a change in the volume of multilateral counter-terrorism, even if the competitive dynamics of cooperation have endured in many ways. Since 9/11, there has been an unprecedented uptick in international counter-terrorism cooperation, with the UN central to these developments. In practice, this has involved the elaboration of new rules and norms in the preventive domains of counter-terrorism. These, in turn, have garnered support from a wide range of institutions, which have been adapted to the tasks of counter-terroism. In advancing these measures, however, political disagreements have arisen over the role of the Security Council and the extent of UN engagement on counter-terrorism.

Chapter 4 looks beyond the UN to illustrate two main points. First, that the volume of multilateral activity on counter-terrorism is by no means limited to UN fora. Indeed, there are now significant links between UN action and that pursued by regional and other organizations. Second, the kinds of competitive political dynamics that characterize cooperation at the UN also reach beyond it. In this regard, in addition to simply describing what different institutions have done, I look briefly at three issue areas—law enforcement and intelligence, terrorist financing and maritime security—to describe the growing number of actors, rules and initiatives in these areas. Recalling Raustiala and Victor, I suggest that "regime complexes" are emerging in some domains of counter-terrorism policy, subject to the vagaries of cooperation and contestation among states.

In concluding, I reflect on the effectiveness of multilateral counter-terrorism and on the future prospects for multilateral counter-terrorism. Although my interpretation of events—drawing, as it does, on realist theories of IR—is broadly skeptical, I find some cause for optimism here. The fact that the historical record exhibits some continuity (i.e. in that competitive political dynamics tend to determine cooperative outcomes) suggests that there may be opportunities to refine existing approaches and selectively venture new ones.

1 Historical precedents for multilateral counter-terrorism

Anti-anarchist cooperation and the League of Nations

The origins of multilateral counter-terrorism lie in efforts to suppress anarchist violence in the late nineteenth century. These measures comprised diplomatic initiatives, as well as cooperation among police services. Although such efforts were discussed as early as the 1870s, those initial attempts were not successful and yielded only the unilateral deployment of certain national police services abroad (an approach pursued by Britain, Italy and Russia).[1] It took a period of sustained anarchist violence in the 1890s to induce states to consider cooperation more seriously. In this chapter, I trace the emergence of multilateral counter-terrorism through three key developments in the pre-World War II period. The first of these, the 1898 International Anti-Anarchist Conference in Rome, represents the first attempt by states to coordinate law and policy to combat political violence. Despite this, anarchist activity continued and the effort was renewed through the 1904 St. Petersburg Anti-Anarchist Protocol, signed in secret by more than 10 states. The protocol set an ambitious program for cooperation, including the establishment of anti-anarchist bureaus in participating states, rules for expelling anarchists, and norms for communication and information exchange regarding anarchist activity. A reduction in anarchist crimes in the early twentieth century, and the intervention of other pressing events, saw the issue decline in importance on the international agenda. But it re-emerged after 1934 in response to the double assassination of Yugoslavia's King Alexander and French foreign minister Barthou by a Croatian nationalist in Marseilles. Coordinated efforts this time occurred through the League of Nations and, after a period of negotiation, the members concluded the Convention for the Prevention and Punishment of Terrorism in 1937. The convention is novel in that it provides a definition of "terrorism," a feat not achieved in any subsequent international treaty or resolution. While the convention attracted 24 signatories, only one member (India) ratified it, meaning that it never entered into force and has the status of a "dead letter."[2]

Why do these historical precedents matter for our understanding of multilateral counter-terrorism today? In concluding the chapter, I contend that there are several lessons from history here, not least because the pre-World War II record of multilateral counter-terrorism provides early evidence of what we can now recognize as broad trends that pertain over time. Specifically, history shows that: states are constrained by competing political agendas and are, therefore, unable to achieve broad-based consensus on counter-terrorism cooperation; where cooperation does succeed, it is generally pursued at an operational level, thereby minimizing political sensitivities; where it occurs, multilateral counter-terrorism builds on, and subsequently shapes, cooperative endeavors in related domains; the need to define terrorism has a politicizing effect on cooperation, yielding unworkable definitions or, later, stalemate; attempts to advance multilateral counter-terrorism are often direct responses to attacks, but the issue inevitably recedes from importance as cooperation stumbles and other priorities emerge. In sum, history matters in that the contemporary record of multilateral counter-terrorism sometimes resembles patterns of cooperation that first emerged more than 100 years ago.

Cooperation against anarchism

By the 1880s, anarchist ideas had gained wide circulation in Europe, the Americas and beyond. In particular, the anarchist attempt to legitimate the use of violence as a tool of social change—"propaganda by the deed"—attracted many adherents and served to inspire acts of violence by individuals and groups, inducing a previously unseen degree of hysteria in many countries.[3] As Richard Bach Jensen points out, this sense of hysteria was out of proportion to the number of fatalities actually claimed by anarchists. He estimates that, for the period 1880–1914, and not counting Russia, anarchists killed only about 160 people, while injuring another 500.[4] Rather, the fear they stirred reflects that anarchist tactics were unique (often involving bombing and the use of dynamite), their violence was random and caused mass disruption, and the media served to publicize their acts. They targeted the symbols of religious and bourgeois life, and claimed more heads of state (seven in Russia, Europe and the United States between 1894 and 1912) than any comparable practitioners of political violence.[5] Still, despite perceptions at the time, it cannot be said that anarchists ever formed a unified political movement as such, and Rick

Coolsaet observes that, "The [so-called] Black International only ever existed in the minds of police officers and the press."[6] This leads many contemporary observers to compare the anarchists to today's "al Qaeda movement," a position I argue against, below.

However organized, anarchist violence increased in the 1890s, prompting two kinds of responses from states.[7] First, at the national level, many states sought new legislation to enable them to suppress anarchism. Such laws criminalized the use of explosives and also attempted to suppress anarchist propaganda. Second, states sought stronger bilateral ties among police services. There was some precedent for this, as Britain, Italy and Russia had already stationed officers abroad. The Russians (faced with threats from nihilists and revolutionary socialists) had sought broader cooperation in the 1870s and 1880s, but had not been able to advance the idea. For their part, the British (threatened by Irish nationalist Fenians) and the Italians (whose diaspora was notoriously radical) each had their own reasons to develop international policing networks. Still, there remained a sense that these responses were inadequate given the apparent scope of the anarchist threat. But what to do? Here, there was no consensus. Rather, some states, especially Britain and Switzerland, invoked the ire of others for their relatively liberal policies regarding sanctuary for political refugees and asylum. Similarly, extradition and expulsion policies were a source of contention, as states sought to utilize these sovereign prerogatives to their own advantage.

These pressures were brought to a head when Empress Elizabeth of Austria was stabbed in the heart by an Italian anarchist as she boarded a ferry on Lake Geneva on 10 September 1898. Rome was soon under pressure to act and did so promptly, issuing invitations for a European conference to counter anarchism. These invitations were quickly accepted by the European powers, although Britain considered declining. British hesitation reflects that anarchism was considered to be more of a problem for the continent. However, concern about the presence of émigrés gave London a stake in the debate about expulsion and extradition, commending attendance.[8] Importantly, the invitations from Rome requested that delegations comprise not only diplomats, but police officers, and technical and administrative staff, such as officials from justice and interior ministries. Indeed, attendees included the national police heads of Russia, France and Belgium, in addition to the municipal chiefs of police forces from cities such as Berlin, Vienna and Stockholm.[9]

The conference commenced on 24 November 1898, with 54 delegates from 21 countries. It lasted a month and concluded on 21 December. The conference addressed three main tasks: the definition of "anarchism," the development of an international agreement on the treatment of anarchists and the elaboration of technical arrangements to coordinate anti-anarchist activities among states.[10] The first of these tasks yielded a broad definition of "anarchist acts" as those "having as [their] aim the destruction through violent means of all social organization." Anarchists were those that committed such acts. Some delegations, especially the Germans and Russians, who tended to take on leadership roles over the conference, would have preferred a more precise definition.[11] Others, especially the Swiss and British, expressed reservations that a broad definition would limit states' discretion and impinge upon individual rights to freedom of expression. At issue here was whether or not anarchist crimes would be defined as "political" crimes, and therefore be non-extraditable. The broad definition of "anarchist acts" (with its reference to "social organization") reflects the irony that influential delegations went out of their way to treat anarchism (with its obviously political motivations) as being non-political, to facilitate extradition.[12]

With the task of defining "anarchism" accomplished, albeit in a satisficing way, the conference divided into committees on legislation and administrative matters, respectively, with a subcommittee of the latter dealing with questions of extradition and expulsion. The agenda in the legislative committee was set by the representative of Monaco, who was acting on behalf of France, which hoped to avert any confrontation on these matters with its ally, Russia. A series of proposals was eventually adopted by delegates, including prohibitions and punishments attached to: the use of explosives for illegitimate purposes, membership in anarchist associations, provocation or support for anarchist acts, spreading anarchist propaganda, publicizing anarchist trials and assisting anarchists. There were also proposals concerning conditions for the incarceration of anarchists and a measure to adopt the death penalty for anarchist crimes, although the latter was approved with several delegations abstaining.[13]

Several states indicated that they would introduce new legislation to implement this program. But what was the impact of this agreement in practice? An initial point to note here is that these provisions were adopted as recommendations only—a trade-off made necessary by dissonant views about the definition of anarchism. But even with this in mind, the results were very modest. Jensen notes the irony that Great Britain—which did not sign the protocol that emerged from Rome—was the only European power to draft legislation to implement it, and even that initiative never made it into law.[14]

If the work of the legislative committee did not translate in substantive changes, the committee on administrative matters was rather

more successful. Participants there agreed on a set of operational proposals, including that states should monitor anarchist activity, establish
central agencies to oversee this task and, subsequently, exchange information among national agencies. Regarding the latter, a secretive group
of police chiefs and others met over the course of the conference, agreeing
to exchange lists of expellees on a monthly basis. Moreover, it was out
of this group that the conference agreed that the *portrait parlé* system
for identifying criminals should be adopted as standard practice by states.
This system utilized a numeric code to record anthropometric measure-
ments, thereby enabling identification information to be transmitted by
telephone or telegraph. This scheme was eventually superseded by the
move to fingerprinting in the early 1900s.[15]

On the question of extradition, delegates eventually agreed that
crimes related to anarchism should be treated as non-political crimes
and, therefore, that they be subject to extradition agreements. But
again, this consensus did not translate into significant change at the
operational level. More important in this regard was the specific
agreement among delegates that attempts against the lives of heads of
state should be extraditable. This measure—the so-called "Belgian" or
attentat clause—had gained currency in 1856 after a failed attempt to
blow up a train carrying Napoleon III. It would later become standard
practice. A further effect of Rome was the facilitation of contacts
among police services, enabling relationships to develop and providing
a basis for future cooperation.[16]

In sum, the outcomes from Rome were underwhelming, although there
were some tangible results in terms of operational cooperation (especially regarding *portrait parlé* and the *attentat* clause) and the promise
of more in the future. Indeed, it soon emerged that further action
would be required to quell anarchist activity, which persisted into the
new century. Most glaringly, in July 1900, King Umberto of Italy was
assassinated by anarchists. This was followed by the assassination of
President McKinley of the USA in September 1901. These shocking
events triggered a range of responses, including prompt action by states
to reform policing practices (especially regarding the protection of
heads of state), as well as the expansion of existing bilateral arrangements, such as officer exchanges, among police services. The McKinley
assassination brought the United States into debates about international cooperation to suppress anarchism. Previously, the United States
had largely avoided anarchist attacks, giving the impression that—
despite the presence of native and foreign anarchists—anarchist violence was someone else's problem. By contrast, the attack by US-born
anarchist Leon Czolgosz, led the new president, Theodore Roosevelt,

to declare: "Anarchy is a crime against the whole human race; and mankind should band together against the anarchist. His crime should be made an offense against the law of nations ... It should also be so declared by treaties among civilized powers. Such treaties would give to the Federal Government the power of dealing with crime."[17]

The renewed attention to anarchism was viewed as an opportunity by Russia and Germany, who were seeking to press the case for more meaningful anti-anarchist cooperation in the wake of Rome. In late 1901, the Russians and Germans addressed a memorandum on the topic to European states, which was also shared with the United States. The memorandum sought action on many of the unimplemented elements of the Rome agreement, especially the creation of central anti-anarchist bureaus by states, information exchange, international regulations for the expulsion of anarchists, and measures to strengthen criminal laws.[18] Within the United States, Roosevelt's rhetoric was not enough to convince Congress to pass broad anti-anarchist legislation. Rather, familiar concerns for states' rights and the centralization of power in the federal government limited legislative action to measures to bar the entry of anarchists from abroad. Believing that such a response was unsatisfactory, the Russian and German ambassadors presented a more detailed proposal to Washington, emphasizing administrative measures for expulsions and, again, the creation of central bureaus. However, as Jensen argues, the United States did not possess a national police force, and federal law enforcement agencies did not emerge until the twentieth century. Therefore, even if the United States was inclined to revisit its tradition of isolationism, and to overcome its wariness of the European powers, it could not credibly undertake to implement the Russian/German proposal.[19] In later chapters, I illustrate the extent to which this situation was reversed in the twentieth century, as the USA transformed its role from skeptical follower to assertive leader.

Despite US reticence, the Russian/German proposal won adherents within Europe, at least in the East. On 14 March 1904, 10 states (Russia, Romania, Serbia, Bulgaria, the Ottoman Empire, Austria-Hungary, Germany, Denmark and Sweden-Norway) signed the secret St. Petersburg Anti-Anarchist Protocol. The protocol set out procedures for expelling anarchists, as well as calling for the creation of central anti-anarchist offices in each country and regular communication on anarchist activity on a police-to-police basis.[20] In addition to the United States, several other states elected not to sign. For example, the Italians were concerned that the expulsion clause would mean that Italian anarchists abroad would be forced to return to Italy—a prospect Rome wished to avoid.[21] The British response was interpreted on the continent as part of an ongoing attempt by liberal states to tolerate the presence of anarchists as a kind of "insurance payment" against attacks in England.[22] The Swiss were wary of a secretive agreement that tied it to the conservative powers, but eventually accepted the protocol with reservations in 1907.[23]

If the Rome Conference had not succeeded in mobilizing states to pass new laws and broaden the bases of cooperation, what effect did the St. Petersburg Protocol have? For Jensen, the primary impact of the protocol should be assessed by looking at the effects it had on police cooperation. Combined with the bilateral agreements that were becoming more common on the continent, both the St. Petersburg and Rome initiatives were part of a trend towards increasing levels of operational collaboration and information exchange.[24] Similarly, Mathieu Deflem characterizes Rome and St. Petersburg as unsuccessful (as they did not yield legislative change at the national level), but notes that relative successes (the adoption of the *portrait parlé* system and agreement on the Belgian extradition clause) were, in essence, operational matters. For Deflem, this reflects that these initiatives built upon pre-existing networks of practical cooperation among police services and this, in turn, substantiates his "bureaucratization" thesis, i.e. that police cooperation developed and became more effective as a result of professionalization and increasing contacts among experts in different states.[25] I return to this theme, below. Suffice it to note here that, even if operational contacts were trending in one direction, political differences were prone to undermine the rules and norms established by the 1904 protocol as Europe edged closer to World War I. Efforts to expand the reach of the protocol were unsuccessful during this period and some states began to insist that communications pertaining to expulsions go through diplomatic channels, rather than being police-to-police. In this period, too, some governments sought alternative ways to reduce the threat posed by anarchism, including non-coercive measures such as removing prohibitions against organized labor and providing alternative outlets for political expression.[26] For several reasons, then, anarchist violence began to recede from the high point of the 1890s. The mixed record of international cooperation against anarchism is part of the explanation for this, but only part.

Counter-terrorism and the League of Nations

If anarchism showed signs of receding in the pre-World War I period, it made something of a resurgence after that conflict, with attacks occurring in Spain, the United States, Italy, France, Argentina, Brazil, and Portugal.[27] However, these attacks did not prompt states to revisit the Rome and St. Petersburg agreements, and multilateral counter-terrorism as such did not advance in the immediate post-World War I period. But the topic was soon on the agenda of relevant post-war institutions, including inter-governmental and civil society bodies.

Regarding the latter, the International Association of Penal Law undertook a series of conferences on the "Unification of Penal Law." It was at the third such conference, held in Brussels in 1930, that the term "terrorism" entered into more common usage.[28] A committee of the conference commenced work on a definition of the term. Over successive conferences (in 1931 and 1934), participants debated various aspects of the definition, especially whether terrorism should be defined with reference to political motivations. (In doing so, they clearly took note of the definition of "anarchism" agreed to in Rome in 1898.) The task gained a sense of urgency after the assassinations of King Alexander and Foreign Minister Barthou. The text approved by the sixth conference defines "terrorism" in two parts.[29] First, it provides a broad statement defining as a terrorist:

> Any person who, by wilful acts directed against the life, physical integrity, health or freedom of a Head of State or his or her spouse, a person exercising the prerogatives of the Head of State, Crown Princes, members of a Government, persons possessing diplomatic immunity, or members of constitutional, legislative or judiciary bodies, has endangered the community or created a state of terror calculated to cause a change in or impediment to the operation of the public authorities or to disturb international relations.

Second, in the subsequent article, a non-exhaustive list of specific terrorist acts is enumerated. These include impeding railways, maritime, river or air communications, using explosives, poisoning drinking water, destroying public buildings, and so on. Thus, even if the first part of the definition contains a tautology (defining terrorism by reference to a "state of terror") and is otherwise vague, the enumeration of specific crimes gives some substance to the definition. The text went on to espouse the principle of "extradite or prosecute," envisioning that states would try terrorists, deliver them to an international court, or extradite them to be tried elsewhere.

The work of these conferences provided the backdrop for action against terrorism by the League of Nations, which had emerged out of the Paris Peace Conference in 1919. Despite the travails of the League, which failed to win the backing of powerful states, had a fluctuating membership, and was ultimately unsuccessful in preventing the slide back to war in 1939, one might expect that states would acknowledge a common interest in acting against non-state violence. But, when Romania raised the matter of terrorism in League fora in 1926, it did not prompt action. Rather, it was only after 1934 that cooperative efforts were increased. Following the October killings in Marseilles, the French petitioned the League to elaborate a convention on terrorism. In December 1934, after much debate, the Council of the League established an expert committee (the Committee for the International Repression of Terrorism, or CIRT) to draft a preliminary convention. CIRT comprised 11 states and met in three sessions from April 1935 to April 1937.[30] In November 1937, a diplomatic conference was convened to consider two conventions—on the Prevention and Punishment of Terrorism and on the creation of an international criminal court to try offences under the former treaty. Once concluded, the former convention attracted 24 signatories, but only one ratification.[31] Although the convention never entered into force, it is significant for three reasons.

First, unlike any subsequent agreement of this type, the convention provides a definition of terrorism. The approach taken reflects that of the sixth conference on the Unification of Penal Law, cited above. Article 1(2) of the convention defines "acts of terrorism" broadly as "criminal acts directed against a state and intended or calculated to create a state of terror in the minds of particular persons, or a group of persons, or in the public." Article 2 then elaborates the several acts that signatories are to criminalize in so far as they constitute "acts of terrorism," so defined. On this definition, as Ben Saul notes, specific motives (whether political or otherwise) drop out: rather, the key elements are the intention of the act, the target and the means used. The definition is tautological (defining "terrorism" by referring to a "state of terror") and unclear in several other ways, e.g. it suggests that a subjective belief about a state of terror among a small group might be considered "terrorism." Further, certain clarifications (such as a proposal referring to political motivations and another on attacks on property) were rejected in the course of drafting the convention. The fact that a two-part or hybrid approach was taken reflects a disagreement in the drafting process as to whether to adopt a generic or enumerative definition.[32] Thus, while it is significant that states agreed upon a definition, the dilemmas they encountered in doing so, and the shortcomings of the outcome they achieved, are likewise noteworthy.

Second, it is worth reflecting further on the failure of the convention to enter into force. In this regard, it is interesting that not all states considered that it was necessary to act against "terrorism" per se and that, rather, it would suffice simply to criminalize the kinds of acts that terrorists do.[33] A more fundamental point of contention concerned the extradition provisions in the convention (Art. 8). Although the convention specified that terrorism may be considered a "non-political" crime, and therefore extraditable, states had absolute discretion in implementing this provision (see Art. 8(4)). In the political climate of the day, states took a guarded view of such prerogatives and were eager to maintain close control over provisions related to extradition and asylum.[34] The principle of "extradite or prosecute" is a fine sentiment, but could not guarantee the freedom of action that skeptics of the convention sought. For others, such as the United Kingdom (UK), failure to ratify reflected the perception that there would be no support in the legislature, and in the wider public, to make the necessary changes to domestic law.[35]

Third, beyond defining terrorism, the convention set out a broad and aspirational range of actions for states to take in suppressing it. For example, it contained provisions regarding the fraudulent use of passports, as well as measures to regulate the possession of firearms. In these provisions, we can see the expansion of the counter-terrorism imperative into other fields of state activity, such that the effort to cooperate against terrorism had spillover effects in related domains (or would have, had the convention entered into force). Relatedly, and perhaps recalling the anti-anarchist campaign, the convention urged enhanced police cooperation. So, just as drafters sought to influence developments in other domains, they aspired to capitalize on other developments to advance counter-terrorism.

Lessons from history?

Why is it important to consider the historical precedents of multilateral counter-terrorism? For several observers, the answer is self-evident on the basis of apparent similarities between the early anarchists and today's jihadi terrorists. This argument cites as evidence the organizational attributes of both sets of terrorists (decentralized networks), as well as their tactical decisions (such as selecting symbolic targets) and the sense of fear they inspired in the populace.[36] But this claim falls wide of the mark. It elides the obviously divergent prognoses of anarchism and jihadism, and does not accurately reflect the level of organizational sophistication achieved by al Qaeda in the pre-9/11 period, as well as the role of technology (especially the internet) since.[37] Nonetheless, there are five reasons why pre-World War II attempts at counter-terrorism cooperation are worthy of our attention.

First, there is a lesson in the failure to develop and maintain broad-based cooperation against political violence. This failure can be attributed to political disputes that limit counter-terrorism cooperation over time. Such disputes often centered on contending views of extradition policies, as well as fundamental differences between liberal and illiberal states. Ironically, while much was invested in treating anarchism as a "non-political" crime, the politics surrounding extradition surfaced often enough to preclude genuine consensus.[38] More broadly, Jensen views it as a puzzle that the Rome and St. Petersburg programs went largely unexecuted, but reflects that "national self-interests and rivalries edged out international concerns ... The European states were much too divided in political thought and practice to make possible any ... alliance [against anarchism]."[39] Even though the 1937 convention may appear to transcend politics (in so far as the agreement emerged at all and, moreover, contained a definition of terrorism), the extradition issue was again a point of contention. Also, of course, politics reasserted itself as the convention went unimplemented in the lead-up to World War II.

Second, there is a lesson in the contrast between political dissension (which stymied broad-based cooperation) and operational-level consensus (which facilitated that cooperation that did occur). Again, Jensen reflects that "The areas in which the protocols of 1898 and 1904 had repercussions were those where policy changes could be decided largely outside of public purview, and dealt with as technical, bureaucratic questions rather than as political issues."[40] Similarly, acknowledging this distinction, the 1937 convention called for a range of operational measures, although these had little effect. Still, regarding the provisions for police cooperation, one contemporary observer remarked that,[41]

> cooperation of police forces is already, to a large extent, effective without the existence of any international treaty obligation, and has been, is, and will be, of great value. Indeed, it may be surmised that for the prevention of terrorist outrages such cooperation is likely to be far more effective than the stiffening of the law for the infliction of punishment, usually after the event, on men and women of a fanatical temper."

A third lesson is that the problem of responding to terrorism builds on, and advances, cooperation in other, related fields. Responses to terrorism are a product of cooperative mechanisms already in existence: in turn, cooperation against terrorism produces spillover effects for cooperation in other domains. In the pre-World War I period, anarchism was treated as a criminal matter and helped move along police cooperation. As Mathieu Deflem argues in his history of policing,[42]

> The anti-anarchist conference of Rome in 1898 and its follow up meeting in St. Petersburg in 1904 represent remarkable threshold cases in the transformation of international policing in Europe. On the one hand, these efforts clearly have a foot in the 19th century as they remained largely framed in a politically sensitive framework of national governments and international formal law. Yet, on the other, they also reveal the growing influence of a developing European police culture that was moving towards the institution of international police practice on the basis of professional expertise.

In this regard, Rome and St. Petersburg undergirded more regular contacts between police and law enforcement officials in the early part of the twentieth century which, in turn, resulted in the founding of the International Criminal Police Commission in Vienna in 1923, the forerunner to today's Interpol.[43]

In turn, the 1937 convention built upon past collaborations among lawyers and diplomats, especially in arriving at a definition of terrorism. But a fourth lesson concerns the dilemmas of defining terrorism, for which the League's experience is a critical reference point for future practice. As Saul contends, "The League anticipated most of the legal issues which would plague the international community's response in the following seven decades."[44] For example, the dilemmas of selecting between a generic or enumerative definition, or integrating both, have been revisited since.

A final lesson is that the urgency attached to counter-terrorism tends to subside over time, as disagreements emerge and other issues command attention. In the pre-World War II period, states were quick to put aside their efforts to cooperate against non-state threats once they perceived that other states posed the bigger threat. In this regard, the rise of "garrison states"[45] across Europe both suppressed the threat of terrorism and yielded the kind of bloody conflict that could only result from the mobilization of the coercive power of the state. Counter-terrorism cooperation again receded from the international agenda as the world went to war.

2 Multilateral counter-terrorism and the United Nations, 1945–2001

With the League of Nations having failed to prevent the outbreak of World War II, the allied states redesigned the institutions of global governance, founding the United Nations in October 1945. Although terrorism had attracted the attention of the League, it was not a significant concern for the new organization, which faced a range of emerging challenges, not least the onset of the Cold War. While the first reference to terrorism in the Security Council occurred in 1948 (in a resolution condemning the assassination of the UN mediator in Palestine, Count Folke Bernadotte, by Jewish extremists), there was only scant attention to terrorism in UN fora in the first 20 years of its existence. In the 1950s, passing references to terrorism were made in the Draft Code on Offences against the Peace and Security of Mankind, prepared by the International Law Commission, and in debates surrounding the definition of "aggression," which began at that time. In the 1960s, terrorism was raised briefly in the context of the Declaration on Principles of International Law Concerning Friendly Relations and Cooperation among States, finally approved by the General Assembly in resolution 2625 (XXV) (24 October 1970).[1] But it was only late in that decade that terrorism reappeared on the international agenda, as a consequence of an increase in aircraft hijackings. Over the next three-plus decades (that is, prior to 9/11) there were something in the order of 100,000 terrorist attacks across the world.[2] These attacks utilized diverse and often innovative tactics, as terrorists took advantage of technological advances in planning and executing acts of violence. These attacks were motivated by a variety of causes and this period spans the "anti-colonial," "new left" and "religious" waves of terrorism, as summarized by Rapoport.[3] They also prompted a diverse range of responses from states, who evolved a means of cooperating against terrorism in spite of their disagreements on fundamental issues, such as whether political violence could be justified under certain circumstances and, in turn, how to define "terrorism." The UN was integral to these developments. Its organs were the fora in which the views of states frequently clashed and, less frequently, coalesced. The UN—or, more correctly, the officials and bodies that comprise the UN system—were also important as actors in this period, prompting and facilitating negotiations.

This chapter recounts the pattern of multilateral counter-terrorism within the UN system prior to 9/11. Once again, my approach is chronological, but I draw attention to four key themes. First, the enduring attribute of counter-terrorism cooperation in this period was the failure to achieve a definition of terrorism and, in turn, the inability of states to achieve broad-based cooperation. Still, the broader trajectory was towards increasing (even if incremental) levels of cooperation over time. This was especially so towards the end of, and after, the Cold War. As this suggests, the structure of international relations exerted a broad constraint on counter-terrorism cooperation. But more immediately determinative of outcomes—and the issue on which Cold War rivalry rather piggy-backed for a time—was the politics of the Middle East. For much of this period, outcomes reflected entrenched positions either in support of Israel, or sympathetic to the various Palestinian groups that utilized violence.

Second, when cooperation occurred, the form that it took was distinctive. In short, being unable to achieve broad-based cooperation without a definition of terrorism, a "piecemeal approach" evolved, whereby states agreed that certain terroristic acts (hijacking, hostage-taking, bombing, etc.) should be subject to prohibitions. The main contribution of UN bodies to counter-terrorism during this period was the conclusion of 12 international instruments (summarized in Appendix A), which cover a range of specific acts and manifest the piecemeal approach. Third, a further consequence of the failure to define terrorism was a "spillover effect," whereby states sought to engage regional organizations, as well as other bodies outside of the UN system, to advance cooperation. Indeed, as if underscoring the limitations of multilateral approaches, and continuing a historical trend, the preference for many states was to cooperate against terrorism using bilateral or minilateral mechanisms primarily.

Finally, in spite of the constraints, I argue that patterns of cooperation in the pre-9/11 period were a key factor in determining the approach of states after those attacks. While the volume of multilateral activity against terrorism increased dramatically after 9/11, there is a sense in which later developments are "path dependent," in that their form and content is contingent upon pre-9/11 measures.[4] The signature achievements of the UN in the post-9/11 period—including Security Council resolution 1373 (28 September 2001), the General Assembly's 2006 "Global Counter-terrorism Strategy" and the proliferation of new rules and norms through specialized bodies within the UN system—have their roots in the pre-9/11 era. I develop this claim more fully in Chapter 3, but suffice it to note here that any attempt to explain the evolution of the UN's response to 9/11 requires an account of what came before.

The re-emergence of multilateral counter-terrorism

From its inception until the late 1960s, the UN system was virtually silent on the topic of terrorism. But an increase in the number of terrorist incidents, especially those utilizing the tactic of aircraft hijacking, led states to seek cooperative responses.[5] While the sense of urgency on this issue peaked towards the end of the decade, it was in 1963 that the first of the terrorism-related international conventions emerged. The Convention on Offences and Certain Other Acts Committed aboard Aircraft 1963 (the Tokyo Convention) had come about to fill a jurisdictional gap concerning offences committed on planes above the high seas.[6] This was a particular concern for the United States, which had found that it lacked jurisdiction to secure convictions for offences that had taken place over the high seas, even in US-registered planes. With others, the United States requested that the matter be put to the International Civil Aviation Organization's (ICAO) Legal Committee. The Committee recommended a convention in 1959. It was only late in the negotiations that the United States and Venezuela—whose planes had been targeted for several hijackings in the Caribbean—suggested the inclusion of a provision on the "unlawful seizure" of aircraft. Article 11 of the Tokyo Convention does not create a separate offence for hijacking, but rather commits states to "take all appropriate steps to return control of the aircraft to its lawful commander," in the event that one should occur. It is contemplated that the various acts involved in unlawfully seizing a plane would be covered by the jurisdictional provisions of the convention, thereby facilitating legal action against hijackers by the state of registration. As such, the convention impacts extradition arrangements (by clarifying that the state of registration, in addition to any state in which an incident occurs, can claim jurisdiction), but it otherwise creates no extradition obligations.

In all, the Tokyo Convention is modest in terms of its impact on terrorism. The drafters did not consider the suppression of terrorism a primary objective of the convention and the term is not mentioned in it. Nonetheless, the jurisdictional provisions, and the idea that states would act against unlawful seizures, set a precedent. In this regard, FitzGerald observes that, "it seems plausible to suggest that if the Tokyo Convention had been widely accepted and implemented by states prior to the escalation of hijackings in the period 1967–70, the need for a specific convention for the suppression of the unlawful seizure of aircraft might not have been so desperately felt."[7] As that remark suggests, the convention did not attract a lot of signatories and only entered into force when ratified by the 12th state to do so (the United States), in 1969. This order of priorities was soon revised. Indeed, although the Tokyo Convention was not yet in force, the ICAO Assembly referred the question of unlawful seizure specifically to the organization's Legal Committee in late 1968. By December 1970, the Convention for the Suppression of Unlawful Seizure of Aircraft was put before a diplomatic conference in The Hague. Later that month, it was opened for signature, entering into force in October 1971, after 10 states had ratified it.

The Hague Convention exceeds the provisions of the Tokyo Convention in several ways. Most importantly, it defines "unlawful seizure" as an offence and commits states to imposing "severe penalties" as punishment. The Hague Convention has a broader approach to jurisdiction, for example, requiring that states of actual landing take measures against hijackers where necessary. Here, the idea was to remove as many safe havens for hijackers as possible.[8] Similarly, the Hague Convention incorporates the principle of "extradite or prosecute," missing from the Tokyo Convention. Notably, the offence of "unlawful seizure" is limited to aircraft "in flight," defined as the time between the closure of the cabin doors following embarkation, and their opening prior to disembarkation. This reflects the fact that a separate convention—which would later become the 1971 Convention for the Suppression of Unlawful Acts against the Safety of Civil Aviation (Montreal Convention)—was being negotiated at the same time. Apparently as a pragmatic measure, an Extraordinary Session of the ICAO Assembly in June 1970 charged the Legal Committee to begin work on a convention to cover those incidents beyond "unlawful seizure ... in flight." That convention was opened for signature in September 1971 and entered into force in January 1973, following the 10th ratification and thereby concluding an intense period of rule-making.

The Montreal Convention defines a series of offences that fall short of "unlawful seizure" while in flight, as well as prohibiting acts likely to endanger the safety of an aircraft committed while it is "in service." The latter phrase is defined as the period from the commencement of preflight preparations until 24 hours after the conclusion of the flight. As with the Hague Convention, the Montreal Convention strives to establish universal jurisdiction over the relevant offences and adopts the "extradite or prosecute" principle. But also like the Tokyo and Hague conventions, no mention is made of "terrorism." Taken together, the three conventions began the process of institutionalizing multilateral counter-terrorism in the post-World War II period. They were endorsed by resolutions of the UN General Assembly and Security Council.[9] Within ICAO, the conventions were complemented by other institutional mechanisms with the aim of suppressing hijacking. These included the establishment of the Committee on Unlawful Interference in 1969 (to investigate incidents), the issuance of the restricted *Security Manual for the Safeguarding of Civil Aviation against Acts of Unlawful Interference* (first published in 1971) and the development of Annex 17 to ICAO's founding Chicago Convention (which sets out Standards and Recommended Practices on the topic of unlawful interference).[10]

Despite such advances, some observers were inclined to view these measures with a skeptical eye. ICAO reportedly had only one staff member committed to aviation security for much of the 1970s and 1980s.[11] Although all three conventions entered into force, rates of ratification remained modest and several critical states—i.e. those that were often implicated in hijackings—had not signed. In addition, compliance soon emerged as a problem. Yet the attempt to impose sanctions through ICAO against non-implementing states foundered in 1973, along with efforts to strengthen anti-hijacking measures.[12] Contemporary scholars attributed this failure to the Arab-Israeli dispute, which prompted a bloc of Arab states to oppose further action to suppress hijacking.[13] Interestingly, the idea of sanctions against safe havens for hijackers was subsequently revisited in 1978, when the G7 group of states issued the Bonn Declaration on International Terrorism. In light of these problems, several states relied on "self-help" to respond to hijackings, including Israel's use of commandos to free hostages aboard an Air France flight hijacked to Entebbe, Uganda, in June 1976.[14] In sum, the re-emergence of multilateral counter-terrorism was characterized by the relatively prompt conclusion of three conventions and the establishment of related initiatives to suppress hijacking. But these developments were accompanied by the appearance of political divisions among states. These divisions would exert a constraining effect on cooperation over time.

The 1970s: cooperation without consensus

In the early morning of 5 September 1972, eight members of the PLO's "Black September Organization" stormed a dormitory housing Israeli athletes competing at the Olympic Games in Munich. Two athletes were killed immediately and another nine taken hostage. A lengthy nego-tiation ensued, with the terrorists demanding the release of some 236 Palestinian prisoners in Israeli jails, as well as other terrorists elsewhere (including the founders of the German group, the Red Army Faction, Andreas Baader and Ulrike Meinhof), in exchange for the hostages. A deal was eventually struck and arrangements made for the terrorists and hostages to be transported to Cairo, where the exchange would occur. However, once on the tarmac, and with two terrorists inspecting the air-craft provided, the West German police opened fire, which was returned by the terrorists. A standoff followed, eventually broken by the deto-nation of a hand grenade inside one of the helicopters in which the hostages were being kept. A bloody shoot-out occurred. Three terrorists survived and subsequently surrendered to police. But all nine hostages were killed, along with a West German police officer.

Beyond the shocking nature of the attack, Hoffman suggests that this incident is remarkable for two reasons.[15] First, although the attempt to take hostages was a tactical failure, the media coverage devoted to the crisis as it unfolded made it a strategic success. A relatively obscure group had shot to prominence. Palestinian terrorist groups attracted new members and their cause achieved levels of attention that were previously unseen. Second, it prompted states, especially in Europe, to improve their counter-terrorism capacity, especially the capability of police forces. As a consequence, the idea of special forces dedicated to counter-terrorism became more common.

The impact of the Munich disaster on counter-terrorism, however, extends well beyond national-level responses. Indeed, the events at Munich set in train a series of events that would effectively institution-alize the political divisions that stymied multilateral counter-terrorism for much of the twentieth century. How would the UN respond? It was not immediately obvious that it would. In the Security Council, ter-rorism had already attracted some degree of dissension, as members responded to the May 1972 attack on Lod airport in Israel (in which 26 passengers and 3 terrorists were killed) with a mere statement of concern issued by the president.[16] The Munich crisis brought these divisions into clear view. A draft resolution was circulated by the non-aligned members of the Council, but it did not mention either terror-ism or the Munich crisis. In response, the United States exercised its veto power (the first time it had done so alone, and only its second veto to that point). A US draft, which framed the issues in much starker terms, was not put to the vote at all, while a more moderate Western European draft drew vetoes from China and the Soviet Union, as well as negative votes from Guinea, Somalia, Sudan and Yugoslavia.

It was in light of this stalemate that Secretary-General Kurt Waldheim took steps to put the issue on the organization's agenda, acting through the General Assembly. Waldheim initially consulted with select middle powers to include an item on terrorism on the Assembly's schedule. Being unsuccessful, he took the "unusual and courageous" step of proposing the item himself. Waldheim judged it to be worth the risk, given that the alternative was organizational inaction.

The politics of these developments are telling. The Secretary-General's proposal was initially titled, "Measures to prevent terrorism and other forms of violence which endanger or take human lives or jeopardize fundamental freedoms." In the General Committee, that proposal was approved by a vote of 15 in favor, 7 against, and 2 abstentions, with the negative votes cast by Asian and African members. Prior to the item being included on the agenda proper, however, an intervention by Saudi Arabia altered the title of the item to read: "Measures to prevent terrorism and other forms of violence which endanger or take human lives or jeopardize fundamental freedoms, and study of the underlying causes of those forms of terrorism and acts of violence which lie in misery, frustration, grievance, and despair and which cause some people to sacrifice human lives, including their own, in an attempt to effect radical changes." It was in this form that the item was referred to the Assembly's Sixth Committee (Legal). In making these amendments, the Saudis and their supporters aimed to preserve the legitimacy of "national liberation movements"—in Asia and Africa, but especially in the Middle East—and to avoid having the use of violence towards such ends being labeled as "terrorist." Strategically, this approach was designed to deflect attention from the use of violence to emphasize the grievances that motivated it, arguing that such injustices would need to be remedied before acting to suppress the violence that results. This position was put most clearly by the PLO chairman, Yasser Arafat, in his speech to the General Assembly, 18 months after the Munich attack:[18]

> Those who call us terrorists wish to prevent world public opinion from discovering the truth about us and from seeing the justice on our faces. They seek to hide the terrorism and tyranny of their acts, and our own posture of self-defence … The difference between the revolutionary and the terrorist lies in the reason for which each fights. For whoever stands by a just cause and fights for the freedom and liberation of his land from the invaders, the settlers and the colonialists, cannot possibly be called terrorist … This is actually a just and proper struggle consecrated by the

United Nations Charter and by the Universal Declaration of Human Rights. As to those who fight against the just causes, those who wage war to occupy, colonize and oppress other people, those are the terrorists. Those are the people whose actions should be condemned, who should be called war criminals: for the justice of the cause determines the right to struggle.

As indicated, this position united a broad coalition of Third World, communist and non-aligned states from Africa, Asia, Europe and the Middle East (hereafter, the "Third World bloc"). On the opposite side of the argument, Western states and their allies sought to affirm the principle that certain violent tactics are not justified by any cause, as innocents are the victims. There was little scope to reconcile these positions. The Sixth Committee, in considering its workload in the autumn of 1972, asked the Secretariat to prepare a study "on the problem of terrorism, including its origins." That study—lumbered as it was with the unwieldy name of its originating request, above—took the Western view, concluding that, "terrorism threatens, endangers or destroys the lives and fundamental freedoms of the innocent, and it would not be just to leave them to wait for protection until the causes have been remedied and the purposes and principles of the [UN] Charter have been given full effect."[19] This aspect of the Secretariat's study was not well received by some delegations.[20] The ensuing discussion in the Sixth Committee, with the goal of developing a resolution, played out along predictable lines. Initially, the United States circulated a draft and also proposed a convention on terrorism, carefully worded so as to avoid being a lightning rod for dissension.[21] However, both were greeted skeptically by the Third World bloc and the United States did not put the draft resolution to a vote in the Sixth Committee. Instead, the United States threw its support behind a compromise proposal from 14 states. This coalition did not include any African states and had only one Asian member, Iran. However, after a vote, a counter-proposal, from 16 Arab, African and allied states was considered first, and subsequently adopted (76 to 34, with 16 abstentions). Importantly, the Soviet Union sided with the Third World bloc in this debate, having flip-flopped somewhat on terrorism issues to this point.[22] The Soviets had an important stake in this debate, not least because they were occasionally victims of terrorism. Having suffered hijackings of domestic flights, the Soviets had taken a relatively strong position in ICAO debates. But they also perceived that support for Palestinian groups in the Middle East could advance Soviet interests against the West. Moreover, the Soviets were eager to keep the US proposals on terrorism in check, responding skeptically to the proposal for a convention. In this way, the broader division of the Cold War came to be manifested in the UN's response to terrorism.

And so the die was cast. In late 1972, resolution 3034 (XXVII) (18 December 1972) was adopted by the General Assembly with a vote of 76 to 35 and 17 abstentions (again, it bore the politicized name of the initial agenda item). The text of the resolution "expresses deep concern" over acts of violence while, in several paragraphs, urging states to find solutions to the "underlying causes" of such violence, reaffirming the right to self-determination and the legitimacy of struggles for national liberation, and condemning "colonial, racist or repressive regimes." Nonetheless, the resolution established two new mechanisms. First, the resolution requested that states submit reports to the Secretary-General, containing proposals for responding to terrorism. Second, the resolution created an Ad Hoc Committee, comprising 35 members, to receive reports from the Secretary-General, and develop its own recommendations. The task before the Ad Hoc Committee—to study causes as well as develop ideas for prevention—ensured that political differences were at the forefront. It duly reproduced and reaffirmed them. For example, when the Committee met in 1973, members of the Third World bloc suggested that "state terrorism" should be the priority.[23] Over time, the Committee submitted two major reports to the Assembly,[24] which were endorsed in a series of Assembly resolutions.[25] The latter, produced by the Sixth Committee, placed a premium on preserving space for the legitimate use of violence against "racist, colonial or alien regimes."[26] Although numerous states submitted reports to the Secretary-General, who in turn reported to the Committee, the debate in that forum was essentially repetitive. For example, the Committee reported in 1979 that,

> legal formulations, no matter how perfect, would never suffice to solve the problem of terrorism unless action was taken to remove its underlying causes. The restoration of the legitimate rights of the Arab people of Palestine ... and the provision of support to the liberation struggle of peoples under the colonial yoke were some ways in which a real solution to that problem can be found.[27]

The recommendations put forward in that report—balancing condemnation of terrorism with an emphasis on the elimination of its causes—underscore the modesty of the Assembly's role.[28] The item, which maintained its long title until 1991, was kept on the agenda on a biannual basis, but the committee was not asked to continue its work beyond 1979.

The early experience in the Committee soon led certain participants and outside observers to the view that comprehensive international action to suppress terrorism through the UN was unlikely. In turn, the logic of acting to prohibit specific offences gained some appeal, building on the precedent set by the ICAO conventions.[29] Indeed, some contemporary scholars suggested that cooperation would be facilitated by going further and discarding the term "terrorism" altogether. Writing in 1974, Franck and Lockwood judged the prospects of a general convention against terrorism to be negligible, arguing that, "'Terrorism' is an historically misleading and politically loaded term which invites conceptual and ideological dissonance."[30] A virtue of imposing prohibitions against certain acts in a piecemeal fashion, they suggested, was that this controversial term could be avoided altogether.

Further support for this view could be found in the shape of the Convention on the Prevention and Punishment of Crimes against Internationally Protected Purposes, concluded in 1973. The negotiations on this treaty are the exception that proves the rule concerning impediments to multilateral counter-terrorism in this period.[31] Work on this matter had begun in 1970, under the aegis of the International Law Commission (ILC), where it had been raised by the Netherlands. Following the April 1971 murder of the Yugoslav ambassador to Sweden in Stockholm, the General Assembly adopted resolution 2780 (XXVI) (3 December 1971), requesting that the ILC draft an agreement on the topic. The ILC concluded this task 11 days prior to the seizure of Israeli athletes at the Munich Olympic Games. The Sixth Committee in 1973 proceeded upon this basis, being uniquely positioned to avoid the confounding political issues of the day. The fact that it was the Yugoslav ambassador who had been murdered ensured buy-in from the Third World bloc. The convention, which establishes certain offences against state officials and property, was opened for signature on 14 December 1973 and entered into force on 20 February 1977. Importantly, this was not the first multilateral convention on this topic, the Organization of American States (OAS) having concluded the Convention to Prevent and Punish Acts of Terrorism taking the Form of Crimes against Persons and Related Extortion that are of International Significance, in 1971.

For its part, a similar pattern of competitive interaction came to characterize debates among states in the Security Council.[32] Any action on terrorism was highly politicized. In 1973, the Council passed a resolution condemning Israel for the interception and diversion of an Iraqi Airways plane, mistakenly thought to be carrying George Habash, leader of the Popular Front for the Liberation of Palestine.[33] In 1976, responding to the Israeli rescue of hostages aboard an Air France plane hijacked to Entebbe, Uganda, Council members split over whether to criticize the hijackers or the Israelis. No resolution was issued. In 1979, the Council declined to use its powers under Chapter VII of the UN Charter to impose sanctions on Iran following the hostage crisis at the US Embassy in Tehran, although it had threatened to do so and had called for the release of the hostages.

This latter dispute—entailing as it did the use of the veto by the Soviets to block a resolution proposed by the United States—was particularly revealing. At that time, negotiations for the latest "piecemeal" convention, on hostage taking, were being concluded by an Ad Hoc Committee working to the Sixth Committee of the General Assembly. However, the negotiations that led to the 1979 International Convention against the Taking of Hostages tested the limits of the piecemeal approach. The matter had been introduced to the Assembly in 1976 by West Germany which, subsequent to the Olympic Games disaster, had experienced further hostage crises, including a siege at its embassy in Sweden in 1975.[34] The Assembly decided to develop a convention on the topic and duly established an Ad Hoc Committee to draft it, although some states raised concerns at this stage that such moves risked conflating terrorists and national liberation movements.[35] In turn, members of the Third World bloc introduced the idea of "state terrorism" into the committee's negotiations at the outset, arguing that it would be wrong to condemn certain actions by national liberation movements, without addressing the problem of "seizure or detention, not only of a person or persons, but also of masses under colonial, racist or foreign domination."[36] Such matters dominated the first session of committee meetings, which had before it a draft convention prepared by the West Germans.

At the second session a procedural innovation—the creation of working groups whose deliberations would not be recorded—permitted states more room to maneuver.[37] However, the respective positions proved irreconcilable and some delegations wondered whether the idea should be dropped entirely. Still, the General Assembly renewed the committee's mandate and a third session was scheduled. At that meeting, by virtue of a series of discussions in a subgroup of a working group, a compromise was struck. The Third World bloc conceded to the Western view of the relationship between the new convention and the Geneva Conventions and Protocols (which prohibit the taking of hostages in armed conflict), thereby closing any loopholes that might legitimate hostage-taking by national liberation movements. (Under an earlier resolution of the General Assembly, armed conflicts involving national liberation movements were to be regarded as falling under the Geneva Conventions and Protocols).[38] In turn, the Western states agreed to the inclusion of an article affirming the "territorial integrity and political independence" of states, as sought by the Third World bloc, reacting to the incident at Entebbe. While the wording of the relevant clauses has led some commentators to conclude that the convention endorses or permits hostage-taking by national liberation movements,[39] that interpretation is questionable.[40] Like prior conventions, it incorporates the "extradite or prosecute" principle. Unlike other conventions, the word "terrorism" is used, having been included in the preambular language as part of the bargain struck among states. The convention came into effect on 3 June 1983, after the 22nd ratification was deposited.

A further convention was negotiated in the 1970s, pursuing the logic of the piecemeal approach. In 1974, in his address to the General Assembly, the US Secretary of State, Henry Kissinger, underscored the need to safeguard nuclear materials. The issue was subsequently taken up by the International Atomic Energy Agency (IAEA) in a series of meetings at its headquarters in Vienna, from 1977 to 1979.[41] The 1980 Convention for the Physical Protection of Nuclear Material sets minimum standards for the transport of nuclear material and requires states to prohibit nuclear theft and sabotage. But these provisions are a watered-down version of what had been proposed initially. The rules concerning transit pertain to international movements only, as language on the domestic regulation of nuclear materials was resisted by some states as being a breach of their sovereignty.[42] While the convention builds on the series of non-binding IAEA standards that had emerged in the area,[43] rates of ratification were low, with fewer than 70 states ratifying before 9/11. Although the convention was opened for signature in March 1980, it did not enter into force until February 1987, following the 21st ratification.

By the end of the 1970s, states acknowledged a fundamental disagreement on how to respond to terrorism, but evolved a means of responding that was tolerable to both sides of the debate. Several bodies within the UN system were engaged as part of this response. Further, the failure to achieve consensus on broad-based cooperation through the UN led states to seek other venues for multilateral action. The OAS and the G7 both advanced terrorism-related measures in this period. Similarly, European states pursued both legal and operational initiatives, including the 1977 European Convention on the Suppression of Terrorism.[44] Each of these attributes of multilateral counter-terrorism would become more recognizable over time.

The 1980s: politics and pragmatism

The trend over the course of the 1980s was for multilateral counter-terrorism to broaden and deepen, albeit at an incremental pace and subject to the kinds of competitive dynamics related above. With that said, the early 1980s was a period of stasis on terrorism within the UN. There was a sense of routine regarding the biannual General Assembly resolutions passed at this time.[45] Although the Ad Hoc Committee on Terrorism was no longer in operation, its final report was cited in these resolutions and the Secretary-General maintained the duty to report on the implementation of the Committee's recommendations. This yielded a series of reports which, although often light on substance, indicate that several other UN organs—beyond those mentioned earlier—had begun to think of their contribution to the effort to suppress terrorism. For example, the International Labour Organization, the Universal Postal Union and the UN Educational, Scientific and Cultural Organization (UNESCO), as well as the Council of Europe, all provided information on the relevance of their work to counter-terrorism.[46] Perhaps more enduring than the substance of the reports, they represent an early attempt at establishing an institutional mechanism for monitoring responses to terrorism among states and across the UN system. This monitoring and reporting function would be reinvigorated in the 1990s and again after 9/11.

Another feature of the early 1980s was the Soviet-led effort to introduce the topic of "state terrorism" into the General Assembly. This item was discussed in the First Committee of the General Assembly (Disarmament and International Security), yielding a resolution.[47] As noted above, the concept of "state terrorism" had appeared before in Assembly debates, and the Soviet decision to raise it again can be interpreted in terms of Cold War competition. Still, this was clearly not a pressing concern for the Soviets, and Peterson notes that the resolution did not place the item on the Assembly's agenda for future sessions.[48]

The tone of multilateral counter-terrorism changed somewhat over the course of 1985—a "banner year" for international terrorists—precipitating a stronger state response.[49] That year saw an increase in the number of incidents, an increase in the number of fatalities and, importantly, an increase in the number of states that were victimized by terrorists. Among the 782 incidents recorded in 1985 were a series of hijackings, both in the air and at sea, as well as hostage crises and bombings. For example, in June, gunmen hijacked TWA flight 847 from Athens to Rome, eventually forcing it to land in Beirut. One hostage (a US Navy diver) was killed and it was 17 days before the others were released. In October, the most brazen act of maritime terrorism witnessed to that point occurred, with the hijacking of the Italian cruise ship, the *Achille Lauro*, in the Mediterranean Sea, after its departure from Alexandria. Infamously, wheelchair-bound US tourist, Leon Klinghoffer, was shot in the head and chest before being thrown overboard. The hijackers surrendered to the Egyptian authorities two days after seizing the vessel. In November, an Egyptair 737 was hijacked to Malta. The hijackers killed several passengers, before the plane was stormed on the tarmac by Egyptian commandos. Sixty further fatalities were incurred. In December, machine gun and grenade attacks killed more than 20 people in apparently synchronized attacks on the El Al ticket counters at the Rome and Vienna airports. In terms of influencing the international response to terrorism, a further attack of note was the September kidnapping of four Soviet embassy officials in Beirut, one of whom was killed. All of these incidents were attributed to Middle Eastern terrorists, with Palestinian and Lebanese groups especially active. The most deadly attack that year, recording 329 casualties, occurred after Air India flight 182, en route from Montreal to London, exploded over the North Atlantic Ocean in June. Sikh extremists were responsible.

This increase in terrorist violence changed the nature of the discussion in the Sixth Committee of the General Assembly as it debated its next resolution on terrorism in the fall of 1985. The Cuban delegation submitted to the committee a draft resolution that more-or-less reproduced earlier resolutions, albeit with a stronger emphasis on "state terrorism."[50] A Western coalition submitted an alternative draft, proposing a departure from past practice. Out of the ensuing negotiation, resolution 40/61 (9 December 1985) emerged. This resolution is remarkable for three reasons. First, the resolution included a previously unseen operational paragraph, stating that the Assembly, "*Unequivocally condemns*, as criminal, all acts, methods and practices of terrorism wherever and by whomever committed" (para. 1, emphasis in original). This was the strongest statement yet in support of the view that terrorist violence could not be justified under any circumstances. Second, the resolution was adopted unanimously by the Assembly. Cuba alone had expressed opposition to the draft in the Sixth Committee, but reversed that position in the Assembly proper. At last, it seemed, an international consensus against the use of violence might be emerging. Certainly, the resolution received the enthusiastic endorsement of the superpowers, being supported "wholeheartedly" by the Soviets, and greeted as a "symbol of new times" by the United States.[51] Third, the resolution gave momentum to the piecemeal approach, by encouraging further rule-making on terrorism within ICAO, and by requesting that the International Maritime Organization (IMO) study the problem of maritime terrorism, with a view to more concrete actions. The resolution also continued the practice of requesting that the Secretary-General provide a report to the Assembly on the implementation of the resolution.

The sense of optimism surrounding these developments was underscored by a Security Council resolution passed later that month, which "*condemns unequivocally* all acts of hostage taking and abduction."[52] Of course, there is always reason to question how far these resolutions actually reflected a consensus among states. Neither resolution defined terrorism, such that different states could interpret them in different ways. Moreover, although the Cold War was in its final days, the Soviet Union had not yet distanced itself from states such as Libya and Syria, whom the United States regarded as state supporters of terrorism. Still, these resolutions—and General Assembly resolution 40/61 in particular—did set in motion processes in ICAO and IMO that resulted in new rules and norms.

Given the prevalence of attacks targeting aircraft in the mid-1980s, ICAO had been active on terrorism prior to the UN resolutions. In July 1985, the ICAO Council instructed the Committee on Unlawful Interference to undertake a complete review of Annex 17 (Security) to the Chicago Convention. In consultation with member states, other international organizations and a group of experts, amendments were adopted in December that year. Importantly, in light of the bombing of Air India 182 (and a related baggage explosion at Narita Airport in Japan), the new Standards and Recommended Practices (SARPs) prescribed measures concerning unaccompanied baggage.[53] Following General Assembly resolution 40/61, ICAO advanced several further initiatives. In March 1986, the ICAO Council, acting on the advice of the Committee, established a 15-member expert body, the Aviation Security Panel. The Panel was charged with reviewing relevant SARPs and other technical advice, including the *Security Manual*. Through a Council resolution in June that year, ICAO recommended that states include a "model clause on aviation security," in bilateral air services agreements. These clauses, which soon appeared in several such agreements, had the effect of underscoring state obligations under ICAO conventions and rules, as well as committing states to assist each other should an incident occur. In order to ensure consistency with other measures, no provision concerning sanctions was inserted into the model clause, although that was debated.[54]

In September and October 1986, the ICAO Assembly adopted two important resolutions on aviation security. The first of these consolidated

Assembly resolutions, effectively unifying ICAO policy on the topic. The resolution restated ICAO's condemnation of all forms of unlawful interference wherever and by whomever perpetrated. In a second resolution, upon the initiative of Canada, the Assembly delegated to ICAO's Legal Committee the task of developing an international instrument to address the problem of acts of violence at airports. The process of developing such an instrument was notably smooth in comparison to past multilateral action on terrorism, and the measures were adopted as a protocol to the Montreal Convention.[55] Negotiations concluded in February 1988 and the Protocol for the Suppression of Unlawful Acts of Violence at Airports Serving International Civil Aviation came into force in August 1989. Indeed, ICAO reported an increase in the number of signatories to its other conventions over this period, too.[56]

As with ICAO, IMO initiated action to suppress political violence prior to the UN resolutions. IMO's highest governing body, the Assembly, adopted a resolution on "Measures to Prevent Unlawful Acts Which Threaten the Safety of Ships and the Security of Their Passengers and Crews" in November 1985. The Assembly also delegated to IMO's highest technical body, the Maritime Safety Committee (MSC), the task of developing technical measures to strengthen port and on-board security. This initiative resulted in MSC Circular 443 on "Measures to Prevent Unlawful Acts against Passengers and Crew on Board Ships," issued September 1986. This circular had a limited scope, in that it applied only to passenger ships on international voyages, and the port facilities that serve them. But it also contained a series of recommendations (for governments, port authorities, ship owners, masters and crews) that would provide a touchstone for post-9/11 developments. In particular, the circular recommended that each ship and port facility develop a security plan, designate a security officer, undertake a security survey and seek opportunities for training.[57]

The paragraph in UN General Assembly resolution 40/61 requesting IMO to act had been proposed by the Italians, and supported by Austria and Egypt (as well as the European Community). It was these three states that prepared an initial draft of a convention for the suppression of unlawful acts against the safety of maritime navigation, and requested that the item be placed on the agenda of the IMO Council (the executive organ of IMO, with member states elected by the IMO Assembly), held in November 1986. As with developments in ICAO at this time, the process of drafting and adopting a new convention proceeded consensually. With the IMO Council having established a drafting committee, work began on a convention. As a compromise arising out of the definition of "ships," the committee decided early on to develop an accompanying optional protocol to cover acts against fixed platforms at sea.[58] By June 1987, the Council referred drafts to the Legal Committee. In March 1988, following a conference on the final drafts in Rome, the Convention for the Suppression of Unlawful Acts Against the Safety of Maritime Navigation and the Protocol for the Suppression of Unlawful Acts Against the Safety of Fixed Platforms Located on the Continental Shelf were opened for signature. The main objective of the convention and protocol is to facilitate the prosecution and extradition of persons committing acts of violence at sea, including seizing ships by force, threatening passengers and crew, and placing devices likely to destroy or damage ships or platforms. The convention and protocol entered into force in 1992.

A further initiative of IMO at this time was the commencement of training programs, regional seminars and workshops to increase awareness and disseminate methods and procedures for implementing IMO measures on maritime security. In this regard, the MSC sought the assistance of the United Nations Development Programme (UNDP) and donor countries. In addition to recipient states and donors, these workshops often brought together multiple international organizations (including ICAO, the International Association of Airport and Seaport Police, and the UN High Commissioner for Refugees, among others) as well as regional organizations, non-government and private sector bodies (key players in international shipping). In these developments, we can observe the emergence and institutionalization of a professional network mobilized around the issue of maritime security.

The relative consensus engendered in the 1985 resolutions of the General Assembly and Security Council reappeared on several occasions over the balance of the 1980s. Subsequent resolutions of the General Assembly again "unequivocally condemned" terrorism as criminal and made a broader request to specialized organizations within the UN system to consider actions against terrorism—a further extension of the piecemeal approach. The Universal Postal Union, the World Tourism Organization and the IAEA were mentioned specifically,[59] and all duly reported their activities to the Secretary-General.[60] In the Security Council, the 1988 abduction and subsequent hanging of a US Marine serving as a military observer with the UN Truce Supervision Organization (under the UN Interim Force in Lebanon), yielded two resolutions condemning hostage-taking.[61]

The response to the December 1988 bombing of Pan American flight 103 over Lockerbie, Scotland, provides further evidence of consensus in this period. Subsequent to a special request from the United States and the UK, a special meeting of the ICAO Council was convened in

February 1989. Later that year, the Council delegated to the ICAO Legal Committee responsibility for drafting a convention on the marking of plastic explosives. The urgency of ICAO's work on this topic was underscored in resolutions from both the General Assembly and the Security Council, and by the September 1989 explosion of UTA flight 172 over Niger.[62] The Convention on the Marking of Plastic Explosives for the Purpose of Detection was subsequently opened for signature on 1 March 1991, although it did not attract enough signatories to enter into force until June 1998.

These instances of consensus were punctuated by moments of contention, reviving the tone of cooperation from earlier in the decade. General Assembly resolution 42/159 (7 December 1987) was adopted only after a Syrian proposal for a conference on terrorism had been effectively set aside in the Sixth Committee. The title of the Syrian proposal set out its objective, that is, the "Convening, under the auspices of the UN, of an international conference to define terrorism and to differentiate it from the struggle of peoples for national liberation." It was supported by Yemen, Algeria and Kuwait, on behalf of the Group of Arab States, but opposed by the United States and others, for whom the reaffirmation of 40/61, and the extension of counter-terrorism measures through the specialized agencies, were the priority.[63] In February 1986, the United States used its veto to oppose Security Council resolutions condemning the interception of Libyan aircraft by Israel, aircraft mistakenly thought to be carrying terrorists. It did so again in April, and was joined by France and the UK, when other Council members sought a resolution condemning US military strikes on Libya in response to the bombing of a discotheque in Berlin frequented by US servicemen.[64]

It is perhaps for these reasons that the incremental progress made was generally greeted with skepticism by contemporary observers, who noted that the implementation of rules and norms by states was weak and, therefore, multilateral measures were not likely to be effective against the terrorist threat.[65] After all, at no stage had the international community succeeded in defining "terrorism" (meaning, again, that different states could interpret measures in different ways). Similarly, oft-repeated language concerning the rights of those resisting various forms of oppression could be interpreted as a "saving clause" in conventions and resolutions.[66] In her 1989 monograph, *Terrorism and International Cooperation*, Martha Crenshaw struck a decidedly skeptical note, arguing that[67]

> Although the international community appears to recognize the need for cooperation against terrorism, national interests have dominated

the treatment of the issue and unanimity has been rhetorical rather than practical ... At the global level, collaborative measures are formal and redundant, adopted as a reaction to events. There can be no doubt that sensitivity to the political implications of the issue of terrorism has limited international cooperation. The search for juridical solutions in the United Nations has not been notably successful.

She goes on to reflect that the inadequacy of UN fora had led states to seek other means for cooperating, including through regional organizations (especially the OAS, the Council of Europe and the European Community), the G7, NATO (which established a working group on terrorism in 1987), Interpol, and networks of professionals (such as in law enforcement, where operational-level cooperation was more likely to occur). Further, she noted, states were inclined to avoid large membership bodies to seek cooperation with smaller groupings of like-minded states, or bilaterally.[68] In speculating on the conditions for future cooperation, she drew upon realist theories of international relations, suggesting that only a significant—and unlikely—realignment of the costs and benefits of cooperation would yield more collaborative outcomes.[69]

This is a somewhat damning indictment of the importance of the UN in this period. Nonetheless, the end of the Cold War would soon provide the opportunity to revisit these claims. Moreover, in retrospect, the significance of UN measures in this period was not their impact or effectiveness, but rather that they help explain the form and outcomes of cooperation in subsequent years, including after 9/11.

The 1990s: the Security Council leads, competition follows

As the Cold War began to thaw, and then ended, the promise of more effective multilateral cooperation against terrorism loomed.[70] To some extent, this promise was borne out, as two shifts in the UN response to terrorism occurred in this period. First, the Security Council rose in prominence as an actor, increasingly making use of its powers under Chapter VII of the UN Charter (i.e. conceiving terrorism as a threat to "international peace and security") to pass resolutions binding on the membership of the world body.[71] Second, beyond the focus on norm-building and rule-making—which had comprised much of the substance of the UN's response to date—further tools were added, giving the UN a more operational role. In particular, sanctions against supporters of terrorism were imposed by the Security Council on three occasions over the decade: against Libya in 1992, Sudan in 1996 and the Taliban in 1999.[72] While significant, however, neither of these developments should be interpreted as a complete departure from past patterns of interaction on terrorism in the UN, as a durable consensus remained elusive and, across the multiplicity of fora within the UN system, instances of cooperation were offset by familiar disagreements about whether and how to respond to terrorism.

The first reference to terrorism in the Security Council in the 1990s came in the preamble of resolution 687 (3 April 1991). That resolution, following the first Gulf War, specified the conditions that Iraq must meet in order to have the recently imposed (August 1990) comprehensive sanctions lifted. In it, the Council deplored Iraq's threat to use terrorism in response to the outbreak of conflict. Beyond this reference alone, the initial experience in implementing a multilateral response to Iraq's invasion of Kuwait served to underscore the potential for cooperative action through the UN. That sense of optimism appeared again in the January 1992 meeting of the Council held at heads of state level, the first such meeting since the founding of the UN. The statement that emerged from that gathering noted the "momentous changes" in the international system and committed members of the Council to a broad range of principles, including norms of collective security, peacemaking, disarmament, arms control, and non-proliferation. Also included was an expression of "deep concern" regarding international terrorism and an undertaking that the international community should "deal effectively with all such acts."[73]

In his address to the Council on that occasion, US president George H. W. Bush endeavored to translate such broadly stated principles into specific actions. He described collective action against Iraq as a "testament to the UN's mission," adding that "we must deal resolutely with ... renegade regimes." He then drew attention to the role of Libya in the destruction of Pan Am 103 and UTA 772, demanding that it "heed the call of the Security Council."[74] This latter comment was a reference to Security Council resolution 731 (21 January 1992) (introduced by France, the UK, and the USA) which had condemned the bombings, and called on Libya to accede to requests (from the sponsoring states) to bring those responsible to justice. Although resolution 731 was adopted unanimously, efforts to enforce it only occurred with abstentions from five Council members, including China. Resolution 748 (31 March 1992) imposed a first round of sanctions on Libya, including aviation bans (i.e. denial of take-off, landing, overflight and the servicing of aircraft), an arms embargo, diplomatic sanctions (including a call to reduce staffing at embassies in Libya) and a travel ban on Libyan nationals involved in terrorism.

In response, the Gaddafi regime made some gestures at complying with the Council's demands. In its public statements within the UN and elsewhere, Libya continued to reject terrorism. Nonetheless, a stalemate emerged and Western states sought further sanctions.[75] Resolution 883 (11 November 1993) tightened the aviation ban and added limited sanctions on oil-transporting equipment, as well as freezing Libyan assets abroad. This resolution again attracted abstentions from China and three other Council members. It also received less support among European states, which relied upon Libyan oil exports. Despite the additional measures, Tripoli failed to forward the relevant suspects for trial. That situation prevailed until mid-1998, when Organization of African Unity states announced their willingness to flout the UN sanctions if a settlement could not be reached within a few months. Negotiations ensued, leading to an agreement that Libya would hand over two suspects for trial under Scottish law in the Netherlands. This agreement was enshrined in Security Council resolution 1192 (27 August 1998), but it was not until April 1999—when the Secretary-General confirmed that the suspects had arrived at The Hague—that the sanctions were suspended. The sanctions were not formally removed until 2003 (with resolution 1506 (12 September 2003)), after Libya accepted responsibility for the acts in question, disavowed terrorism and agreed to compensate victims. Both France and the United States abstained from that resolution and the latter maintained sanctions upon Libya (as a "state sponsor of terrorism," designated by the State Department) until June 2006.

Like the Libya sanctions, Security Council measures against Sudan were designed to compel the release of suspected terrorists, this time those involved in the "terrorist assassination attempt" on Egyptian president Hosni Mubarak, in Addis Ababa in June 1995.[76] With China and Russia abstaining, resolution 1054 (26 April 1996) imposed diplomatic sanctions and travel restrictions on Sudanese government officials. Sudan took the position that the requested suspects were not in the country and, moreover, that it condemned terrorism. Further sanctions, including an aviation ban, were threatened with resolution 1070 (16 August 1996) (China and Russia again abstaining), but these never went into effect. Concerned about the humanitarian consequences of sanctions elsewhere, especially in Iraq, the Council commissioned a "pre-assessment report" on the likely humanitarian effects of the sanctions. That report was enough to persuade Council members not to activate the tougher measures. In the meantime, though, Sudan had taken steps to restore its reputation, tarnished by the UN sanctions and by its inclusion in 1993 on the US State Department's list of "state sponsors of terrorism." Indeed, as evidenced in the Secretary-

General's report pursuant to resolution 1070, Sudanese government officials admitted to having had an "open-door" policy that, "in the name of pan-Arabism, might have enabled some terrorists to enter the country easily." Those same officials pointed out that the government,[77]

> had adopted a number of new measures, such as reinstating the regulation requiring all foreigners to have entry visas, reviewing the status of all foreigners who had entered the country at a time when no entry visas were required, requesting a number of Egyptians, Palestinians and "Arab Afghans" (including Oussama Ben Laden) [sic] to leave the country (which they had), and undertaking very close scrutiny of applications for visas to enter, leave or reside in the Sudan.

By most accounts, bin Laden left Sudan for Afghanistan in May 1996.[78] In turn, the measures imposed by resolution 1054 were formally lifted in 2001 (resolution 1372 (28 September 2001)) after the Non-Aligned Movement and African states petitioned the Council on Sudan's behalf. While Council members agreed that Sudan had met its obligations under 1054, the United States abstained and Sudan remains on its list of state sponsors.

Unlike the Libya and Sudan examples, the final case of terrorism-related sanctions imposed by the Security Council in the 1990s is ongoing. In the next chapter, I detail the contemporary dilemmas surrounding the targeted sanctions imposed on the Taliban, al Qaeda and related individuals and entities. But it is important to note that these measures emerged out of growing Security Council concern for the situation in Afghanistan in the late 1990s.[79] The Council finally turned to sanctions, passing resolution 1267 (15 October 1999) unanimously. The resolution imposed targeted financial sanctions on persons and entities designated by the Sanctions Committee (created under the resolution), in addition to an aviation ban. The resolution demanded that the Taliban ensure that territory under their control was not being used by terrorists and that Osama bin Laden be extradited to a country where he faced prosecution. To be sure, following the bombings of the US embassies in Nairobi and Dar es Salaam in August 1998, bin Laden was now highly sought after by the United States. Subsequently, resolution 1267 was supplemented with an arms embargo, travel ban and other measures with resolution 1333 (19 December 2000) (China and Malaysia abstaining). That resolution also established a committee of experts to report on the implementation of the sanctions. Acknowledging considerable challenges in this regard, the Council unanimously adopted resolution 1363 (30 July 2001), establishing a monitoring group based in New York and a Sanctions Enforcement and Support Team, comprising up to 15 persons, to be deployed to states bordering Afghanistan. Preparations to establish the Group and Team were underway when the terrorist attacks of 9/11 occurred.

An intuitive question in reflecting on the use of multilateral sanctions in the cause of counter-terrorism is "do they work?" That question can be difficult to answer as it presupposes that a straightforward cause-and-effect relationship can be discerned in complex situations such as these.[80] Nonetheless, the Council's efforts at this time are generally interpreted to have had mixed effects. Of the three cases, Libya is most often portrayed as a success, as the demands of the Council were eventually acceded to by the targeted state.[81] The Sudan sanctions were perhaps "more symbolic than real," but seem to have at least been influential in convincing Khartoum to expel bin Laden.[82] Regarding the Taliban case, implementation was weak prior to 9/11 and the effects of the measures are difficult to specify. But even if the impact of sanctions on terrorists and their sponsors were limited, it is important to see the use of sanctions by the Council in this period in its broader context. That is, they were part of an historical uptick in the use of sanctions by the Council—hence, Cortright and Lopez's characterization of the 1990s as the "sanctions decade."[83] More than this, these sanctions regimes were part of a trend from comprehensive sanctions (such as those imposed on Iraq, which had unintended humanitarian consequences) to targeted sanctions. In turn, states have sought to refine the tool of targeted sanctions.[84]

As I argue below, over time, the 1267 sanctions reflect a good deal of institutional learning within the Council. To be more precise, despite the challenges they still face, the 1267 or "al Qaeda-Taliban" sanctions today are a much more sophisticated instrument (in terms of procedures for listing targets, and for reporting on and monitoring implementation) than they were when first imposed in 1999. In sum, while I have pointed out several areas in which counter-terrorism spilled over into related domains (a consequence of the spread of the piecemeal approach), the use of multilateral sanctions to act against terrorism reflects the opposite trend, i.e. developments in the practice of multilateralism (the increasing use of targeted sanctions) became relevant to counter-terrorism cooperation.

Beyond sanctions, there are further examples of the Council's increasing willingness to discuss terrorism issues after the Cold War. Presidential statements were issued in response to terrorist violence in 1994 (condemning attacks in Buenos Aires and London), and in 1995 and 1996 (condemning attacks in Israel designed to undermine the Middle East peace process). With resolution 1189 (13 August 1998), the Council condemned the bombings of the US embassies in Kenya and Tanzania. Russia took advantage of its presidency of the Council to draw attention to terrorism, having suffered an increase in violence related to the situation in Chechnya. Resolution 1269 (19 October 1999) condemned terrorism in general terms and, with language reminiscent of General Assembly resolutions on the topic, called on states to take a range of counter-terrorism measures (such as denial of financing and safe haven) and to sign the anti-terrorism conventions. While its Russian sponsors considered the resolution "a kind of anti-terrorism manifesto"—and although it was adopted unanimously—other delegations prefaced their vote by drawing attention to the need to differentiate between terrorism and national liberation movements, and by reminding the Council of the urgency of the problem of state terrorism, especially as practiced (in their view) by Israel.[85]

It is also interesting to note instances where the Security Council was silent on certain counter-terrorism actions. For example, the United States did not seek approval in the Council before launching military strikes against Iraq in 1993 (in retaliation for an assassination attempt against former president George H. W. Bush), and against Afghanistan and Sudan in 1998 (responding to the bombing of the US embassies in Kenya and Tanzania). As Ed Luck reminds us, these latter actions, pursued by the Clinton administration, reflect a preference for unilateralism that contrasts sharply with the post-9/11 record of the George W. Bush administration.[86]

The General Assembly Responds

How, then, did a more active Security Council affect the debate on terrorism in the General Assembly? The first General Assembly action on terrorism in the 1990s, culminating in resolution 46/51 (9 December 1991), was in many ways a continuation of measures adopted in the 1980s. In both preambular and operational paragraphs, language referring to the legitimacy of struggles for national liberation and self-determination was maintained. The resolution again avoided the issue of convening an international conference to define terrorism, as distinct from national liberation movements (the Syrian proposal), by asking the Secretary-General to seek the views of member states on the matter. Also, requests to the specialized organs within the UN system—to take action within their domains—were continued. In other ways, however, the resolution foreshadows a change in the dynamics of cooperation, for example, by discarding the long title (inherited from 1972) in favor of simply "Measures to eliminate international terrorism." When the item was taken up two years later in the Sixth Committee, Algeria and India put forward the view that a general convention on terrorism was needed, as a next step in strengthening the international legal response to terrorism. As no consensus could be found on this proposal, the matter was put out for consultation. No resolution was adopted in 1993 (breaking the biannual cycle) and the Secretary-General was asked to solicit states' opinions on the idea.[87] As the subsequent report reflects, member states remained split, with the Algerian and Indian position attracting some support, but being firmly opposed by the United States and European Union.[88] In the view of the latter states, who cited past experience, any broad discussion of terrorism would be counterproductive, in sharp contrast to the relative success of the piecemeal approach. These positions were reconciled in informal consultations that resulted in the "Declaration on Measures to Eliminate International Terrorism," annexed to General Assembly resolution 49/60 (9 December 1994). While the declaration (adopted without a vote in both the Sixth Committee and the Assembly) is largely repetitive of prior resolutions, it assigns further tasks to the Secretary-General, including collecting data on the status of multilateral, regional and bilateral agreements, as well as national counter-terrorism laws (to be submitted by states), and reviewing the existing international legal framework with a view to identifying areas for further action.

In spite of this compromise, the arguments concerning a general convention on terrorism, and a conference on defining terrorism, reappeared a year later, in the negotiations that led to resolution 50/53 (11 December 1995). That resolution did little beyond reaffirming the declaration. Seeking to advance the issue, India went so far as to circulate a draft comprehensive convention on international terrorism in the Sixth Committee in 1996.[89] In retrospect, this was one of several developments at the time that resulted in the further (but again incremental) broadening and deepening of the General Assembly's consideration of terrorism. For example, over the course of the early 1990s, several regional, affinity-based and other multilateral groupings became more active on the issue of terrorism. Beyond the Council of Europe and the OAS, the Organization of African Unity, the Organization of the Islamic Conference, and the South Asian Association for Regional Cooperation all made statements on terrorism-related issues (the last having concluded a convention in 1987). Similarly, the Non-Aligned Movement (NAM) had endorsed the General Assembly's declaration. Perhaps more importantly, however, the G7 group of states had by this time institutionalized a series of ministerial-level meetings on terrorism, elaborating detailed multilateral counter-terrorism plans in July 1996, with Russia participating.[90] The effect of the G7 agreement was to expand the scope of multilateral counter-terrorism, to issues such as terrorist financing, travel document security and terrorist bombing, thereby extending the logic of the piecemeal approach to a wider range of actions. This shift was duly reflected in the Secretary-General's report in September 1996, as requested under preceding General Assembly resolutions.[91] There, the Secretary-General suggested a range of issues that states might consider as topics of new terrorism-related conventions. However, in deference to the disagreement among states concerning a general convention, the Secretary-General rather hedged his bets, noting that the rise in concern for terrorism in related multilateral fora might lead states to "review whether a more global approach to counter-terrorism could be taken in addition to the sectoral efforts that have been made so far."[92]

These developments yielded three outcomes of note in the Sixth Committee, reflected in resolution 51/210 (17 December 1996).[93] First, that resolution broadened the Assembly's counter-terrorism agenda. For example, it includes the most detailed language on terrorist financing then seen from the Assembly, including references to the possible abuse of charities by terrorists. Second, the Assembly established both an Ad Hoc Committee and a Working Group of the Sixth Committee (the former meeting in the spring, the latter in the autumn) to advance new legal instruments against terrorism. These fora were to be open to all member states, as well as UN specialized agencies. The primary tasks assigned to these bodies were the development of conventions on terrorist bombing and the suppression of acts of nuclear terrorism. The emphasis on terrorist bombing resulted from a US proposal and should be viewed in light of the truck bomb attack on US military officers in Dhahran, Saudi Arabia, in June 1996, as well as the 1993 attack on the World Trade Center in New York City. The proposal on acts of nuclear terrorism came from Russia. Importantly, through informal consultations it was agreed that, following the conclusion of these two instruments, the Ad Hoc Committee would "address means of further developing a comprehensive legal framework of conventions dealing with international terrorism" (para. 9). So, once again, a satisficing approach was taken to the issue of whether or not a comprehensive convention on terrorism was needed.

Finally, following a UK proposal, resolution 51/210 adds a supplementary declaration to the 1994 declaration. The supplementary measures address the relationship between international refugee law and terrorism, clarifying that states should ensure that asylum seekers are not connected to terrorism in any way before granting refugee status. In addition, the supplementary declaration restates that the principle of "extradite or prosecute" should apply to terrorists, whether or not an extradition treaty is in existence between states.

The period following resolution 51/210 was very productive for the Assembly. Two conventions were negotiated through the Ad Hoc Committee and Working Group. First, the elaboration of the International Convention for the Suppression of Terrorist Bombings proceeded in prompt fashion.[94] Working from a French draft, submitted on behalf of the G7 (with Russia), the Ad Hoc Committee encountered few points of controversy, although last-minute negotiations were required to clarify the application of the convention to the armed forces of states. Beyond defining and prohibiting the act of bombing, the convention introduces several innovations. For example, in addition to including the principle of "extradite or prosecute," the convention facilitates the temporary transfer of suspects from their state of nationality to a requesting state (willing to pursue a prosecution), on the understanding that, if convicted, any sentence could be served in the state of nationality. Further, the convention takes a maximal approach to jurisdiction, permitting states to pursue prosecutions concerning attacks on their facilities (e.g. embassies) abroad. Finally, the convention is the first to use the word "terrorism," although it is not conclusively defined. The convention was opened for signature in January 1998 and entered into force in May 2001.

Second, the International Convention for the Suppression of the Financing of Terrorism also emerged at this time. The initiative in this regard was once again taken by the French, who aimed to close a perceived gap in international law and circulated a draft convention on the topic in November 1998. The issue was subsequently assigned to the Ad Hoc Committee in resolution 53/108 (8 December 1998), where it was accorded priority over the commencement of debate on a general convention against terrorism. Working from the French draft, the Committee and Working Group were able to conclude negotiations within a year and the Assembly adopted the convention with resolution 54/109 (9 December 1999). The convention creates the offence of terrorist financing, which is defined in Article 2:

> Any person commits an offence within the meaning of this Convention if that person by any means, directly or indirectly, unlawfully and wilfully, provides or collects funds with the intention that they should be used or in the knowledge that they are to be used, in full or in part, in order to carry out:

(a) An act which constitutes an offence within the scope of and as defined in one of the [international instruments related to terrorism]; or

(b) Any other act intended to cause death or serious bodily injury to a civilian, or to any other person not taking an active part in the hostilities in a situation of armed conflict, when the purpose of such act, by its nature or context, is to intimidate a population, or to compel a government or an international organization to do or to abstain from doing any act.

While this latter phrase (subparagraph (b)) effectively creates the offense of "terrorism" (for the purpose of prohibiting the financing of such acts), the drafters included it in the knowledge that the existing conventions did not cover the variety of terrorists' tactics.[95] The convention attracted only four signatories prior to 9/11, and subsequently entered into force in April 2002.

Despite these achievements, the Committee and Working Group also provided fora for states to disagree on several issues. The debate on a convention for the suppression of acts of nuclear terrorism stands out in this regard. The Russian draft met resistance on several points, as some states felt that the debate on the comprehensive convention ought to take precedence, that the definition of "nuclear terrorism" ought to include the actions of states, that the IAEA (which participated in the negotiations) was the more appropriate forum to develop the convention, and that the elimination of nuclear weapons altogether ought to be pursued.[96] The division among states was somewhat familiar here, generally pitching NAM states against supporters of the proposed convention, including Western states and Russia.[97] These issues proved difficult to overcome and negotiations ground to a halt, with no formal or informal consultations pursued in the spring 1999 meetings of the Ad Hoc Committee.[98] A series of bilateral and informal consultations took place on-and-off in subsequent years, but the political will to address stated differences did not emerge until after 9/11.

The Committee and Working Group also encountered other political disagreements, including the issue of whether a high-level conference on terrorism should be convened under UN auspices. This proposal came out of the NAM Heads of State meeting in 1998 which, along with its successor meetings, was cited in the preambular language of multiple Assembly resolutions.[99] Resistance to this initiative (in the Committee) echoed that a decade earlier, in response to the Syrian proposal (for a conference to define "terrorism" as distinct from national liberation movements), namely, "it was felt that a conference might provide an invitation to embark on a rhetorical exercise on issues that have historically confounded practical solution, thus distracting the Ad Hoc Committee from continuing to take pragmatic measures."[100] While the matter had been assigned to the Committee in 1999, by 2000 the Assembly resolved only to keep it on the Committee's agenda.[101]

Further evidence of political dissension in the period can be found in the abstentions of Lebanon and Syria from the aforementioned Assembly resolutions in 1999 and 2000. For more than a decade, resolutions under this heading had been adopted without a vote. In a reminder that fundamental differences were never far from the surface, the Syrian delegate explained the 2000 abstention by arguing that "a clear distinction should be established between terrorism as a crime and the legitimate struggle of peoples against foreign occupation, as in the case of the struggle against Israeli occupation. Occupation and State-sponsored terrorism [are] the most odious forms of terrorism."[102]

Political differences were also evoked by the consideration of the Indian draft comprehensive convention on international terrorism, which finally commenced in the Working Group in the fall of 2000.[103] States were divided about the utility of such a convention, with many preferring the less politically charged piecemeal approach.[104] In light of this, and past attempts to tackle terrorism per se, it is perhaps not surprising that several issues proved immediately contentious, including: the definition of terrorism; the scope of the convention (i.e. whether acts of resistance to foreign occupation, and state terrorism, would be included); and the relationship between the comprehensive convention and the existing, piecemeal instruments.[105] Discussions on these points were underway in the Committee and Working Group when 9/11 occurred.

A further effect of resolution 51/210 was to continue the gradual integration of the specialized agencies, and other multilateral bodies, in the UN's response to terrorism. The annual reports submitted by the Secretary-General—as requested under the "Measures to eliminate" resolutions—document states' implementation of necessary measures, as well as the actions of a wide range of international and regional organizations.[106] These reports confirm that the number of international and regional organizations drawn into the remit of multilateral counter-terrorism continued to grow. Moreover, the roles played by these bodies became more diverse. Those with longer involvement in counter-terrorism—especially the IAEA, ICAO and IMO—maintained the tasks of developing and disseminating (through training and related assistance) technical rules and standards, often working within highly specialized professional communities. In this way, they made important advances regarding "preventive" aspects of counter-terrorism. As noted above, the IAEA's expertise was drawn upon in the failed negotiations for a convention on the suppression of acts of nuclear terrorism. The International Committee of the Red Cross, Interpol, and the Asian-African Legal Consultative Organization, among others, also participated in these and other negotiations. In 1997, the General Assembly itself enhanced the capability of the UN Secretariat on counter-terrorism by deciding to create the Terrorism Prevention Branch within the Office of Drug Control and Crime Prevention (now the UN Office on Drugs and Crime). The Office had been established as a result of the consolidation of the UN's criminal justice organs, which had addressed terrorism on several occasions in the past.[107] However, the Branch was assigned two staff members only, limiting its range of activities to servicing other organizations, and some preliminary research and analytical tasks.

As the example of the Terrorism Prevention Branch underscores, the limited capacity of some bodies involved in multilateral counter-terrorism at the time means that their impact was limited to declaratory statements. Similarly, other activities had a very broad scope, making it difficult to measure their actual influence in suppressing terrorism. For example, UNESCO's "Towards a Culture of Peace" project ran education and other programs to eradicate violence and promote reconciliation. It is obvious that the involvement of such bodies in the broader counter-terrorism effort did not then succeed—and has not now succeeded in suppressing terrorist activity. However, suffice it to note here that an expanding web of institutions was becoming involved in multilateral counter-terrorism, developing a repertoire of responses to terrorism that would be called upon amid the urgency of the post-9/11 period.

Assembly action on "human rights and terrorism"

An additional branch of General Assembly activity on terrorism in the 1990s concerns a series of resolutions titled, "Human Rights and Terrorism," assigned to the Third Committee (Social, Humanitarian and Cultural). In its Declaration and Program of Action, the 1993 Vienna Conference on Human Rights asserted that,[108]

> The acts, methods and practices of terrorism in all its forms and manifestations as well as linkage in some countries to drug trafficking are activities aimed at the destruction of human rights, fundamental freedoms and democracy, threatening territorial integrity, security of States and destabilizing legitimately constituted Governments.

The international community should take the necessary steps to enhance cooperation to prevent and combat terrorism.

Without a vote, the Third Committee recommended a resolution unequivocally condemning terrorism as an activity "aimed at the destruction of human rights."[109] The matter was included thereafter in the Committee's deliberations on "Human rights questions" and two subsequent resolutions (in 1994 and 1995) were adopted without the need for a vote in the Committee or the Assembly.[110] However, that consensus fractured over time, with the effect that later resolutions in this stream were adopted with abstentions from many states, including the United States and the European Union (EU) states.[111] To put this development into context, it is apt to note that the item was taken up in the highly politicized Commission on Human Rights (then under the Economic and Social Council; now re-formed as the Human Rights Council, under the General Assembly) in 1994. In this forum, several Western states, along with others, voiced opposition to the view that terrorist groups could "violate human rights" as such, arguing that human rights obligations are imposed upon states, and that state and non-state actors should not be equated.[112] This view hardened over time. The Commission's annual resolution on the issue—often proposed by Turkey—was first subjected to a vote in 1997, when more than 20 states abstained.[113] By 2000, the Western bloc actively voted against the proposed resolution, arguing again for a clear distinction between state obligations to observe human rights and the criminal acts of terrorists.[114] Also playing on this tension were the series of reports submitted by a Special Rapporteur, appointed by the Sub-Commission on Prevention of Discrimination and Protection of Minorities upon a request of the Commission first made in 1994.[115] These reports were wide-ranging, exploring the causes of terrorism and tending to take the view that there were indeed important linkages in fact and law between terrorism and human rights violations, i.e. contrary to the position taken by the United States, the EU, and others.[116] Against this background, the United States and its allies argued that terrorism ought to be dealt with in the Sixth Committee only.

Conclusion

What ought we to conclude from the pattern of cooperation on terrorism in UN fora in the post-World War II, pre-9/11 period? Consistent with Crenshaw's skeptical view, quoted above, many observers at the time interpreted the UN's role to be very modest indeed. For example, recall Pillar's reflection that, "Much multilateral diplomacy is essentially mood music [to other instruments of counter-terrorism], but even mood music can be helpful in reaching more specific goals."[117] Multilateralism, he claimed, was useful for three reasons: to provide a "formal structure for making demands and implementing responses"; to help build international norms against terrorism; and to facilitate the development of common standards (e.g. for aviation security, the marking of explosives, etc.) that help prevent terrorism.[118] On this view, the nature of international organizations limits their capacity to play more than a bit-part in responding to terrorism. More stridently, Wilkinson argued that, "The huge gulf between the rhetoric and the reality of international cooperation against terrorism is a powerful illustration of the extent to which the realist paradigm actually dominates and shapes the perceptions of the majority of political leaders and their citizens in the contemporary international state system."[119]

Indeed, there was plenty of reason to doubt the effectiveness of the UN as a tool of counter-terrorism. Although UN mechanisms recorded several achievements, especially concerning the elaboration of rules and norms, limitations were readily apparent. Rates of ratification of the terrorism-related conventions were quite modest, and implementation did not always follow. (The latter problem also impacted the effectiveness of the sanctions that the Security Council imposed upon supporters of terrorism.) Without an agreed-upon definition of terrorism, states retained the flexibility to interpret multilateral measures in line with their own preferences. Genuine disagreements regarding states' understandings of terrorism and appropriate responses to it emerged with some frequency.

Nonetheless, the pre-9/11 record of multilateral counter-terrorism is instructive for several reasons. For example, increasing levels of cooperation in this period reflect the willingness of powerful states, especially the United States, to use multilateralism to advance their interests. Of course, multilateralism was not seen as a primary tool in this regard, and was utilized quite selectively.[120] When it occurred, the form of cooperation was distinctive, manifesting a piecemeal approach, with outreach to the specialized agencies, an emphasis on norm-building and rule-making, and the elaboration of procedures for states to report on their implementation of UN measures. These elements formed the basis of the post-9/11 response. In other words, in reacting to the 9/11 attacks, states did not have a "blank slate" to work with and, not surprisingly, those measures already in place were adapted and extended in the urgency of the moment.

3 Multilateral counter-terrorism and the United Nations after 9/11

The eleventh of September, 2001, was the second Tuesday of the month. That day had traditionally been set aside to celebrate the International Day of Peace, which is commemorated at UN Headquarters in New York City by a ceremony featuring the ringing of the "peace bell."[1] The 2001 ceremony was postponed. When it was held three days later, UN Secretary-General Kofi Annan observed that, "We ring this peace bell in solidarity with the people and Government of the United States, at this moment of immense suffering and bereavement ... We have lost family, friends and colleagues."[2] As his comments reflect, the attacks of 9/11 were in many ways a deeply personal experience for diplomats and staff at the UN, not least because of a fear that the organization itself might be targeted. Consequently, the initial response of the UN community to the attacks included solemn memorial and prayer services, a blood drive overseen by the UN Medical Service and fundraising for victims of the attacks. As one delegate noted in the General Assembly on 12 September, "We, the United Nations diplomatic community, are not only parking rule violators—we do love this city, we love New York, and we want to help it."[3]

In analyzing multilateral counter-terrorism in the aftermath of 9/11, it is plausible to speculate—but difficult to know—whether, or how much, the experience of that day at a personal level affected the political response from actors within the UN system. Certainly, as I illustrate in the first part of this chapter, the days and weeks immediately after 9/11 were a period of "extraordinary politics," when "political structures are fluid," and, "[b]oth leaders and ordinary citizens feel a stronger-than-normal tendency to think and act in terms of the common good."[4] Such "extraordinary politics" is most clearly manifested in the assertive role of the Security Council after 9/11, especially in passing resolution 1373 (28 September 2001) (Appendix B). This resolution builds on and extends preceding measures, broadening the scope of multilateral counter-terrorism through the UN. Having been passed under chapter VII of the UN Charter, the provisions of 1373 are mandatory for member states. Moreover, the resolution requires that states report on their implementation of its provisions, creating a subsidiary body—the Counter-terrorism Committee (CTC)—to monitor their performance. These attributes of 1373 had the effect of confirming the Security Council as the most prominent of the UN organs on counter-terrorism, setting the agenda for subsequent action. Whereas states had historically been more comfortable with incremental steps toward counter-terrorism cooperation, 1373 represents a bold leap forward: it is difficult to imagine that it could have emerged in the absence of 9/11.

Of course, periods of "extraordinary politics" are temporary and eventually give way to the "more mundane politics of contending parties and interest groups."[5] Although the Council's response to 9/11 initially attracted broad support across the UN system, consensus did not last. Rather, despite several achievements, dilemmas regarding the implementation of 1373 soon emerged and other actors began to question the role of the Council. Indeed, within the Council itself, the unity of purpose that had produced 1373 became fragmented over time, correlative with the divisive debate about war in Iraq. The second part of this chapter tracks the efforts of the General Assembly and the Secretary-General to correct the course set by the Council after 9/11. I show that, in spite of the dramatic post-9/11 developments, the travails of the UN in this period manifest longstanding political disputes among states, such that there is both continuity and change in the pattern of multilateral counter-terrorism. Indeed, in enacting the signature achievement of the Assembly on this issue since 9/11—the 2006 Global Counter-terrorism Strategy (Appendix C)[6]—one could be forgiven for experiencing a sense of déjà vu.

The third part of this chapter asks whether the metaphorical pendulum, having swung both ways, has come to rest in the middle. Here, I point to several signs that a relatively stable equilibrium has indeed been struck. For example, the Strategy has helped make multilateral counter-terrorism more politically palatable for many member states. The operational aspects of the Security Council's response have been rationalized and rendered more effective in recent years. Related to this, the volume of norm-building and capacity-building activity that has occurred through the specialized agencies of the UN—and their wide-ranging contacts with organizations beyond the UN—has been quite remarkable. Beyond the "piecemeal approach" of earlier eras, counter-terrorism is now more institutionalized than ever before. With that said, there remains a measure of predictability about the dynamics of cooperation at the UN, as political scraps and incendiary rhetoric are far from a thing of the past. Several longstanding disputes remain, not least concerning the way in which to define "terrorism." More recently, new disputes have emerged, for example, over how to implement the measures elaborated by the Council and Assembly. In other ways, too, instances of cooperation remain undergirded by competition among states regarding the elaboration of norms and the allocation of resources in the effort against terrorism. As a result of these quarrels, it is too early to argue that multilateral counter-terrorism in the post-9/11 period represents a genuine break from the past. In concluding the chapter I suggest that, between incremental steps and a bold leap forward, the UN system has shown itself to be surprisingly nimble in the post-9/11 period, learning from and adapting to events, all the while subject to vicissitudes of cooperation and contestation among states.[7]

The Security Council responds to 9/11

The Security Council meeting on 12 September 2001 began with a minute of silence. Subsequently, the Secretary-General and the Council members gave short addresses, expressing their shock and revulsion at the attacks, passing on their condolences to the United States and pledging to redouble the efforts of the international community in suppressing terrorism. Several members noted that, although the United States was the target, the violence that day constituted a broader attack, against humanity, freedom and the values of the UN Charter. Indeed, the initial response of the Council is notable because of its implications under the Charter. Resolution 1368 (12 September 2001) was passed unanimously, with delegates standing in unity (rather than raising their hands, as is usual) to indicate their approval of the pre-negotiated text. In both preambular and operational paragraphs, the resolution characterizes terrorist acts as "threats to international peace and security," confirming that terrorist violence could be dealt with under Chapter VII of the Charter. Under that chapter (see Art. 39), the Council may decide to act using force (Art. 42) or means other than force (Art. 41) to respond to such threats. In addition, Article 51 affirms that states possess an "inherent right of individual or collective self-defence if an armed attack occurs." Resolution 1368 explicitly recalls this right. While the Council had acted under Chapter VII to impose sanctions on the supporters of terrorism in the 1990s, this was the first time that the Article 51 right of self-defense had been cited in the context of violence by a non-state actor. It was under this provision that the

United States, and later its allies, formally notified the Council of its intention to use force against the Taliban regime in Afghanistan, beginning in October 2001. But, as some commentators have noted, this approach provides a potentially broad mandate to states seeking to use force against terrorists.[8] Indeed, in notifying the Council regarding the war in Afghanistan, the United States portentously stated that, "We may find that our self-defense requires further actions with respect to other organizations and other States."[9] This precedent has been cited by other states to justify armed action against non-state adversaries.[10] With that said, despite the attempt to link Saddam Hussein and terrorism, resolution 1368 did not comprise a central plank of the US justification for war against Iraq in 2003.[11] Here, recall that the United States had *not* sought multilateral approval prior to using force in response to terrorist attacks in the 1990s. For this reason, Ed Luck points to resolution 1368 as evidence that the Bush administration, despite oft-heard allegations of a proclivity for unilateralism, had a clear initial preference for pursuing counter-terrorism multilaterally.[12]

Further evidence of this can be found in resolution 1373 (28 September 2001), which was introduced by the United States. That resolution has a broad scope and requires states to implement counter-terrorism measures in such areas as financial regulation, migration and customs controls, travel document security, movements of arms, explosives and nuclear, chemical and biological materials, and the use of communications technologies. In addition, the resolution calls for bilateral, regional and international cooperation on law enforcement, administrative and judicial matters, in extradition proceedings, and as regards the exchange of information regarding terrorism. The resolution also establishes a subsidiary organ of the Council, the Counter-Terrorism Committee (CTC), to which states are required to submit reports on their implementation of the measures. Above, I described the passage of 1373 as extraordinary. In identifying its unique attributes, it is apt to note those aspects of the resolution that were not so new.

First, many of the substantive provisions of 1373 are drawn from elsewhere and an analysis of the text reveals many similarities to existing measures. For example, the paragraphs on terrorist financing resemble those in the 1999 Terrorist Financing Convention and in prior resolutions of the General Assembly and the Council.[13] Other provisions, too, had found earlier expression in Assembly and Council resolutions, including those regarding the obligations of states (not to organize, assist, instigate, participate or acquiesce in terrorist acts), the importance of cooperation (including language urging states to sign the relevant international instruments), the integrity of asylum processes (to ensure they are not abused by terrorists) and the links between terrorism and other forms of crime.[14] In this sense, 1373 represents a consolidation of existing norms. Second, the mechanism created to enforce 1373—the establishment of a subsidiary organ of the Council, to which states would submit reports—had precedents in the Council resolutions imposing sanctions throughout the 1990s, and in Assembly practices in the 1980s and 1990s. Regarding the latter, recall the succession of reports submitted by the Secretary-General pursuant to the Assembly resolutions on "Measures to Eliminate Terrorism," discussed in Chapter 2.[15] Regarding the former, the practice of states submitting reports on their implementation of sanctions to subsidiary organs of the Council had been utilized on multiple occasions, even if compliance was irregular and reports often lacked substance.[16] Third, like other UN pronouncements on terrorism, resolution 1373 contains no definition of "terrorism" and, therefore, leaves the term open for interpretation. Rather, the resolution sidesteps such political questions, elaborating things that states should do—a further extension of the logic of the piecemeal approach.

In these ways, while the language of 1373 is not exactly "cut and pasted" from existing measures, it is very much a product of what came before it. In other ways, however, 1373 is of course different. Many of the existing measures had been elaborated in fora other than the Council and were of a non-binding or discretionary character. In contrast, 1373 binds member states (by virtue of having been passed under Chapter VII), obliging them to enact the broad counter-terrorism program set out therein. In this regard, it is important to note that 1373 does not consolidate *all* of the terrorism-related norms that had been elaborated across the UN system up to that point. Rather, the drafters were more selective. For example, the linkage between human rights and terrorism—the subject of ongoing disagreement in the Third Committee of the Assembly—was left out.[17] On the flip side, 1373 did include several existing measures that were not yet in force, or that were contained in treaties that many states had not signed or ratified (such as those reflecting the Terrorist Financing Convention).[18] In this way, the elaboration of such a broad framework for counter-terrorism in one fell swoop by the Council threw into relief the labors of the Assembly in negotiating a comprehensive convention on the topic. Overall, with 1373, the ability of the Council to exercise binding authority meant that it could bypass or trump developments in other parts of the UN system. These attributes set 1373 apart, suggesting that the cadence of multilateral counter-terrorism had changed.

In addition, the unique nature of 1373 provided a propitious environment in which to implement the resolution. The resolution attracted broad endorsement, both within the Council and beyond it. In the General Assembly debate on terrorism in early October 2001, member states were almost uniformly warm towards 1373, with only the Tanzanians questioning whether such an assertive role for the Council was desirable.[19] Words were followed with action. The first chair of the CTC, British ambassador Sir Jeremy Greenstock, tapped into this consensus, elaborating an initial work program by late October. That plan emphasized: the establishment of contact points in states and international organizations (with whom to liaise on the resolution); the appointment of a core of experts in the various substantive areas covered by the resolution, to aid the CTC; the circulation of guidance to states, to help them fulfill their obligation to report to the Committee; the identification of "best practices," to give operational expression to the specific requirements of 1373; and the role that the Committee may play in effectively brokering technical assistance, by linking potential donors and recipients.[20]

The plan also called for transparency in the work of the CTC, concerning relations with other actors in the UN system as well as internal procedures (which were set out formally in a separate document).[21] Early challenges to the implementation of the resolution were identified and addressed with this ideal in mind. For example, the Security Council, meeting at the ministerial level, passed a separate resolution (1377) in November expressing its "determination to proceed with the implementation of [1373] in full cooperation with the whole membership of the United Nations," and noting in particular that "many States will require assistance in implementing all the requirements of … 1373."[22] In this regard, the Council gave a clear mandate to the CTC to develop its roles in identifying "best practices" to guide implementation, and in facilitating technical assistance. In this context, too, the question of human rights was soon raised. On this point, Greenstock, the CTC chair, was clear that the Committee had no mandate to monitor the human rights record of member states. However, other methods were sought to address concerns surrounding this issue.[23] For example, the practice of having the High Commissioner for Human Rights brief the CTC commenced in February 2002. In September of that year, the Office of the High Commissioner circulated "further guidance" for states reporting under 1373, intended as a human rights-focused supplement to the guidance previously issued by the Committee.[24] In his October address to the CTC, High Commissioner de Mello raised the concern that many states were "enacting anti-terrorism legislation that is too broad in scope (namely, that allows for the suppression of activities that are, in fact, legitimate), or … seeking to fight terrorism outside the framework of the court system."[25] He urged the CTC to appoint a human rights advisor. This specific idea did not materialize for several years. In the interim, the CTC undertook to remain cognizant of human rights concerns in the course of its work and took measures to regularize its interaction with the Office of the High Commissioner for Human Rights.[26] Subsequently, with resolution 1456 (2003)—passed in a special session at the foreign minister level—the Council addressed the relationship between human rights and counter-terrorism directly, stating that, "States must ensure that any measures taken to combat terrorism comply with all their obligations under international law ... in particular international human rights ... law."[27]

The early achievements of the CTC gave much cause for optimism about the prospects for multilateral counter-terrorism. After one year in operation, Greenstock reported to the Council that the CTC enjoyed high levels of cooperation and support from member states.[28] The Council positively reviewed the structure and work of the Committee twice in 2002. State compliance with the reporting requirement was far higher than that achieved by any previous subsidiary organ of the Council and, by the end of May 2003, all states had submitted at least one such report. The number of signatories to the existing UN conventions and protocols related to terrorism increased over this period, as called for in 1373. CTC experts made progress in identifying relevant "best practices" and in establishing a means to facilitate technical assistance, in the form of a matrix, compiling requests for assistance and the response of donors. By July 2003, the CTC was aware that 159 states were receiving capacity-building assistance of some kind, whether in legislative drafting, financial law and practice, policing and law enforcement, or immigration and customs controls.[29] Recognizing that the Committee could not oversee implementation of 1373 by itself, the CTC introduced innovative mechanisms to reach out to other international organizations, as well as regional and subregional bodies. In March 2003, more than 65 such organizations met in New York to discuss cooperation and coordination among the growing number of actors in the field of multilateral counter-terrorism. The statement that emerged from that meeting identified information sharing, complementarity (i.e. avoiding duplication), independent effort (that is, each body acting to pursue its own mandate) and political momentum as the keys to sustainable collaboration.[30] Follow-up meetings were subsequently held in October 2003 (in Washington, D.C., in collaboration with the Organization of American States' Inter-American Committee against Terrorism)[31] and in March 2004 (in Vienna, in collaboration with the Organization for Security and Cooperation in Europe (OSCE) and the UN Office on Drugs and Crime). Among the attendees were specialist and functional organizations, both within and outside of the UN system. Recall that several regional and specialist organizations had been engaged in multilateral counter-terrorism for many years, both through the development of the terrorism-related conventions and as part of the General Assembly's counter-terrorism work. In the post-9/11 period, under the aegis of the CTC, this collaboration was remade on a much grander scale. More broadly, achievements recorded by the CTC led to claims that a "new paradigm for the international community to combat international terrorism" had emerged.[32] This is a sharp contrast to the pessimistic conclusions drawn by Crenshaw, Wilkinson and Pillar, respectively, in discussing the pre-9/11 period, quoted in Chapter 2.

Following 9/11, the Security Council also acted to extend the reach of the financial sanctions, travel ban and arms embargo first imposed with resolutions 1267 (1999) and 1333 (2000). Resolution 1390 (28 January 2002) broadened the category of persons and entities that could be included on the list of targets to cover "Usama bin Laden, members of the Al-Qaida organization and the Taliban and other individuals, groups, undertakings and entities associated with them." Resolution 1390 also reassigned the Monitoring Group that had been established under resolution 1363 (2001). No team would be deployed to assess the implementation of the sanctions on Afghanistan's borders and the group would work from New York. Several procedural refinements were made to the sanctions, to advance their effectiveness and fairness. For example, targets were permitted to request exceptions in specified circumstances.[33] Further, the Sanctions Committee (the subsidiary organ of the Council, created under 1267 (1999)) was requested to improve circulation of the list of targets and was mandated to undertake country visits to monitor the implementation of the measures on the ground, while states were requested to improve the quality of identifying information they forwarded to the Committee with listing requests.[34] In the context of the evolution of the Council's use of sanctions, these moves were quite progressive, integrating lessons from the Stockholm Process on Implementing Targeted Sanctions, which reported in February 2003.[35]

With that said, it was not all smooth sailing for the revised sanctions regime. The monitoring group reported on four occasions in 2002, each time noting the significant challenges to the full implementation of such measures, including some apparent reluctance among states to forward names to the Committee to be added to the list.[36] By mid-2003, the group noted that states were reporting on court challenges to the sanctions measures (in particular the assets freeze on targeted individuals), especially in the European Union and the United States.[37] Moreover, the group itself raised hackles in some quarters, as its wide-ranging reports were perceived by some to lack rigor and to venture off topic.[38] On the whole, however, the sanctions acquired a new vigor after 9/11. Certainly, despite hesitation among some states, the list of individuals and entities to whom the sanctions applied grew notably in this period, with many names having been put forward by the United States.

While these achievements were unprecedented, the political momentum that undergirded the Council's initial response to 9/11 began to dissipate over the course of 2003, such that, by early 2004, both the CTC process and the al Qaeda-Taliban sanctions were in need of a make-over. We can point to three reasons for this. First, it is apt to recall the unprecedented scope of 1373. Put simply, 1373 sets the bar very high and, with the benefit of hindsight, the task of implementing it was always likely to exceed the capacities of many member states. The same might be said for the targeted sanctions, which require a highly advanced technical capacity to monitor the financial sector and control the movement of goods and people across borders. Despite early successes, there is nothing in the history of multilateral counter-terrorism (and nothing in the past experience with targeted sanctions) to suggest that states could achieve such high standards without a sustained, resource-intensive effort, entailing high levels of political commitment. As such, there is a sense of inevitability about the loss of momentum here, as the full impact of the Council's action became more widely appreciated across the international community.

Second, far from engendering the kind of political will necessary to fulfill the ambitious agenda it had set, the Council often had the opposite effect on the broader membership. The fact that counter-terrorism cooperation had evolved so quickly—and as a consequence of a non-democratic body—led to claims that the Council was being unduly intrusive in the domestic affairs of states, and that it had assumed a "legislative" role for itself.[39] The political sensitivities concerning terrorism in the pre-9/11 era could not simply be set aside by the assertive exercise of Chapter VII powers and, as I describe further below, too many states were displeased by the substance and pace of change. In addition, intervening events sharpened divisions and attenuated the authority and credibility of the Council. Although it is difficult to know for certain how much the discordant debate in the Council concerning Iraq in 2002 and 2003 impacted multilateral counter-terrorism, there can be little doubt that it helped undermine the broad consensus that emerged after 9/11.

Third, by late 2003 or so, several technical problems in implementing both 1373 and the sanctions were well known. Regarding the former, in January 2004, the chair of the CTC reviewed its progress by reporting to the Council on "Problems encountered in implementing 1373."[40] In frank terms, the report drew attention to significant deficiencies in states' implementation of the resolution in each of its substantive areas. Moreover, the report noted that the Committee itself was poorly placed to advance its mandate much further, given its structure and working methods. For example, without further expertise on the coordination and provision of technical assistance, the CTC could not adequately perform its role as facilitator, for which there was an established need. Similarly, the division of labor that had evolved within the CTC meant that there were inconsistencies in the assessment of states' reports. The chair's review concluded that, "the implementation of Resolution 1373 is encountering serious problems, both at the States and at the Counter-Terrorism Committee levels. These should be tackled in a comprehensive way due to the intimate interaction between them and the urgency of the task."[41]

Related concerns were afflicting the implementation of the sanctions. In its final report, in December 2003, the monitoring group again noted the difficulties many states faced in this regard.[42] Of particular concern was the list—the key operational mechanism for multilateral action against al Qaeda, the Taliban and their associates. Earlier improvements, enacted with resolution 1455 (2003), did not go far enough, it seems. On country visits, members of the group found that officials in capitals were not well informed, or not aware at all, of UN-imposed measures. Many states remained reluctant to forward names to the Sanctions Committee for the purpose of listing. Those that did did not always provide adequate identification information. States were facing legal challenges to their implementation of the sanctions against listed individuals, and one state (Sweden) reported that it had delisted two individuals, while another (Switzerland) had initiated action to delist several individuals according to the procedure that had been established by the Committee. These cases illustrated the kinds of concerns that human rights advocates continued to articulate regarding the negative impacts of multilateral counter-terrorism, further weakening the legitimacy of the Council's response. In sum, the monitoring group warned that, "Without a tougher and more comprehensive resolution—a resolution which obligates States to take the mandated measures—the role played by the United Nations in this important battle risks becoming marginalized."[43]

Beyond the discrete problems with the CTC process and the al Qaeda-Taliban sanctions, their overlapping mandates created confusion in many permanent missions and capitals.[44] In addition, states were concerned about the burdens imposed by reporting requirements. Many claimed to be suffering from "reporting fatigue" and rates of compliance slackened over time. Both the CTC and the Sanctions Committee were conscious that their work ought to be better coordinated, but specific mechanisms for doing so were not well established. Moreover, rather than acting to simplify matters in the short term, the Council actually added to its counter-terrorism machinery on two occasions in 2004.

The first of these measures, resolution 1540 (28 April 2004) addresses the problem of weapons of mass destruction (WMD) (that is, nuclear, chemical and biological weapons) proliferation with regard to non-state actors, including terrorists. It obliges states to refrain from supporting such actors in their attempts to "develop, acquire, manufacture, possess, transport, transfer or use nuclear, chemical or biological weapons and their means of delivery" (para. 1). In addition, it requires states to "adopt and enforce appropriate, effective laws" to ensure that non-state actors are not able to gain WMD (para. 2). Here, recall that the domestic control of nuclear materials had been a point of contention in negotiating the 1980 Convention for the Physical Protection of Nuclear Material. In this way, 1540 is a further example of the Security Council exceeding existing measures in an issue area long subject to broader multilateral action. Also, the resolution created another subsidiary organ of the Council to monitor its implementation (the "1540 Committee"), provided for the formation of another expert group to assist the committee (i.e. matching those under 1373 and the al Qaeda-Taliban sanctions regime), and imposed a further reporting requirement on states. The assertive role of the Council attracted critical attention in the lengthy negotiations over the resolution.[45] Some states objected to the idea that non-proliferation should be dealt with in this way without also calling for disarmament. Further, the sponsors of the resolution, the USA and the UK, offered reassurances that such measures, passed under Chapter VII of the UN Charter, would not form the basis of a case for the use of force against those alleged to be non-compliant. Still, the resolution was passed unanimously as states acknowledged that, despite existing counter-proliferation and arms control measures, there was a gap in international law concerning the risk of WMD terrorism. The focus on non-state actors is of particular relevance in this regard.[46]

The Council's response to terrorism was further broadened through a Russian-initiated resolution—resolution 1566 (8 October 2004)—passed in the wake of the hostage crisis and massacre of more than 330 people, including 186 children, at School Number One in Beslan, North Ossetia. The Council established a working group to identify "practical measures" that could be pursued by the Council against "individuals, groups or entities involved in or associated with terrorist activities" but not already identified by the al Qaeda-Taliban Sanctions Committee (para. 9). The group, which would comprise members of the Council, would also consider the establishment of a fund for victims of terrorism, financed through voluntary commitments (para. 10). (This latter idea was not itself new and had appeared, for example, in General Assembly resolutions under the title "Human rights and terrorism" since the mid-1990s.) Beyond the creation of the group, no formal subsidiary organ of the Council was instituted and no reports were requested from member states. The group has not been particularly active since its inception.[47]

How, then, did the Security Council respond to the apparent crises afflicting 1373 and the al Qaeda-Taliban sanctions? Regarding the CTC, the "problems encountered" report was followed within a month by a "Proposal for the Revitalisation of the Counter-Terrorism Committee."[48] The proposal represented a significant departure from existing practice by reorganizing the expert staff attached to the Committee in the form of a "Counter-Terrorism Committee Executive Directorate" (CTED), headed by an executive director. In effect, the executive director would oversee the day-to-day tasks involved in monitoring the implementation of 1373, under the strategic direction of the Committee. The proposal was endorsed with resolution 1535 (26 March 2004), which created CTED as a special political mission and provided that its experts and staff would be international civil servants, rather than contracted experts. In these ways, the Council moved to shore up the resource and staffing dilemmas that had constrained CTC action to that point. Javier Rupérez, the Spanish ambassador to the United States, was appointed as the first executive director by mid-2004 and an organizational plan was submitted to the Council in August.[49] Regarding the sanctions, resolution 1526 (30 January 2004) introduced a further series of measures designed to improve their implementation. Most notably, the monitoring group was replaced by an Analytical Support and Sanctions Monitoring Team ("Monitoring Team"), comprising up to eight experts under the direction of a coordinator. Among its designated tasks, the Team was mandated to undertake field visits to analyze implementation of the sanctions on the ground and to make recommendations to the Sanctions Committee on this basis. In March 2004, British diplomat Richard Barrett was appointed as coordinator.

These efforts to reform the Council's post-9/11 initiatives served to illustrate the seriousness of the Council in leading multilateral counter-terrorism. However, in the short term at least, problems persisted. For example, the process of forming CTED proved more challenging than first anticipated due to unwieldy budget and personnel processes.[50] Indeed, with UN budget decisions made by the highly politicized Fifth Committee of the General Assembly, the resourcing of CTED was subject to criticism from some developing states, whose priorities lay elsewhere.[51] As a result, CTED did not become fully staffed until September 2005, only becoming operational that December. For this period, the task of building the capacity of states to suppress terrorism across the globe was impeded by the need to build the international bureaucracy that could oversee the effort. In the meantime, the Council had acted again to extend the CTC's mandate. Resolution 1624 (14 September 2005) is unique in the history of multilateral counter-terrorism, in that it requires states to prohibit incitement to terrorism, also calling upon states to strengthen border controls and promote "understanding among civilizations."[52] The CTC was mandated to monitor states' implementation of the resolution. In a separate resolution, the Council urged greater cooperation between the CTC and regional and subregional organizations.[53]

The first two reports submitted by the Sanctions Monitoring Team, for its part, provided stark reminders of the challenges presented in implementing those measures.[54] Of particular concern to the new Team was the list of individuals and entities. On review, the Team found that the list contained inconsistencies and inaccuracies, and that deceased persons remained on it. In order to generate more consensus around the list, and to have more states submit names, the Team recommended that the Committee provide states with better guidance on its scope, by defining what it means to be "associated with" al Qaeda or the Taliban (the Team suggested a broad interpretation, knowing that the Committee would review all requests for listing). The Team noted that at least 13 lawsuits had been filed around the world on issues relating to the sanctions, and recommended that the procedures for being removed from the list be revisited to ensure fairness and efficiency. For all of these reasons, the Team commented that the credibility of the list was being questioned by many states, as reflected in the general disinclination to forward names and in declining willingness in terms of reporting and implementation.

Several of the Team's suggestions were picked up in resolution 1617 (29 July 2005), which introduced further procedural innovations designed, once more, to enhance the legitimacy and effectiveness of the measures. For example, that resolution defines "associated with," thereby clarifying the scope of the sanctions.[55] It also imposes the requirement that states forwarding names for the list do so using a "statement of case," describing the basis of the request. Further, the resolution provides a template, in the form of a "checklist," to assist states in fulfilling their obligation to report to the Committee on the implementation of the resolution, especially regarding their actions against listed individuals and entities. Finally, the resolution renews the mandate of the Monitoring Team, requesting that it work further to improve the integrity of listing and delisting procedures.

Over the course of 2004, political problems also impacted the work of the newly established 1540 Committee. Pakistan was a member of the Council at the time and felt as though the resolution was aimed at itself (although it nonetheless voted in favor of 1540). Pakistan subsequently used its membership of the 1540 Committee to obfuscate its work, which did not begin in earnest until Pakistan rotated off the Council.[56]

In sum, the years following 9/11 represented an unprecedented era of activity in multilateral counter-terrorism, led by the Security Council. Beyond amply demonstrating its willingness to act, the Council also showed an ability to innovate and respond to problems. Exceeding past responses, the Council sought to carve out genuinely operational roles for itself, imposing broad requirements on states and following through with mechanisms to monitor and facilitate implementation. With this said, the Council's response does not reflect a shared vision among its members—or even among its permanent five members—as to what role the body should play in multilateral counter-terrorism, beyond asserting leadership. In this regard, as Rosand et al. have observed, improvisation trumped strategy.[57] Not surprisingly, the Council met resistance in various forms, leading some observers to doubt that a "new paradigm" for counter-terrorism had emerged and suggesting instead that the post-9/11 period was really just a continuation of the pattern of cooperation from the pre-9/11 period.[58] To put this resistance to the Council in context, it is necessary to trace developments within other parts of the UN system.

The General Assembly: responding to the response of the Security Council

If the immediate post-9/11 period was characterized by bold and assertive action in the Security Council, the record of the General Assembly is more modest. In its first plenary meeting after 9/11, on 18 September, the Assembly passed a resolution condemning the attacks, offering condolences to the people of the United States, and calling for international cooperation to bring the perpetrators of the attacks to justice and, more generally, to eradicate international terrorism.[59] In the following weeks and months, the states in the Assembly expressed support for Council resolution 1373 and, through the Sixth Committee, came closer than ever to concluding the comprehensive convention on international terrorism.[60] These actions, however, were not a harbinger of a new and lasting consensus on terrorism within the Assembly, nor a signal that the leadership role staked out by the Council was acceptable to the broader membership of the UN. Over time, the Assembly's work on terrorism became more diverse as states sought new ways in which to influence the course set by the Council. Still, despite identifying shortcomings in the Council-led approach, it was only with the intervention of the Secretary-General, Kofi Annan, that the Assembly was able to formulate a more robust response of its own, in the form of the 2006 Global Counter-terrorism Strategy. Even then, in terms reminiscent of the past, many states were frank that the Strategy does not meet their interests. In other words, as the Council put a premium on the operationalization of its response, the Assembly's efforts remained mired in politicization—perhaps an unavoidable consequence of being the most democratic organ of the UN.

Beyond condemning the 9/11 attacks, the resolutions passed by the General Assembly in the autumn of 2001 were remarkable only insofar as they mirrored Assembly practice from the pre-9/11 period. The resolution on "Measures to Eliminate International Terrorism" that year referred to Council resolutions 1368, 1373 and 1377 and urged states to provide technical assistance to those in need.[61] The Sixth Committee's Ad Hoc Committee and Working Group were renewed, but debate on key items (the comprehensive convention, the convention for the suppression of acts of nuclear terrorism and the convening of a high-level debate on terrorism under the auspices of the UN) took on a familiar hue soon enough. The pre-9/11 stalemate concerning the resolutions on "Human Rights and Terrorism" continued, with many Western (and other) states abstaining on such measures.[62] Although consensus had been sought, many members remained unhappy about the characterization of the relationship between human rights breaches and terrorist acts. One new measure taken in 2001 was a request (out of the Fifth Committee (Administration and Budget)) that the Secretary-General develop a proposal to strengthen the Secretariat's Vienna-based Terrorism Prevention Branch (TPB) of the UN Office of Drug Control and Crime Prevention.[63]

In 2002, three new resolutions were added to the Assembly's work on terrorism. Out of the Third Committee, a Mexican-initiated resolution on "Protecting Human Rights and Fundamental Freedoms while Countering

Terrorism" was adopted without a vote (in both the Committee and the Assembly).[64] Unlike the "Human Rights and Terrorism" resolutions, the focus of the new measures was on the duty of states to observe human rights in formulating and implementing counter-terrorism policies. This approach was capable of achieving consensus, but several states noted concerns in explaining their votes, including that the resolution did not refer to 1373 (as remarked by the Danish delegate, on behalf of the EU), that the Sixth Committee is the appropriate forum for discussing terrorism (the United States) and that a shortcoming of the new resolution was its failure to acknowledge the root causes of terrorism (Pakistan and Indonesia).[65] Also out of the Third Committee, a Russian-initiated resolution on hostage-taking was adopted without a vote.[66] In the First Committee, the Indians introduced a resolution on "Measures to Prevent Terrorists from Acquiring Weapons of Mass Destruction."[67] The resolution cited recent action taken by the IAEA (including the establishment of an advisory group on nuclear security) and called for the Secretary-General to report on measures undertaken by international organizations concerning the linkage between terrorism and the proliferation of WMD. Also that year, the Assembly, in its now-annual "Measures to Eliminate" resolution, noted the Secretary-General's report on "Strengthening the Terrorism Prevention Branch of the Secretariat."[68] That report recommended a modest increase in staffing (three professional positions and two general service posts) to pursue an expanded work program, including the facilitation and provision of legislative drafting and capacity-building assistance, as well as the identification and dissemination of best practices. In these ways, the report noted, the work of the TPB would aid the implementation of 1373. This proposal was subsequently adopted.[69] Also in 2002, it became clear that 1373 and the work of the CTC had overtaken reporting requirements imposed on states by the Assembly under the "Measures to Eliminate" resolutions. The Secretary-General's report under this stream duly referred readers to the CTC website for more detailed reports on states' counter-terrorism measures.[70]

In 2003, the work of the Assembly diversified further still, with the Third Committee producing a resolution on "Strengthening International Cooperation and Technical Assistance in Promoting The Implementation of the Universal Conventions and Protocols Related to Terrorism within the Framework of the Activities of the Centre for International Crime Prevention."[71] Just as the TPB had received more resources and a broadened mandate, the Centre (also part of the Vienna-based UN Office of Drugs and Crime) had launched a "Global Program against Terrorism," bolstering the capacity of the UN itself to be a provider of

certain forms of technical assistance. The resolution had been introduced to the Third Committee by the Economic and Social Council
(ECOSOC), receiving unanimous support.

Also of note in the Assembly in 2003 was the gradual sharpening of
the criticism that multilateral counter-terrorism was giving rise to significant breaches of international human rights law. While the resolution on "Human Rights and Terrorism" was subject to the familiar
political division, action under the title "Protecting Human Rights and
Fundamental Freedoms while Countering Terrorism" was more telling.
In his report with this name (as requested in the previous year's resolution), the Secretary-General noted that the human rights bodies of
the UN were now monitoring breaches of a range of well-established
human rights principles (including the right to life, freedom from torture, conditions and treatment in detention, the right to a fair trial and
freedom of expression) arising from state counter-terrorism actions.[72]
In this regard, the Commission on Human Rights had passed a succession of resolutions requesting that the High Commissioner assume
an active role on this issue (beyond merely liaising with the CTC) and
renewing the mandate of the Special Rapporteur initially appointed by
the Sub-Commission on the Promotion and Protection of Human
Rights in the mid-1990s, who had been working at the margins of the
debate ever since.[73] The Commission had also received a briefing on
human rights and counter-terrorism from Human Rights Watch, indicating the growing activism on the issue from the NGO sector.[74] In its
2003 resolution on "Protecting Human Rights," the Assembly noted
the Secretary-General's report, the action taken by the Human Rights
Commission, and the passage of Security Council resolution 1456 (which
contained direct language regarding the observation of human rights
law while countering terrorism).[75] This Assembly resolution also extended
the work of the High Commissioner in the area, requesting a report
on whether existing human rights mechanisms within the UN would
be able to address questions concerning the compatibility of national
counter-terrorism measures and international human rights law.

One year later, the High Commissioner's report made clear that, while
actively engaged on the issue, the existing treaty monitoring bodies and
special procedures mechanisms (i.e. Special Rapporteurs with mandates on specific topics) could not cover the field. Rather, the report
concluded that "there are significant gaps in the consideration of national
counter-terrorism measures by the UN human rights system," and, as
such, "the UN has been unable to address the compatibility of national
counter-terrorism measures with international human rights obligations
in a comprehensive and integrated way."[76] To put together the report,

the Commission had resolved to create a one-year position—an independent expert to assist the High Commissioner on the issue of protecting human rights while countering terrorism.[77] The Commission also requested that the independent expert report on ways to strengthen the promotion and protection of human rights while countering terrorism. This step, which was "noted with appreciation" by the Assembly, ensured that the human rights issue would remain on the agenda, providing an institutional focus for member states to elaborate their concerns about the unintended consequences of the Security Council's assertiveness.[78]

In addition to advancing the debate on "protecting human rights," the General Assembly in 2004 maintained its focus on weapons of mass destruction (duly noting the passage of Security Council resolution 1540 (2004)) and strengthening international cooperation and technical assistance relating to the terrorism conventions and protocols.[79] The reports of the Secretary-General on these issues serve to illustrate the increasing depth and breadth of multilateral action against terrorism, with multiple specialist bodies of the UN, as well as regional and subregional organizations, engaged in efforts to regulate WMD and provide counter-terrorism assistance.[80] Although political divisions continued to dominate the debate on "human rights and terrorism," perhaps the signature achievement of the Assembly at this time was progress, in the Working Group and Ad Hoc Committee of the Sixth Committee, towards the completion of the International Convention for the Suppression of Acts of Nuclear Terrorism. Recall that that process had begun almost a decade earlier but progress had slowed as the priorities of the Committee (to focus on the nuclear or the comprehensive convention) and the scope of the convention (entailing, as that does, an implicit understanding of what constitutes "terrorism") were in dispute. By early 2005, however, sufficient political will to move forward on nuclear terrorism had gathered, partly as a result of developments in other parts of the UN system—specifically, the Secretary-General's High-Level Panel report on "Threats, Challenges and Change" and his 2005 report, *In Larger Freedom*, described below.[81] The convention defines radioactive and nuclear material and creates a series of offences, including the possession or use of such materials with intent to cause death or injury, to damage property, or to compel a person, international organization or state from doing or refraining from an act.[82] Signatories are required to criminalize these acts and to extradite or prosecute persons alleged to have committed them. The Assembly approved the convention in April 2005. It was opened for signature in September of that year and entered into force in July 2007. To date, it is the only new convention that states have agreed to since the attacks of 9/11 (although protocols under the IMO Suppression of Unlawful Acts instruments—i.e. against the Safety of Maritime Navigation and against the Safety of Fixed Platforms Located on the Continental Shelf—were also added in 2005).

To commemorate the sixtieth session of the General Assembly, world leaders gathered at the UN in New York in September 2005. The resulting World Summit Outcome document, passed as a resolution of the Assembly, devotes 11 paragraphs to terrorism, restating existing measures but also urging the Security Council to rationalize the reporting requirements under its three terrorism-related regimes (deriving from resolutions 1267, 1373 and 1540).[83] Again in 2005, the Assembly continued its norm-building regarding "Measures to Eliminate Terrorism," and terrorism and WMD.[84] Out of the First Committee (Disarmament and International Security), a new resolution on "Preventing the Risk of Radiological Terrorism" drew universal support, urging states to sign the new convention and implement a series of measures advanced through the IAEA.[85] But perhaps more influential than these developments were those relating to the protection of human rights while countering terrorism. The independent expert appointed by the Commission on Human Rights reported in February 2005, recommending that, "given the gaps in coverage of the monitoring systems of the special procedures and treaty bodies and the pressing need to strengthen human rights protections while countering terrorism, the Commission on Human Rights should consider the creation of a special procedure with a multidimensional mandate to monitor States' counter-terrorism measures and their compatibility with international human rights law."[86] This proposal was acted upon by the Commission, which created the new position of "Special Rapporteur on the promotion and protection of human rights and fundamental freedoms while countering terrorism," with a three-year appointment.[87] The rapporteur was given a broad mandate to liaise with bodies across the UN system (including the Security Council and its subsidiary organs), to research, analyze and report on the promotion and protection of human rights and fundamental freedoms while countering terrorism, and to identify "best practices" with regard to counter-terrorism in the context of human rights norms. A Finnish law professor, Martin Scheinin, was appointed Special Rapporteur in July and elaborated a framework to implement his mandate, including an emphasis on country visits, in September.[88] These developments were welcomed by the Assembly.[89] In his first statement to the CTC, in October, the Special Rapporteur delivered a frank appraisal of emerging trends. Terrorism, he argued, was being used as a justification to stigmatize political, ethnic, regional or other groups for political gain, to question or compromise the absolute prohibition against torture and all forms of cruel, inhuman or degrading treatment, to limit free speech, to tighten immigration controls and to expand the powers of the police. Having begun his work by reviewing state reports to the CTC, the Special Rapporteur noted that the Committee had been inconsistent in its feedback to states when human rights and counter-terrorism prerogatives came into conflict. Beyond such specific criticism, the institutionalization of a human rights monitor in the field of counter-terrorism was one way for non-Council members to hold the Council accountable in exercising the broad mandate it had given itself after 9/11.

The Secretary-General: negotiating paths of resistance

As I have described it so far, the work of the General Assembly after 9/11 was broad in scope, disaggregated across committees and, to a large extent, derivative of Security Council measures. The failure of the Assembly to endorse the Council-led approach more directly no doubt contributed to its loss of momentum, especially regarding the CTC process, from 2003. For all its activity, however, the Assembly, much like as the Council, did not elaborate a single, coherent strategic response to terrorism. For that to occur, it would take the incremental intervention of the then Secretary-General, Kofi Annan. The role of the Secretary-General is often conceived as having two parts: that of a "secretary," merely responding to the wishes of member states and; that of "general," actively managing the preferences of states and exercising influence towards desired outcomes. Through the numerous reports described above (and in previous chapters), it is clear that there was much work as "secretary" on counter-terrorism issues in the post-9/11 period. But what of his role as "general"? According to Ed Luck (who was writing before 2006), the Secretary-General's "vigorous and courageous statements" following 9/11 were not followed through in the years afterwards, and he "did not make much use of his bully pulpit."[90] In retrospect, however, the main Assembly outcome of this period—the 2006 Global Counter-terrorism Strategy—suggests that the Secretary-General negotiated the space between the Security Council (and the powerful states within it) and the General Assembly (with its near-universal membership) in a studied and deliberate fashion.

In October 2001, following the passage of Council resolutions 1368 and 1373, and Assembly resolution 56/1, the Secretary-General, upon his own initiative, formed a "Policy Working Group on the UN and

Terrorism." The mandate given to the group was very broad: "to identify the longer-term implications and broad policy dimensions of terrorism for the UN and to formulate recommendations on the steps that the UN system might take to address the issue."[91] The members of the group were senior civil servants, past and present, drawn from across the UN system, as well as academic and NGO experts. The group met on several occasions, addressing a range of specific issues in subgroups, and producing a final report in August 2002. The limited membership of the group, especially the fact that it did not draw upon the expertise of member states, perhaps limited the impact of the report.[92] Nonetheless, the report makes two prescient claims.

First, members of the group were clear that any contribution to counter-terrorism by the UN was likely to be modest. "Counter-terrorism activities," the group noted, "are carried out through bilateral and multilateral cooperation among national agencies devoted to law enforcement, intelligence and security. By and large, such measures do not require the organization's involvement."[93] In a similar vein, the group acknowledged that the UN was not "well placed to play an operational role" in counter-terrorism, although the initial experience of the CTC indicated that "there may well be places where the UN system could assist in providing and organizing capacity-building efforts."[94] Overall, the group considered that the UN should identify those areas where it would have a "comparative advantage." An appropriately limited role would have the added benefit that the UN could not then be "perceived to be offering ... a blanket or automatic endorsement of all measures taken in the name of counter-terrorism."[95]

Second, the group set out, through a tripartite strategy, its own view of where the UN's comparative advantage might lie. UN actions could be grouped under the headings "dissuasion," "denial" and "cooperation." Dissuasion here refers to the implementation of the international legal instruments, the protection and promotion of human rights to prevent terrorism, and the elaboration and dissemination of non-legal norms (e.g. that terrorism is unjustifiable under any conditions). Denial refers to the building of state capacity, à la 1373, to create "inhospitable environments" for terrorists. State capacity is of particular importance in relation to the security of WMD materials, and the prevention and resolution of armed conflicts which, according to the group, provide opportunities for terrorists to operate. Cooperation refers to those mechanisms, both within the UN and beyond it, that can assist in building norms, avoiding the duplication of efforts and achieving comparative advantage among the different multilateral actors involved. Here, the group specifically recommended an "international action plan" elaborated through the UN, the creation of a focal point within the Secretariat to coordinate counter-terrorism activities, and the establishment of a senior-level group within the UN system to review the organization's work in the area, with a focus on assessing coherence and effectiveness.

The tone and substance of the group's report were in many ways out of step with the measures advanced in other parts of the UN system and especially in the Council, where the impetus to act gave way to any such consideration of comparative advantage at a system-wide level. Subsequent events in late 2002 and early 2003, especially the fraught debate in the Council concerning the United States' decision to use force against Saddam Hussein in Iraq, made it more difficult to find consensus on principles to inform the UN response to terrorism. With member states divided, the response of the Secretary-General was again to exercise his discretion to commission experts, this time in the form of a High-Level Panel on Threats, Challenges and Change. The Panel was asked to examine current challenges to peace and security, to consider the role of collective action in responding to them, to review the operation of the major organs of the UN and the relationship between them, and to recommend ways of reforming UN institutions and processes.[96] By focusing on security issues, the Secretary-General aimed to piece together some semblance of consensus out of the Iraq debate. Announcing his intention to form the Panel, in an address to world leaders gathered to open the General Assembly session in September 2003, the Secretary-General was sharply critical of the idea of preemption, injecting urgency into the debate by claiming that, "we have come to a fork in the road." In other words, it was time either to affirm the framework of collective security embodied by the UN, or to seek "radical changes."

The Panel comprised former heads of state, foreign ministers, ambassadors, high-ranking military officers and diplomats, who undertook an extensive series of consultations across the globe. The Panel's December 2004 report was broadly influential, both in terms of the institutional reforms it suggested (such as the formation of the Peacebuilding Commission and the refashioning of a Human Rights Council) and the affirmation of key norms (such as collective security and the "responsibility to protect").[97] The report devotes several pages to the discussion of terrorism, with the Panel setting out several operational criticisms of the UN response as it had evolved. For example, the panel noted that the procedures for listing and delisting from the al Qaeda-Taliban sanctions list were in need of reform. The provision of technical assistance ought to be improved, expanding the role of CTED and creating a trust fund for this purpose. Further, the Council ought to consider imposing some set of predetermined sanctions on states that are capable of complying with mandatory counter-terrorism measures, but nonetheless fail to do so.

While these recommendations underscore the existing role of UN organs, and the Council in particular, in responding to terrorism, perhaps the Panel's more important contribution was to frame these operational issues in a broader strategic context. The need for a more coherent strategic approach was made clear through the panel's regional consultations, where it heard that counter-terrorism often did more harm than good, with serious impacts for human rights and good governance. There was a lack of political will regarding UN-led counter-terrorism actions, which were perceived to focus too narrowly on coercive measures. What was needed, according to the Panel, was a "global strategy of fighting terrorism that addresses root causes and strengthens responsible states and the rule of law and fundamental human rights. What is required is a comprehensive strategy that incorporates but is broader than coercive measures."[98] Whereas the Policy Working Group had put forward a tripartite strategy, the Panel opted for five limbs: dissuasion (i.e. targeting the social, political and economic root causes of terrorism), countering extremism and intolerance (through education and public debate), developing the international legal framework (including particular attention to the observation of human rights), capacity-building, and controlling dangerous materials. Moreover, the Panel urged states to conclude the comprehensive convention on terrorism and, once and for all, to define "terrorism," as this would enhance the legitimacy of UN action in the area.

The breadth of the Panel's recommendations gave plenty of room for the Secretary-General to interpret them in his own way. In early 2005, he began to refine the elements of the strategic approach that had been called for by the Panel. In a speech to the International Summit on Democracy, Terrorism and Security in Madrid in early March, he duly elaborated a "5D" strategy:[99]

> first, to dissuade disaffected groups from choosing terrorism as a tactic to achieve their goals; second, to deny terrorists the means to carry out their attacks; third, to deter states from supporting terrorists; fourth, to develop state capacity to prevent terrorism; and fifth, to defend human rights in the struggle against terrorism.

This proposal was also elaborated in the Secretary-General's *In Larger Freedom* report, prepared to update states on the implementation of the 2000 Millennium Declaration.[100] In putting forward his frame-work, the Secretary-General clearly drew upon the precedents set by the Policy Working Group and the High-Level Panel, but also proffered original elements. For example, the Secretary-General did not refer to social, political and economic factors in discussing the "root causes" of terrorism (as the panel had done, and as most member states using the terms had done). Rather, he redefined "root causes" as the belief that terrorist tactics are effective. This is a rather depoliticized use of the term "root causes" and may be interpreted as a concession to those states (especially in the West) that had shied away from it.[101] Similarly, the Secretary-General took a hard line against the concept of "state terrorism"—a rhetorical device long used by states to bring the politics of the Middle East into debates about terrorism—arguing that states could be held accountable in other ways under international law.[102] On the other hand, the Secretary-General insisted that the comprehensive convention ought to be concluded, raising as that did the prospect of further debate on the definition of terrorism. In addition, the Secretary-General's emphasis on human rights in the context of counter-terrorism gave voice to the concerns of those who had resisted the assertive response of the Council after 9/11. In these ways, in putting together the "5D" strategy, the Secretary-General clearly anticipated the need for compromise, attempting to strike a balance between the discordant views of member states.

Momentum towards the development of a strategy was maintained by virtue of the World Summit Outcome document in October 2005, where states welcomed the Secretary-General's framework.[103] Recall that the Assembly also used this document as an opportunity to call for the rationalization of Security Council counter-terrorism mechanisms. The Secretary-General himself had shown some initiative in this regard, establishing a "Counter-Terrorism Implementation Task Force" (CTITF) in his office in July 2005. Bringing together representatives of the 20-plus UN entities working in the domain of counter-terrorism, the aim of the Task Force is to ensure cooperation and coherence at the system-wide level.

To follow up on the World Summit Outcome document, the Secretary-General submitted a report in April 2006 detailing his proposal for a counter-terrorism strategy.[104] The *Uniting against Terrorism* report again elaborates the "5Ds," with a few updates and refinements. For example, the report again calls for better cooperation and information-sharing among the counter-terrorism bodies of the Council, including the streamlining of reporting requirements. But this time, the role of the CTITF is set out and the Secretary-General indicates his intention to institutionalize the Task Force within the Secretariat. Regarding the substance of the proposal, the report eschews the language of "root causes." Rather, it introduces the term "conditions conducive to exploitation by terrorists" (under the heading of "dissuasion"), to frame measures to counter extremist ideology, as well as those to address the kinds of political, social and economic grievances generally intended by the phrase "root causes."

The *Uniting against Terrorism* report kicked off a process of negotiation that would lead to the adoption by the Assembly of the United Nations Global Counter-terrorism Strategy in September 2006 (see Appendix C).[105] The Secretary-General threw his full weight behind the negotiations and was assisted by the then president of the General Assembly, the Swedish foreign minister, Jan Eliasson, as well as the ambassadors from Singapore and Spain. From all accounts, such a high-powered team was required to yield an outcome.[106] Certainly, in passing the Strategy as an annex to a resolution of the General Assembly, several member states took the opportunity to issue caveats and qualifications of their support for the document. According to its critics, the Strategy failed by not resolving the political issues that had long divided states in UN fora. For some delegations, the issue of state terrorism, the right to self-determination (especially for national liberation movements) and a fuller account of the root causes of terrorism (in particular, foreign occupation as a root cause of terrorism) ought to have been included more directly.[107] Similarly, several delegations lamented that the Strategy fails to define terrorism, noting that it should not be seen as a substitute for the comprehensive convention on international terrorism, which would achieve that task at long last. For reasons such as these, the Syrians described the Strategy as "unbalanced and riddled with faults and shortcomings," while the Sudanese remarked that it is "weak and fails to refer to matters without which no counter-terrorism strategy can be developed." The sense of déjà vu here was fulfilled thanks to an untoward exchange among the Israeli, Lebanese, Syrian and Iranian delegates.

The tone of this debate puts into context the consensus generated by the Strategy. Nonetheless, the fact that member states were prepared to compromise to support this "living document" is historically unique. Unlike its antecedents, the Strategy is built around four pillars. (One of the Secretary-General's "Ds"—deterrence—did not make it into the final version, with states apparently unwilling to commit to the principle that sanctions might be used against supporters of terrorism, although that had occurred on several occasions in the past.) The first of these—"Measures to address conditions conducive to the spread of terrorism" (formerly "dissuasion")—again spins the "root causes" argument in a more politically moderate way. While "prolonged unresolved conflicts" are noted as one of several "conditions conducive," the Strategy also makes clear that "none of these conditions can excuse or justify acts of terrorism." This latter statement could be interpreted contrary to the idea that national liberation movements have a legitimate right to struggle. Other measures set out here are broader still, referring to inter-civilizational dialogue, the promotion of a culture of peace, prohibitions against incitement to terrorism (recalling Council resolution 1624 (2005)), the achievement of the Millennium Development Goals and the needs of victims of terrorism.

The second pillar of the Strategy concerns "Measures to prevent and combat terrorism," and covers those actions aimed at denying terrorists the means to carry out attacks. In this section, too, the thrust of the Strategy is to reiterate existing measures, including the principle of "extradite or prosecute," rules against terrorist financing and travel document security, and norms concerning law enforcement cooperation, information-sharing and judicial assistance. Similarly, the Strategy here repeats exhortations to the CTC regarding the elaboration of best practices, and to the al Qaeda-Taliban Sanctions Committee, noting again the need for improved procedures for listing and delisting. More original, however, is the proposal to develop a UN database on biological incidents, towards the broader goal of securing biotechnology from being used by terrorists.

The third pillar of the Strategy concerns "Measures to build states' capacity to prevent and combat terrorism and to strengthen the role of the UN system" (formerly "develop"). Here, the emphasis again is on the importance of capacity-building and the actions of the vast array of agencies within the UN system so engaged are noted and encouraged. While calls to improve cooperation among these bodies were common by this time, the Strategy goes further by welcoming the institutionalization of the CTITF "within existing resources" in the Secretariat, with the task of ensuring "overall coordination and coherence in the counter-terrorism efforts of the UN system."

The final pillar of the Strategy is devoted to "Measures to ensure respect for human rights for all and the rule of law as the fundamental basis of the fight against terrorism." The section again underscores existing commitments to observing human rights while countering terrorism, recalling General Assembly resolutions on the topic. Also, the Strategy is supportive of the reformed Human Rights Council, and argues that the Office of the UN High Commissioner for Human Rights ought to be strengthened. Finally, the Strategy endorses the work of the Special Rapporteur on the promotion and protection of human rights while countering terrorism.

As this description makes clear, the Strategy is largely repetitive of existing measures, but with some original proposals. The remarkable breadth of the Strategy, framing a broad swath of multilateral action as "counter-terrorism" measures, was perhaps necessary to ensure that a symbolic consensus could be achieved, even if deep, substantive disagreements remained among member states. In recounting its development, my point here is simply to note the unprecedented nature of this achievement, and the active role of the Secretary-General in corralling the Assembly towards this outcome. In passing the Strategy, states undertook to review its implementation after two years. Here, it was explicitly noted that implementation would be the responsibility of member states. As such, expectations were bound to be modest, particularly in light of the reservations that many states held. Still, the Strategy had the effect of redressing a perceived imbalance between the principal organs of the UN, as to who should set the counter-terrorism agenda. In this sense, the Strategy brought a sense of legitimacy to UN action against terrorism, in a way that the limited-member Council could not attain. Of course, the Strategy was never likely to be the final word in that debate.

A pendulum coming to rest in the middle? Recent UN action against terrorism

Since the passage of the Strategy in September 2006, two trends in multilateral counter-terrorism at the UN have emerged. On the one hand, we can observe the gradual consolidation of the operational aspects of the UN response, especially within the Security Council. This is most apparent within the three terrorism-related subsidiary organs of the Council and their experts groups, the CTC/CTED, the al Qaeda-Taliban Sanctions Committee and its Monitoring Team, and the 1540 Committee and its Expert Group. To its credit, the Council proper has undertaken no major initiatives in this area, preferring to refine, rather than add to, the counter-terrorism framework it evolved after 9/11. These three committees have shown themselves to be responsive to earlier criticism and have steadily adopted procedural reforms to improve efficiency and effectiveness in implementing their mandates. On the other hand, familiar political divisions are prone to appear on occasions, particularly in the General Assembly. The role of CTITF has attracted attention in this regard, especially in light of the fact that no single UN body was delegated the task of overseeing the

Strategy as a whole. As a result, the perceived gap between the roles of the Council and the broader membership of the UN (which gave rise to the desire for a strategy in the first place) has not been addressed completely. Rather, wariness of the Council's role persists, and critics note that while Council measures have been implemented with renewed vigor, the mandate handed down by the Assembly has benefitted from no such institutional mobilization.[108]

The Council after the Strategy

When the CTC reviewed the performance of CTED in December 2005 (as required under resolution 1535 (2004)), the report was slim, noting that CTED had only recently become operational and outlining a range of issues on which work had begun.[109] One year later, the report was more substantial, noting several initiatives to improve the work of the Executive Directorate and the implementation of resolutions 1373 and 1624.[110] For example, CTED developed a new tool, the "preliminary implementation assessment" matrix (PIA), approved by the CTC in April 2006, as a means of measuring member state implementation of the resolutions. The PIA template offered several benefits. PIAs would enhance consistency in the work of CTED analysts and enable the identification of technical assistance needs, as well as facilitating dialogue with the CTC and member states. Systematizing the gathering of data in this way would also permit the creation of a single database and the sharing of information with other Council committees. Moreover, rather than simply being responsive and relying on state reports, PIAs had the potential to empower CTED, putting the onus back on member states to provide more information or clarify that on record. By the end of 2006, CTED had completed PIAs for nearly 90 member states.

A further advantage of monitoring implementation in this way is that PIAs provide a key point of reference for CTED visits to member states. CTED undertook 10 such visits in 2006 and shared PIAs with states prior to arrival. CTED developed plans to formalize follow-up interactions with national-level experts and became aware of several cases where states had adopted recommendations following visits. To improve coordination, CTED and the al Qaeda-Taliban sanctions Monitoring Team informed each other of and, occasionally, participated in each other's visits. Among the other initiatives advanced by CTED at this time was the development of a *Directory of International Best Practices, Standards and Codes* for implementing resolution 1373. Available online, the directory is a graphic demonstration of the breadth of multilateral counter-terrorism, consolidating as it does measures elaborated by a wide range of international, regional and specialist organizations.[111] In this vein, too, CTED had presented the CTC with a strategy for engagement of international, regional and subregional organizations, and several such bodies had joined in country visits. Within the UN itself, CTED had begun participating in CTITF and acknowledged its role in implementing the Global Counter-terrorism Strategy, within its mandate. In addition, CTED pursued a new communications strategy, for example by taking steps to redesign and update its website, and releasing a press kit.

On two other important issues, the CTC and CTED also recorded advances. On the sensitive question of human rights, the CTC had provided guidance to CTED in May 2006, which was being used in the assessment of states' records of implementation. CTED also maintained liaison relationships with the Office of the High Commissioner for Human Rights, as well as other relevant bodies. Still, in his briefing of the CTC in October 2006, Special Rapporteur Scheinin noted the *Directory of International Best Practices* and argued that human rights standards pertain across all such measures. He offered his assistance in operationalizing such principles, suggesting that measures relating to the incitement of terrorism (resolution 1624) might be a good place to start.[112] With regard to technical assistance, under CTC guidance, CTED again developed a plan to enhance its facilitation role. In fulfilling the plan over the course of 2006, CTED concluded priority needs assessments of 96 states, met with 52 of these, and liaised with 18 donors, while referring 75 requests for assistance to UNODC, 64 such requests to the International Monetary Fund, and 65 reports of country needs to the "Counter-terrorism Action Group" (CTAG) established by the G8 group of states (discussed in Chapter 4).[113] While these numbers appear modest in light of the obvious disparities in state capabilities at a global level, they nonetheless represent a significant increase from past levels of UN engagement on capacity-building assistance for counter-terrorism. In sum, despite the difficulties encountered in the "revitalization" process, CTED, under Executive Director Rupérez, guided by the CTC under Danish leadership, achieved a good measure of vitality.

The record of activity out of CTC/CTED continued over 2007.[114] However, as in the past, challenges came to light. For example, there remained skepticism towards the Council's role in the area, including among developing states that felt unfairly targeted by such measures. Here, lingering doubts about the consistency of CTED assessments across states served to undermine their credibility. Despite the development of a communication strategy, the role of CTED, and its relationship to the Council's other counter-terrorism bodies, was sometimes not well understood both in New York and in national capitals. Moreover, although the Committee and Executive Directorate had been able to advance a range of initiatives, CTC members felt as though there was room to improve their working relationship. While these matters did not require the kind of far-reaching review undertaken as part of the "revitalization" process, there was a growing sense that a reappraisal was necessary. An opportunity to do so arose when Executive Director Rupérez indicated his desire to step down in April, eventually doing so in June. However, a disagreement among the permanent five members of the Council as to whom to appoint in his place meant that the position was not filled until November, when the Australian counter-terrorism ambassador, Mike Smith, became executive director. In turn, Smith was given the opportunity to revamp CTED with resolution 1787 (10 December 2007), which renewed its mandate until 31 March 2008 and requested that the new executive director submit a revised organizational plan within 60 days. After consulting with a wide range of stakeholders, including many member states, the proposed reorganization was designed to address four ongoing criticisms of CTED.[115]

First, regarding the rigor of CTED assessments, the proposal would maintain the practice of organizing CTED experts in regional clusters, but would add five cross-cutting technical clusters. Initially, these would be formed around the issues of: technical assistance; terrorist financing; border security, arms trafficking and law enforcement; general legal issues (including legislation, extradition and mutual legal assistance); and issues raised by resolution 1624 (2005) and the human rights aspects of counter-terrorism in the context of resolution 1373. Further, the proposal called for a quality assurance unit to review all documents prior to their leaving CTED. Second, as this indicates, the CTC and CTED would for the first time devote expert resources to the question of human rights, as had first been suggested in 2002. Third, the proposal argued for more flexibility with regard to CTED country visits, for example, by focusing on particular issues, undertaking ad hoc and follow up visits, and addressing thematic issues at a regional level where specific vulnerabilities exist. Utilizing visits more effectively, alongside the refinement of other monitoring mechanisms (especially the PIA, which would become the primary tool in this regard), would aid implementation at the national level. Finally, the proposal set out plans for a revised communications and outreach strategy, including the formation of a unit within CTED dedicated to this function.

These reforms—in addition to proposals to revise staffing procedures, engage technical assistance donors more actively and further
enhance cooperation with related bodies within and beyond the UN—
were approved by the CTC and the Council. With resolution 1805 (20
March 2008), the Council also renewed CTED until 31 December
2010. Over time, the work of CTED has maintained a brisk pace.[116]
The number of country visits has increased and their scope diversified.
With near-global coverage of PIAs, the CTC and CTED have begun a
"stock-taking" exercise, often engaging member states on their implementation of the resolutions. Two new documents—a global survey of
the implementation of resolution 1373 and a technical guide to the
implementation of that resolution—have been produced. The former of
these provides a global snapshot of states' compliance, amply illustrating the impact of multilateral counter-terrorism at the national level.[117]
The latter document, which was before the Committee at the time of
writing, goes beyond the *Directory of International Best Practices* to
provide more detailed guidance on the provisions of 1373. Here, CTED
experts have played a more active role, by elaborating standards where
existing norms and rules did not exist, or outside organizations could
not be tapped in this regard (such as in areas of law enforcement and
immigration control). Regarding technical assistance, the impact of
CTED is perhaps more difficult to demonstrate. To some degree, that
reflects a change in emphasis, from attempting to orchestrate matches
between potential donors and recipients at a global level, towards a
more targeted and strategic approach, developing relationships with
donors and other key actors in the field (especially the G8's CTAG). In
this way, CTED's analytical products, especially the PIAs and the
global implementation survey, can be leveraged as part of a broader
process. With regard to human rights, Special Rapporteur Scheinin's
most recent report to the CTC notes approvingly the integration of
human rights into the assessment process within CTED.[118] However,
by way of critical reflection, the Special Rapporteur proposes the idea
of joint country missions, noting that the reports from his own country
visits have been utilized by CTED experts. In addition, he notes that
his idea regarding the joint identification of best practices was yet to be
taken up by CTED.

Human rights have remained a key concern for the al Qaeda-Taliban
sanctions regime, too. As ever, the focus of criticism has been the list of
targets maintained by the 1267 Committee. Here, the Council has
continued to introduce procedural reforms to improve the integrity of
the list. In late 2006, the Council established a "focal point" mechanism,
which manages requests for delisting according to specific procedures.[119]

Also at that time, resolution 1735 (22 December 2006) introduced a template to be used by states in forwarding names and "statements of case" to the 1267 Committee. To address due process concerns, states were also asked to specify which parts of a statement of case might be released to the listed individual and interested member states. In a similar vein, resolution 1735 sets out measures to improve notification procedures, to ensure that listed individuals and entities are informed of their designation. To further enhance transparency, resolution 1822 (30 June 2008) directs the Committee to publish narrative summaries of reasons for listing (i.e. the publicly releasable portion of the statement of case) on its website.[120] Moreover, that resolution directs the Committee to undertake a comprehensive review of the names on the list by June 2010, to ensure that it is up to date and accurate. Thereafter, according to the resolution, each listing should be reviewed every three years.

Many of these reforms originated in reports submitted to the Committee by its Monitoring Team.[121] In general, those reports have continued to strike a frank and modest tone about the effectiveness of the financial sanctions, the travel ban and the arms embargo. Here, efforts to improve the integrity of the list are framed as a way of improving the legitimacy and authority of Council actions. As noted earlier, these developments ought to be viewed in the broader context of the Council's gradual refinement of the tool of targeted sanctions, and demonstrate the capacity for learning and policy innovation.[122] In this regard, the experience of the al Qaeda-Taliban sanctions regime has repercussions for current and future efforts to impose multilateral sanctions.

With that said, procedural innovations have not staved off legal challenges to the sanctions regime, and these came to a head in the *Kadi* decision of the European Court of Justice in September 2008.[123] There, the Court held that the EU's procedures for implementing Security Council resolutions infringed the basic rights of the appellants, in particular their right to be heard and their right to effective judicial protection. The immediate effect of the decision was to force the EU Commission to revise the basis upon which the appellants were subject to the sanctions. The Commission duly shared the narrative summary of reasons for listing with the appellants and, after considering their responses, decided to continue the measures.[124] This response is not the final word on the question of listing and delisting, and the appellants in the *Kadi* case may yet seek a further review that would bring before a court the substantive reasons for their designation. Indeed, a more complete judicial review of the evidence used for listing may raise difficulties for the Security Council, given that such evidence is derived from member states that are often wary of sharing sensitive or intelligence information in multilateral fora.[125] Other cases remain before the courts in several jurisdictions and may yet represent a broader challenge to the legitimacy of the Council's response.[126]

In this regard, Special Rapporteur Scheinin has made clear that nothing short of an independent, UN-level mechanism for reviewing listing decisions by the Council can meet due process requirements of a fair trial. The alternative, he has suggested, is to abolish the sanctions regime altogether and permit states to list individuals and entities under national laws.[127] For its part, the Monitoring Team has argued that such a UN-level mechanism is effectively redundant, given the willingness that national and regional-level courts have shown in reviewing the implementation of Council resolutions by states.[128] Most of the problematic listings were those that occurred in the immediate post-9/11 period. Procedural improvements, described above, ought to ensure that more recent listings are less likely to yield legal challenges.[129] In other words, more rigorous procedures ought to have a self-regulating effect on member states that may have erred in the past by forwarding the kinds of designations that attract legal action. Still, the Council has recently established the position of Ombudsperson, to receive requests from individuals and entities seeking to be removed from the list (see resolution 1904 17 December (2009)). This is a significant development in the evolution of listing procedures.

Perhaps as a consequence of procedural reforms and legal action, there are signs that the list is regaining the confidence of the international community, and it has become more dynamic recently. States have been utilizing the statement of case mechanism to forward more names, and the Committee has been active in updating and, in several cases, removing entries.[130] While the technical problems in developing and implementing the list are far from resolved—for example, consistent and detailed identification information across entries has long been, and remains, an issue—the utility of the sanctions seems to be more widely appreciated than in the past. Beyond the list, other aspects of the work of the 1267 Committee and Monitoring Team indicate the relative robustness of this aspect of the Council's response. For example, similar to CTED, the Monitoring Team has rationalized the reporting requirement for states, introducing new, user-friendly tools. In addition, country visits, whether undertaken by the Team alone or jointly with other Council bodies, have proven to be an effective way of increasing awareness and implementation of the sanctions. Moreover, the Team has engaged widely with international, regional and subregional organizations. While these developments are described in greater depth below (and in Chapter 4), one example is apt to note here.

Since 2005, with the support of the Council and the Committee, the Team has collaborated closely with Interpol.[131] Most notably, this has led to the integration of the 1267 list with Interpol's "Special Notice" mechanism, creating "Interpol-UN Security Council Special Notices."[132] In this way, the 1267 list is distributed directly to law enforcement authorities in Interpol's 187 member countries. Further, such Special Notices sometimes include information beyond that contained in the list alone, such as photographs, which is of particular relevance for border officials in implementing the travel ban. Interpol-UN Security Council Special Notices began to be circulated for individuals in 2005 and for entities in 2008. Beyond the special notices, the Team has sought to leverage Interpol tools such as the Stolen and Lost Travel Document database (established in 2002) and the "I-24/7" secure global police communications system.[133]

Such close collaborations with existing bodies are also characteristic of the work of the 1540 Committee and its Expert Group. Recall that 1540 addresses a gap in existing non-proliferation and arms control measures by targeting the role of non-state actors. As such, 1540 is complementary to that large body of rules and norms, with several institutional mechanisms on which to build. Of particular relevance to the Committee's work are the IAEA, the Organization for the Prohibition of Chemical Weapons (OPCW) and the World Customs Organization. Indeed, in 2007 the Committee and the UN Office of Disarmament Affairs (a close internal collaborator) exchanged letters with the IAEA and the OPCW, to formalize cooperative measures concerning the dissemination of best practices and the facilitation of technical assistance.[134] Similar to CTED and the 1267 Monitoring Team, the 1540 Committee and Group have had extensive interactions with these and other specialist bodies, as well as regional and sub-regional organizations.[135] In other ways, too, the 1540 Committee has made up for its slow beginning and has assimilated the experiences of other subsidiary organs. For example, with regard to reporting, the Committee established a reporting template (in the form of a matrix) at the outset, to facilitate dialogue with member states. Also, over time, the Committee has refined its role as a "clearing house" to help match donors and recipients of technical assistance, including the development of a new strategy and template for assistance requests.

Having noted the extent to which the 1540 Committee has adapted some of the more successful practices of other committees, I should add that the implementation of 1540 is constrained by familiar problems—lack of capacity and political will.[136] However, the tone of the Committee's reports is pragmatic on this point, recognizing that the full implementation of 1540 is a "long-term endeavor."[137] The mandate of the Committee and Expert Group has been extended twice, most recently until 25 April 2011.[138] The Committee has been encouraged by the Council to diversify its sources of funding in order to maintain its workload over this period.[139]

Beyond the discrete work of the Council's three terrorism-related committees, a renewed effort has been made to improve coordination among them and, where possible, integrate their operations. The chairs of the three committees have provided joint briefings to the Council since 2005. Over time, the committees and expert groups have evolved several methods for coordinating their activities and sharing information including, as noted above, participating in country visits on a joint basis. Most recently, the three expert groups have collaborated on joint strategies to deal with non- and late-reporting states, and to engage international, regional and subregional organizations.[140] The expert groups have together focused on regions in need of particular assistance, including the Pacific islands (through the Pacific Islands Forum) and subregions of Africa. Other opportunities for collaboration, including joint video conferences with counter-terrorism officials in national capitals, are under consideration. Members of the expert groups in New York meet frequently on a formal and informal basis and the committees publish a table together to clarify the relationship among them.[141] Of course, as cooperation among the committees advances, the question arises as to whether they might be amalgamated or otherwise rationalized to further improve efficiency and effectiveness. However, while Council members have indicated their willingness to review their institutional framework for countering terrorism,[142] the mandates of the three committees are distinctive, and there appears to be little appetite among member states at present to restructure mechanisms that have added more value over time. I return to this point in the conclusion of the chapter.

Everyone's and no-one's: the General Assembly, the Secretary-General, and the implementation of the Strategy

Following the passage of the Strategy in 2006, the General Assembly has maintained a steady workload on terrorism-related issues. Through annual resolutions on "Measures to eliminate terrorism" the Assembly has continued to build norms against terrorist violence.[143] From 2007, the requirement that states provide reports on their implementation of Assembly resolutions under this title was dropped, reflecting a concern for "reporting fatigue" and the prominence of Council requirements in this regard. (International and regional organizations were still invited to report.) Minor political skirmishes have arisen regarding the inclusion of a reference to NATO's counter-terrorism role in preambular language that cites a wide range of international, regional and sub-regional bodies active in the area.[144] Hinting at the insufficiency of the Strategy, Tunisia has consistently argued in the Sixth Committee for the development of a "code of conduct" for the international effort against terrorism, to be drawn up under the auspices of the United Nations, as well as the convening of an international conference. These ideas have been endorsed in other multilateral fora, including the African Union, the Organization of the Islamic Conference and the Non-Aligned Movement.[145] Nonetheless, the Sixth Committee's Ad Hoc Committee is yet to conclude negotiations on the comprehensive convention on international terrorism, and remains divided on the question of whether and when a high-level conference might occur. On these points, one advocate of a high-level conference, Egypt, has argued that it should not be delayed until the completion of the comprehensive convention. Rather, the conference would have a different focus, addressing the "underlying causes of terrorism and the definition thereof."[146]

In resolutions on preventing the use of WMD and radioactive materials by terrorists, out of the First Committee, the Assembly has endorsed substantive measures elaborated in other fora (especially the Council, in the form of resolution 1540, and the IAEA).[147] A similarly declaratory resolution against hostage-taking was sponsored by Russia in the Third Committee in 2006.[148] In 2007, a resolution out of the Third Committee acknowledged the role played by the UN Office on Drugs and Crime, and the TPB in particular, in providing technical assistance towards the implementation of the terrorism-related international conventions and protocols, and the Strategy.[149]

If these developments within the Assembly appear modest, on two issues—human rights and the implementation of the Strategy—its role has been more visible. Regarding the former, successive resolutions under the title, "Protection of human rights and fundamental freedoms while countering terrorism" have provided a forum to endorse the work of Special Rapporteur Scheinin.[150] Above, I have summarized the views of the Special Rapporteur on the issues of listing and the integration of human rights into the work of CTED. But the Special Rapporteur's mandate is much broader and his reports have drawn attention to the wide range of human rights concerns and vulnerabilities that have arisen in the context of the international uptick in counter-terrorism activity since 9/11.[151] This has involved several country visits, including to the

United States (where he visited Guantanamo Bay) and to Israel (where he visited the Occupied Palestinian Territory). The influence of the Special Rapporteur is apparent in many ways, including in the text of Assembly resolutions and the strong support for his role elaborated therein. The Special Rapporteur is also an active participant in CTITF and his work is cited approvingly by human rights NGOs.[152] While the Special Rapporteur has been unable to influence the Council directly on the matters of listing and CTED, his has been a prominent voice in the chorus for reform. In 2007, the Special Rapporteur's mandate was renewed for a period of three years.[153] This suggests that human rights concerns will remain as part of the multilateral counter-terrorism agenda in the years ahead.

With regard to the implementation of the Strategy, we see that the political divisions typical of counter-terrorism cooperation in the Assembly in years past maintain some relevance today. Recall that the Strategy had been developed as a means of reestablishing consensus regarding the UN's response to terrorism, by democratizing the development of counter-terrorism norms and rules (i.e. acting through the Assembly) and by broadening the scope of UN action (e.g. to include "conditions conducive to the spread of terrorism"). Consensus has not been so easily forthcoming, however, and the Strategy itself has been something of a site of contention. To put the Assembly's recent treatment of the Strategy in context, it is necessary first to discuss the role of the Secretary-General and the evolution of CTITF.

Since its creation in 2005, CTITF has become increasingly significant. Although Ban Ki-moon replaced Kofi Annan as Secretary-General from 1 January 2007, he quickly identified terrorism as a priority and has maintained his predecessor's focus on the issue. Over time, CTITF has sought to achieve its goal—"to ensure overall coordination and coherence in the counter-terrorism efforts of the UN system"—in two main ways.[154] First, the Task Force has acted as a forum for exchange and discussion among the several UN agencies engaged in counter-terrorism. This function is neatly illustrated by the CTITF organigram that appears on its website, which depicts the Task Force as if it were a sun, around which some two dozen entities revolve (see Appendix D). A major contribution of the Task Force here is the development of the *UN Counter-terrorism Online Handbook*, released in February 2007, which summarizes the actions of the entities that comprise CTITF and demonstrates the degree to which counter-terrorism has been institutionalized across the UN system.[155]

The second means to the end of better coordination deployed by CTITF has been the creation of working groups on certain thematic issues, fashioned around the "deliverables identified in the strategy" (although the Strategy itself does not use this terminology). By mid-2008, nine such working groups had emerged, on the following topics:[156]

- Preventing and resolving conflicts;
- Addressing radicalization and extremism that lead to terrorism;
- Supporting and highlighting the victims of terrorism;
- Preventing and responding to WMD attacks;
- Tackling the financing of terrorism;
- Countering the use of the internet for terrorist purposes;
- Facilitating the implementation of the UN Global Counter-terrorism Strategy;
- Strengthening the protection of vulnerable targets;
- Protecting human rights while countering terrorism.

At first glance, the convening of such groups may appear to duplicate work already being undertaken in several fora. However, the stated value of the working groups was precisely that they brought together the different entities participating in the Task Force, who took up membership in one or more of the groups. Several of the groups produced interesting reports. For example, the working group on terrorist financing undertook extensive consultation with national money laundering and terrorist financing officials, as well as with private sector actors, academics and civil society groups. The tone of the final outcome, which argues for "proportional measures, commensurate to risks," stands out in a field often characterized by alarmist rhetoric.[157] The working group on terrorists' use of the internet also consulted widely with states, convening a workshop and conducting research interviews. Their report demystifies the topic by providing a typology of different uses of the internet by terrorists, emphasizing the important roles played by civil society and the private sector, as well as the development of counter-narratives.[158] The working group on radicalization utilized a similar approach, developing a report that attempts a comparative assessment of different national approaches to counter-radicalization, usefully advancing the emerging scholarly debate in the area.[159] With regard to the working group on victims of terrorism, the Secretary-General himself convened a symposium on the topic in New York in September 2008, highlighting the human consequences of terrorism, as well as discussing ways of assisting victims.[160]

Despite the work of the groups, the review of Strategy implementation in mid-2008 unearthed serious concerns among states as to the role of the Task Force. In his report to the Assembly, the Secretary-General noted that, although the primary responsibility for implementation lies with member states, CTITF and other UN entities (including Council bodies) had made meaningful contributions.[161] However, in the course of providing briefings to states, the Secretary-General found that, "Member States have ... an interest in greater systematization, so as to be able to provide guidance to the Task Force on its activities and to create a stronger communication channel between the Task Force and the membership."[162] Here, the Secretary-General was quick to note that, however systematization proceeds, it should not consume the bulk of CTITF's energies and it must reflect the pool of resources made available to the effort. The resource question was particularly pressing. Although CTITF had indeed been institutionalized within the Secretariat (as called for in the Strategy), it had been reliant upon voluntary contributions and temporary staff support—an unsustainable arrangement, according to the Secretary-General. Nonetheless, the Secretary-General held out the promise that, "The United Nations system, through the Task Force, if staffed and resourced to do so, could provide a strategic interface with global, regional and subregional bodies and civil society on the Strategy."[163]

This latter point was of particular concern for many states who had found that assigning primary responsibility for implementation to the membership at large meant that no single entity within the UN system itself was responsible for the Strategy. In turn, this meant that the original elements of the Strategy (i.e. those elements that do not overlap with existing Council-based mandates) were liable to continued inaction. The Council's ongoing assertiveness, when contrasted with the Assembly's relative idleness, had the effect of underscoring, rather than ameliorating, the perceived imbalance that prompted the Strategy to begin with. These concerns had also been raised in 2007–8 in the course of the "International Process on Global Counter-terrorism Cooperation," cosponsored by the governments of Costa Rica, Japan, Slovakia, Switzerland and Turkey, and supported by the Center on Global Counter-Terrorism Cooperation. Among the main findings of the process was that "There needs to be a forum within the UN to allow Member States to fulfill their leading role in overseeing UN Strategy implementation efforts and allow them a regular opportunity to review and determine the policy direction of Strategy implementation efforts, including the work of the Task Force."[164]

This and other arguments were put more forcefully in the debate in the General Assembly on the Strategy in September 2008.[165] Several delegations noted that in creating working groups around cross-cutting themes, the Task Force had strayed from its core mandate—the four pillars of the Strategy. There was a sense that the Task Force was being selective in focusing on those parts of the Strategy of particular concern to powerful states. Here, the practice of resourcing the Task Force out of voluntary contributions was seen to have unduly influenced its work. The link between CTITF and the broader membership of the UN needed to be reconceived, to allow more consultation and participation, and affirm member states' ownership of the Strategy. Moreover, a feeling of "politics as usual" crept into the debate as several delegations took the opportunity to raise the distinction between terrorism and legitimate rights of resistance to foreign occupation, as well as the prospect of an international code of conduct and a high-level UN conference on the topic. In sum, if the consensus around the Strategy was fragile to begin with, the first two years of its existence did little to bolster it.

Not surprisingly, the resolution that emerged from the Assembly debate in September 2008 sought to remake the relationships between the Assembly and the Task Force, and the Task Force and the Strategy.[166] In the preamble to that resolution, the Assembly sets out that the "Counter-Terrorism Implementation Task Force shall carry out its activities within the framework of its mandate, with policy guidance offered by Member States through interaction with the General Assembly on a regular basis." In operational paragraphs, the Assembly urged the Secretary-General to "make the necessary arrangements to carry out the institutionalization of the Task Force, in accordance with resolution 60/288" (para. 11), while deciding to "interact with the Task Force on a regular basis, in order to receive briefings and reports on its current and future work, assess the work being undertaken on the Strategy implementation efforts, including the work of the Task Force, and to offer policy guidance" (para. 12). Since then, promised reforms of CTITF have begun to be implemented. The position of director has been created and Jean-Paul Laborde, from TPB in Vienna, has assumed the role. CTITF now resides in the Department of Political Affairs within the Secretariat and its (increased) budget will be secured through regular UN budgetary processes, rather than voluntary contributions. In these ways, the Task Force is described as having entered a "new operational phase," suggesting that it has outgrown its original coordination function and will become an actor in its own right in the evolving UN counter-terrorism effort.[167]

The system-wide effort in perspective

Before moving on to discuss developments beyond the UN, it is important to reflect on the institutionalization of counter-terrorism across the

UN system as a whole, as this constitutes perhaps the most notable achievement in multilateral counter-terrorism in the post-9/11 period. Recall that, going back to the 1980s, there have been efforts to draw on the expertise of UN specialized agencies in combating terrorism. While incremental steps were taken in that direction over time, the period since 9/11 has seen an unprecedented increase in the breadth and depth of engagement.[168]

Those UN agencies with a history of involvement in counter-terrorism have expanded their work in the area. For example, ICAO has continued to set standards for aviation security (Annex 17 of the Chicago Convention, with accompanying advice for implementation in the form of an updated *Security Manual*), while also revising rules covering baggage screening, the security features of passports and the threat to civil aviation from Man-Portable Air Defense Systems ("MANPADS"). These standards are now part of the CTC *Directory of International Best Practices*. Compliance with ICAO standards has improved as a consequence of the Universal Security Audit Programme, now in its second six-year cycle. ICAO's technical assistance programs have remained active, often addressing deficiencies detected through audits. IMO's main achievements since 9/11 have included the elaboration of a new body of rules regarding ship and port security—the "International Ship and Port Facility Security Code" (ISPS Code), annexed to the 1974 Safety of Life at Sea Convention and operational from 1 July 2004.[169] In 2005, states acting through IMO added a Protocol to the Convention for the Suppression of Unlawful Acts against the Safety of Maritime Navigation—as well as the accompanying Protocol on Fixed Platforms Located on the Continental Shelf—to criminalize the use of such vessels for acts of terrorism. According to IMO, its technical assistance program has trained some 6,000 national-level officials on methods for ensuring maritime security. As noted above, the IAEA has a critical role in the implementation of Security Council resolution 1540 (2004), as well as the 2005 International Convention for the Suppression of Nuclear Terrorism. Soon after 9/11, the agency developed its own plan of action for protection against nuclear terrorism. The agency's current *Nuclear Security Plan* (2006–9) aims to: assess nuclear security needs on a global scale; implement measures to prevent malicious acts involving nuclear and other radioactive material; and enhance capabilities to detect, interdict and respond to illegal acts involving nuclear and other radioactive material and associated facilities.[170] Specific measures undertaken include the development of an Illicit Trafficking Database, and a vigorous technical assistance program. Within the UN system, TPB has been similarly active, especially in pursuing its "Global project on strengthening the legal regime against terrorism." Since that project began in January 2003, TPB has trained more than 6,700 officials from 150 states.[171]

Other organizations, with less of a history in counter-terrorism cooperation, have also joined the effort after 9/11. For example, the International Monetary Fund and the World Bank have incorporated counter-terrorist financing rules into their reviews of countries' compliance with standards and codes in regulating the financial sector. As I describe in Chapter 4, the Bank and Fund are now part of a "web of institutions" that comprise the counter-terrorist financing regime.[172] A key achievement of the World Customs Organization has been the 2005 elaboration of a framework of standards to secure and facilitate global trade (the "SAFE Framework").[173] Under the framework, states agree to harmonize advance electronic cargo information, employ a consistent risk management approach in assessing security threats, undertake inspections of outbound cargo when reasonably requested to do so and provide incentives for the private sector to meet security standards. The framework also contemplates the need for technical assistance in implementing its measures. One hundred and fifty seven states have agreed to implement the Framework.[174] In this context, WCO is particularly active in the implementation of resolution 1540. So, too, is the Organization for the Prohibition of Chemical Weapons (OPCW). While formally independent of the UN, OPCW's work is often integrated with it. For example, OPCW participates in CTITF by virtue of its role as implementing body for the 1993 Chemical Weapons Convention. Further, OPCW is active in providing a range of technical assistance including on-site help in establishing national authorities, legislative drafting and other forms of capacity-building. Cooperation among police forces has steadily grown over time, especially in the post-9/11 period. Interpol's 1956 constitution contains a provision designed to ensure neutrality, which had the effect of limiting the organization's role concerning political offences such as terrorism.[175] However, in the 1980s and 1990s, this provision was reinterpreted to permit the organization to participate in counter-terrorism cooperation. Today, as noted above, Interpol has several operational roles, including the Database on Lost and Stolen Travel Documents, the Interpol-UN Special Notices and the I-24/7 communications system. Among other measures pursued by Interpol, Project Geiger gathers and analyzes data on the theft of radiological materials, complementary to IAEA's Illicit Trafficking Database. Further, in 2002, Interpol created a "Fusion Task Force"—a network of law enforcement contact officers and database designed to identify members of criminal groups engaged in terrorist activity. Interpol-derived standards on these and other matters appear in the CTC *Directory of International Best Practices*, and Interpol also undertakes a variety of training and capacity-building exercises.[176]

Different parts of the UN Secretariat are also more engaged in counterterrorism than at any time in the past. The Office of Disarmament Affairs supports the 1540 Committee and Expert Group, while promoting the implementation of relevant international instruments and facilitating technical assistance. The Office of Legal Affairs provides workshops for states to assist them in signing and implementing treaties. The Office also services the Sixth Committee of the General Assembly and publishes compendia on "International Instruments related to the Prevention and Suppression of International Terrorism," and, "National Laws and Regulations on the Prevention and Suppression of International Terrorism." The Department of Peacekeeping Operations works in post-conflict environments to rebuild criminal justice systems and establish the rule of law. Through these actions, it aims to reduce opportunities for terrorists to recruit and operate. By extension, the broad scope of the Strategy means that the work of agencies such as UNESCO (to advance respect for diversity and promote tolerance) and the UN Development Programme (especially programs relating to the rule of law, access to justice and human rights) is now framed as a contribution to counter-terrorism.

This is only a partial survey of UN agencies involved in counterterrorism. A more complete analysis of the institutionalization of counterterrorism across the UN system would require a much longer treatment than I can provide here. Of course, without a more studied approach, the impact and effectiveness of these measures cannot be explored. Similarly, the specific political dynamics that pertain to each agency's involvement are beyond the scope of the chapter. However, suffice it to note that there is evidence of consensus on some issues (e.g. the ISPS Code attracted high levels of support and compliance) and contention on others (e.g. human rights), as well as much in between. Still, what is striking about multilateral counter-terrorism at the UN after 9/11 is the volume and scope of activity, which is historically unique. As such, there is reason to at least question whether the skeptical view of multilateral counterterrorism—as articulated by Crenshaw, Pillar, and Wilkinson before 9/11—still holds today. It is to that debate that I now turn.

Conclusion

The role of the UN in counter-terrorism cooperation since 9/11 manifests elements of both change and continuity from the pre-9/11 period.

As I have demonstrated in this chapter, there has been a *lot* of activity in UN fora and, if measured quantitatively, multilateral counter-terrorism after 9/11 is historically exceptional. The qualitative attributes of cooperation over this period suggest more of a mixed record. The UN system has proven itself to be quite capable in certain aspects of counter-terrorism, especially concerning "preventive" measures. Of particular note here is the mobilization of UN mechanisms to elaborate norms and rules, and to provide or coordinate training, technical assistance, and other forms of capacity-building support. On the other hand, political quarrels are never too far away and manifest in different ways over time. The fact that the UN effort has advanced in fits and starts since 9/11 reflects that states waver between relative consensus and disunity fairly consistently.

What are we to make of this record? Not surprisingly, scholarship on the UN and terrorism has grown since 9/11.[177] Some observers point to the essentially competitive nature of counter-terrorism diplomacy at the UN as a sign of continuity with the pre-9/11 period.[178] Here, the apparent rivalry between the Security Council and the General Assembly on the issue is interpreted as an example of "forum shopping," as states seek to advance their own interests through the UN.[179] Others point to the self-correcting measures undertaken in UN fora—e.g. the Council's integration of human rights into the work of CTED—to argue that the UN has learned from its missteps and shown flexibility in adapting its mechanisms to deal with the problem at hand.[180] Indeed, whatever we might say about the political motivations of the states involved, the ability of the UN system to make successive adjustments and to change course reveals a nimbleness that challenges the stereotypical view of the UN as a slow-moving and clunky bureaucracy.[181] Perhaps, over time, the cluster of actors that comprise the UN system are realizing where their collective "comparative advantage" lies in the field of counter-terrorism, to recall the term used by the Secretary-General's initial Policy Working Group in 2002.[182] Indeed, that document, with its emphases on an international action plan, norm creation and capacity-building, stands up quite well in light of subsequent events.

What, then, of the future? The institutionalization of counter-terrorism across the UN system suggests that the organization will be occupied with it for some time hence. The question is "how?" The current debate concerns the role of an "operationalized" CTITF, and its responsibility for overseeing implementation of the Strategy. There is an argument for further rationalization of UN mechanisms here. For example, Eric Rosand claims that a "single counter-terrorism office or department should be established within the UN Secretariat once CTED's mandate expires at the end of 2010."[183] This new unit would have oversight of 1373, 1624 and the Strategy, and would be well placed to leverage the benefits of the Secretariat's regional offices. According to Rosand, consideration might also be given to consolidating the 1267 Monitoring Team and 1540 Expert Group into this unit. In so far as member states actually desire rationalization, this proposal has merit. The counter-argument here is that further refinement, rather than significant revision, of the institutional structure is preferable. This view acknowledges that any reorganization would not suit the interests of certain states, especially those in the Security Council, who would cede direct control over CTED if it was merged into the Secretariat. Here, we would see CTED (beneath the Council) and CTITF (in the Secretariat) working in parallel, the former pursuing its Council mandate (which overlaps with the Strategy) and the latter monitoring the implementation of those parts of the Strategy not also covered by the Council. CTITF could also maintain its coordination function. This view suggests further that the mandate of the sanctions Monitoring Team (which reflects a core function of the Council—the imposition of sanctions) is distinctive and that, therefore, the current arrangement is likely to continue.

Either way, the debate about how the UN should organize itself is bound to reappear periodically as mandates come up for renewal and ongoing events present new challenges. Other proposals have also arisen. For example, the "International Process on Global Counter-terrorism Cooperation" put forward the useful idea that better connections between national level counter-terrorism officials and the UN ought to be developed.[184] Also, the recurring idea of a high-level conference (perhaps timed to commemorate the conclusion of the comprehensive convention, when and if that occurs) may have implications for the way the UN effort is organized. Further, in debating the renewal of the Strategy, the Saudi delegate, with the support of several others, raised the idea of an international counter-terrorism center, under the UN. Clearly, some member states think that the substance and shape of the UN's role on counter-terrorism should remain on the agenda. That's not necessarily a bad thing. The danger here is that talking about how to organize the UN effort will become a substitute for action. But that danger should be seen in the context of the rather remarkable record of cooperation since 9/11. If those achievements have been undergirded by a willingness to learn and adapt to developments, then we can expect that such flexibility will be required to maintain momentum into the future.

4 Multilateral counter-terrorism beyond the UN

To date, this book has focused mostly on counter-terrorism measures advanced through the United Nations. My doing so reflects that, today, the UN is often at the center of the multilateral effort to suppress terrorism or, at least, that UN bodies are among those now active in many domains of counter-terrorism policy. However, treating the UN effort in this way should not be interpreted to mean that the UN is always the primary actor, or that UN action precedes that advanced elsewhere—far from it. Over time, political constraints upon acting through the UN have led states to seek alternative fora outside of it, including regional and subregional organizations, affinity-based, professional or other limited-membership groupings, military alliances, and ad hoc mechanisms. Especially in the post-9/11 period, the net result of this proliferation of cooperative arrangements is that multilateral counter-terrorism is characterized by multiple and overlapping rules, norms, programs and agencies. As noted in the introduction, contemporary scholars acknowledge that the fields of counter-terrorism embody the present trend towards increasingly diverse forms of multilateralism.[1]

In this chapter, I provide an overview of multilateral counter-terrorism outside of, but often connected to, UN fora. In doing so, I first describe developments at the regional and subregional level. Here, multilateral counter-terrorism most often involves the elaboration of norms and rules, such as through the conclusion of treaties and legal instruments, and the provision of technical and capacity-building assistance. In some regions, the contribution of multilateralism is modest. In others, the effects of institutions are more demonstrable. Second, I turn to other affinity-based groupings, such as the Non-Aligned Movement, the Arab League and the Organization of the Islamic Conference. Given their scope and membership, these groups are more likely to be used as sites to articulate different definitions of the problem of terrorism. In other words, they tend to be used as political organs, rather than as conduits for more substantive responses. Third, I describe how leading states have adapted a military alliance (NATO) and an influential limited-membership group (the G7/G8) to tasks of counter-terrorism. As with other multilateral fora, these mechanisms offer states several opportunities for advancing counter-terrorism cooperation, just as they impose constraints on joint action. Finally, I look at three cross-cutting issues—law enforcement and intelligence cooperation, counter-terrorist financing initiatives, and maritime security cooperation—to illustrate the scale and diversity of cooperation across different domains. My purpose here is to show how the dynamics of cooperation and contestation play out beyond the UN, yielding different outcomes in different fields of counter-terrorism. Before moving on, suffice it to note that my discussion in this chapter is necessarily a survey of developments across a wide range of institutions. The sheer volume of multilateral activity precludes a comprehensive treatment herein,[2] although that task may be taken up by future researchers.

Multilateral counter-terrorism at the regional and subregional levels

Regional and subregional organizations have been sites for multilateral counter-terrorism for many years, including before 9/11. As Eric Rosand et al. note, these bodies offer several comparative advantages in the field, including local knowledge and sensitivity to cultural and contextual issues, enhanced legitimacy and political support, and the capacity to serve as "transmission belts" for UN or other global norms and rules.[3] Of course, regional and subregional bodies face many difficulties, too, not least those relating to lack of capacity and varying degrees of political commitment to suppressing terrorism. In addition, engagement between global bodies, especially those within the UN system, and regional and subregional bodies has sometimes been uncoordinated. This overview of regional and subregional activity highlights major initiatives at these levels, as well as emphasizing links to UN measures.[4]

The first regional convention on terrorism-related issues was the Organization of American States' (OAS) Convention to Prevent and Punish the Acts of Terrorism Taking the Form of Crimes against Persons and Related Extortion that are of International Significance, concluded in Washington, D.C., in February 1971. This convention is perhaps more remarkable for the precedent it set (other such treaties followed it, including at the UN level) rather than for its operational effectiveness.[5] Nonetheless, terrorism remained on the OAS agenda, even if many members were wary of US dominance, especially during the Cold War.[6] In the 1990s there were some moves within the Organization to develop a new convention, and two conferences on terrorism were held. It was out of the latter of these that the idea of forming an Inter-American Committee Against Terrorism (known by its Spanish acronym, "CICTE") emerged.[7] Established in 1999, CICTE aims to promote counter-terrorism cooperation in the Western Hemisphere. CICTE became far more active after 9/11, when the governing organs of the OAS decided to strengthen the legal framework for counter-terrorism in the region. The 2002 Inter-American Convention against Terrorism is broader in scope than its predecessor, covering terrorist financing, border controls, law enforcement cooperation and mutual legal assistance, as well as revising extradition rules. The convention calls for the observation of human rights in the counter-terrorism effort, also asking states to promote cooperation and technical assistance, and highlighting the role of CICTE in this regard.[8] Also in 2002, CICTE established a secretariat based in Washington, D.C. Since that time, it has assumed a prominent role in regional counter-terrorism efforts.[9] Through a regular schedule of meetings and annual work plans, CICTE has developed relationships with a wide range of specialist organizations, and now facilitates and offers technical assistance and capacity-building programs across several tools of counter-terrorism policy. In this regard, CICTE has developed some innovative institutional mechanisms, including a network of "National Points of Contact" (to link directly to national counter-terrorism officials) and a regular newsletter. Indeed, the achievements of the OAS have led to it being described as "perhaps the most developed and effective regional organization in the world outside of Europe."[10]

Critically, CICTE has worked closely with donor countries (the USA and Canada are particularly active in the region, along with France, Italy, the Netherlands, Spain, and the UK), as well as the UNODC's TPB. As analysts from the Center for Global Counter-terrorism Cooperation point out, TPB has a regional presene (five field offices and a network of consultants) that significantly enhances its ability to act in the region. Other UN mechanisms, especially CTC/CTED and the 1267 Monitoring Team, have been rather slower in engaging the region.[11] Meanwhile, at the subregional level, institutions such as the Caribbean Community (CARICOM)[12] and the Central American Integration System (SICA)[13] have much less capacity and are therefore more directly reliant upon bilateral assistance. Among other examples of subregional counter-terrorism cooperation in the region, interior ministers in the MERCOSUR group of states initiated a Standing Working Group on Terrorism after 9/11. This has provided a forum to coordinate counter-terrorism policy, develop contacts and exchange information.[14]

Turning to Europe, the first regional organization to conclude a treaty on terrorism was the Council of Europe.[15] The 1977 Convention on the Suppression of Terrorism aimed to facilitate extradition among member states by removing the "political offense exception" for terrorism offenses.[16] While the convention entered into force a year later, the Council's work on terrorism did not increase significantly until after 9/11. In November 2001, the Council formed a "Multidisciplinary Group on International Action against Terrorism," with two tasks: to revise the 1977 Convention and to identify priority areas for further Council action. The first of these was accomplished by adding a protocol to the convention in 2003, expanding the range of offences covered (i.e. to match those contained in the UN terrorism instruments). Given the mission of the Council—which emphasizes the development of fundamental values such as human rights, democracy and the rule of law across the continent—the group suggested six priority areas: research on the concepts of "apologie du terrorisme" and "incitement to terrorism"; special investigation techniques; protection of witnesses and collaborators of justice; international cooperation on law enforcement; action to prevent terrorists from accessing funding sources; and questions of identity documents which arise in connection with terrorism. In 2003, the Multidisciplinary Group was reformed as the "Committee of Experts on Terrorism" (CODEXTER).[17] Among CODEXTER's achievements since that time are two further conventions—on the "prevention of terrorism" and on "laundering, search, seizure and confiscation of the proceeds of crime and on the financing of terrorism" (both 2005). The former of these goes beyond extradition alone, to criminalize terrorism, provocation, recruitment and training. The latter extends existing rules on the financial aspects of crime to cover terrorist financing.[18] In addition, CODEXTER maintains an active work agenda, including the compilation of country reports (summarizing counter-terrorism developments in the Council's 47 member states), research to identify gaps in international law, and cooperation programs to strengthen the rule of law.

The work of the Council of Europe complements, but is overshadowed by, that of the continent's most prominent regional institution—the 27-member European Union (EU).[19] The predecessor institutions of the EU had cooperated on counter-terrorism prior to 9/11, at both a legal and an operational level.[20] For example, in 1979 the European

Community (EC) states took measures to ensure that the Council of Europe's 1977 convention would be observed consistently in the EC. At the operational level, EC justice and interior ministers began meeting as the "Trevi group" in 1976.[21] An analogous mechanism for police officers was established in 1979, the Police Working Group on Terrorism (PWGT). These groupings were relatively informal and mutually beneficial for states.[22] In 1992, these mechanisms were subsumed under the "third pillar" (justice and home affairs or "JHA") of the EU, as set out in the Maastricht Treaty. That treaty also led to the creation of a European police office—Europol—but only after its founding convention gained enough signatories. Over time, progress in implementing JHA mandates was slow, despite efforts to better coordinate policies on immigration, border control and asylum. Still, the EU and its members had consistently condemned terrorism over this period. In sum, prior to 9/11, EU counter-terrorism cooperation was more political than operational.[23]

Beginning with its reaction to 9/11, EU counter-terrorism cooperation has advanced in response to events. Immediately following the attacks, the EU Council (in which EU member states are represented, and which is not to be confused with the Council of Europe) held an extraordinary session and approved a Plan of Action on counter-terrorism with five priorities: enhancing police and judicial cooperation; developing international legal instruments; putting an end to the funding of terrorism; strengthening aviation security; and coordinating the EU's global action. Several outcomes have emerged from the plan, including improvements in extradition procedures (in the form of the European Arrest Warrant, agreed to in June 2002), an expanded mandate for Europol (including the formation of a dedicated counter-terrorism unit) and measures to ensure legal cooperation (the "Eurojust" mechanism, to aid investigators, prosecutors and judges). In this period, too, the EU succeeded in defining terrorism and also established a peer review mechanism, to evaluate each other's counter-terrorism policies. The plan itself was revised and expanded in 2004 and, following the Madrid bombings in that year, the position of counter-terrorism coordinator was established. In December 2005, after the London bombings in that July, the EU Council approved the EU Counter-terrorism Strategy.[24] The Strategy has four objectives: to *prevent* people from turning to terrorism by addressing conditions conducive; to *protect* EU citizens and infrastructure and reduce vulnerability to attack; to *pursue* and investigate terrorists, including impeding communications, travel and funding for terrorists; and to *respond* to attacks, by managing and minimizing the consequences, coordinating responses and meeting the needs of victims. The counter-terrorism coordinator has subsequently reported progress in advancing these objectives.[25]

In spite of these apparent achievements, critics are quick to point out the shortcomings of EU action. A fundamental concern here is the structure of the EU, which acts as an intergovernmental forum on JHA matters, without exercising legislative or binding authority. In the absence of mandatory measures, implementation gaps have come to characterize the EU's efforts. According to Oldrich Bures, "The recent experiences with Europol and Eurojust indeed seem to suggest that it is one thing for Europe's political elites to make public promises on the international exchange of counter-terrorism intelligence and EU-wide judicial cooperation, and quite another thing for them to persuade the relevant national agencies, over which politicians usually exercise less than perfect control, to comply."[26] With regard to Europol in particular, several alternative fora with smaller, limited memberships have arisen within Europe itself, providing substitutes for states that might be wary of sharing law enforcement and intelligence information with 26 others.[27] In this regard, behind the creation of the coordinator's position lies a political compromise between those states seeking to expand EU-level intelligence capabilities and those (with superior national capacity) content with the status quo. Doron Zimmermann surmises that, "The office of the Union coordinator for counter-terrorism is a political half-way house that is dangerously out of sync with the spirit of the aftermath of Madrid 2004."[28] Further, many of those measures that have been successfully advanced (such as the European Arrest Warrant) had been in train prior to 9/11, giving reason to question the ability of the EU to develop original responses to changed circumstances. Finally, EU-level measures have been subject to legal contestation (recall the *Kadi* decision pursuant to the UN's al Qaeda-Taliban sanctions regime, discussed in Chapter 3) as well as privacy concerns, impeding the EU in its collaborations with key partners, such as the United States.[29]

As this record suggests, there are limitations on what the EU can do to suppress terrorism. Whether these limitations can, in turn, sustain the argument that Europe is "soft on terrorism"[30] or that Europeans (as a matter of strategic culture) prefer "soft" (i.e. criminal justice) over "hard" (military) counter-terrorism tools,[31] is debatable. In this regard, EU action on counter-terrorism ought to be viewed in its broader context. One lesson here is that the EU is but one among many actors in the fields of counter-terrorism where, as we know, bilateral and informal contacts are often valued above formal, institutional cooperation. Pragmatically, it is little wonder that analysts question whether the EU is the right institution for the job, or suggest that the EU might be better at some tasks than others.[32] Here, the EU's current focus on initiatives to prevent radicalization and its efforts to export rules, norms and preventive strategies beyond the region may leverage the strengths of the organization.[33] Moreover, the EU's support for UN measures (especially the UN Strategy), and its willingness to interact with CTED and UNODC, may act as a kind of force multiplier for global initiatives.[34]

In addition to the Council of Europe and the EU, the Organization for Security and Cooperation in Europe (OSCE) is an active participant in multilateral counter-terrorism. The OSCE is the world's largest regional body, with 56 members spanning from North America to Central Asia, but mostly comprising European states. Its mission is to serve as a primary instrument for early warning, crisis management, conflict prevention and post-conflict rehabilitation. In doing so, the OSCE conceives of security along three dimensions—politico-military aspects, economic and environmental aspects, and the human dimension. In line with these prerogatives, the OSCE has evolved a comprehensive counter-terrorism approach, as set out in the Bucharest Plan of Action (December 2001).[35] In 2002, the OSCE established an Anti-Terrorism Unit to oversee the implementation of its comprehensive approach around five priority areas: building political support; enhancing the capacity of states to counter terrorism; identifying cutting-edge threats and options for response; fostering international cooperation on counter-terrorism issues; and promoting security within the framework of human rights. To these ends, the OSCE has collaborated with a wide range of other international, regional and specialist organizations to promote the adoption of treaties, facilitate and deliver technical assistance, and convene fora to build consensus around the nature of the terrorist threat and strategies for prevention.[36] As noted, human rights has been a central focus of the OSCE's work, including through its own human rights organ (the Office for Democratic Institutions and Human Rights), which published a manual on protecting human rights while countering terrorism in 2007.[37] Further, UN measures and bodies have figured prominently in the OSCE's work and advocacy, including a 2007 ministerial statement in support of the UN Global Counter-terrorism Strategy.[38]

Terrorism first appeared on the agenda of the Organization of African Unity (OAU) in 1992, with a decision of the OAU Assembly of Heads of State and Government Summit in Dakar, Senegal, concerning regional cooperation against extremism.[39] However, it was only after the 1998 attacks on the US embassies in Nairobi and Dar es Salaam that more substantive measures were pursued. In 1999, the OAU concluded the Convention on the Prevention and Combating of

Terrorism. The convention is broad in its scope, outlining areas for cooperation and establishing rules regarding jurisdiction and extradition. The convention also provides a definition of terrorism which, though comprehensive, excludes peoples engaged in struggles of national liberation. However, no mechanism for enforcement was included and implementation of the convention was left to member states. As a consequence, implementation was generally weak.

With the transition from the OAU to the African Union (AU) in 2002, and the intervening events of 9/11 and UN Security Council resolution 1373, the AU Commission convened a High-Level Inter-governmental Meeting on the Prevention and Combating of Terrorism in September of that year.[40] That meeting adopted the AU Plan of Action on the Prevention and Combating of Terrorism in Africa. The plan builds on resolution 1373 and expands it in certain ways. For example, the plan calls for the development of a common "Terrorism Activity Reporting schedules," to gather data on incidents, persons, organizations, places and resources of concern. The plan also established the African Center for Study and Research on Terrorism (ACSRT), as a site for research, analysis and training activities. The center is based in Algiers and became operational in 2004. Also in that year, the question of implementation and oversight was addressed with the addition of the 2004 Protocol to the Convention on the Prevention and Combating of Terrorism.[41] The protocol establishes the Peace and Security Council to oversee implementation of the convention, with facilitative and complementary roles given to the AU Commission, the ACSRT and subregional organizations.

If the AU has been active in elaborating rules and mechanisms, there remain serious problems with implementation and "the gap between aspirations and reality is immense."[42] Rates of ratification of the initial convention have been slow over time and the continental effort tends to be dominated by a few states. In light of the vagueness of the negotiation process (with little by way of critical dialogue or reflection), as well as ambiguities in several of the substantive provisions, Ibrahim Wani wonders whether there is much support for continental counter-terrorism action among states. These matters, alongside the limited support given to the institutions administering implementation, "raise serious concerns about the scope of the AU's commitment to counter-terrorism."[43]

Several subregional organizations in Africa are also engaged in counter-terrorism. In the Horn of Africa, the Inter-governmental Authority on Development (IGAD) was initially formed in 1986 with a development mandate, although that has expanded to peace and security issues over time.[44] In 2003, IGAD adopted an Implementation Plan to Counter Terrorism. Three years later, with support from the Dutch and Danish governments, the IGAD Capacity Building Program Against Terrorism (ICPAT) was launched.[45] Staffed with experts from the subregion and supported by an NGO (the Institute for Security Studies), ICPAT is overseen by a steering committee comprising the various stakeholders and represents a unique approach to counter-terrorism cooperation.[46] In a region that is characterized by high vulnerability to terrorism, low state capacity, and (in the past) relative inattention from the UN's counter-terrorism bodies, ICPAT has proven to be a valuable vehicle for counter-terrorism assistance.[47] UNODC and ICPAT established a formal working relationship in 2006. Since then, ICPAT has coordinated capacity-building assistance with a wide range of partners and donors, including a stronger engagement with UN organs.

Other subregional organizations in Africa, constrained by capacity limitations and with priorities other than terrorism, have engaged in some counter-terrorism-related diplomacy, but rarely gone further. In this category fall the East African Community[48] and the Southern African Development Community,[49] while the Economic Community of West African States (ECOWAS) has partnered on occasions with UNODC and CTED to advance legal cooperation in the subregion.[50] Viewed in this context, the success of ICPAT in "overcoming the human and financial resource limitations that ... many other African-based multilateral organizations suffer from," renders it something of a stand-out.[51]

Beyond Africa's formal institutions, a range of cooperative mechanisms of more recent origin have arisen at the behest of the United States, which has grown more concerned about Africa as a source of terrorism or support for terrorism. Reflecting the perceived strategic significance of the continent, the US military developed an African Command (AFRICOM) in 2007.[52] Similarly, since 9/11, Washington has taken steps to increase military, counter-terrorism and security assistance to states in vulnerable regions of Africa, sometimes acting on a minilateral basis. For example, in 2002, the Pan-Sahel Initiative was developed, to enhance the counter-terrorism capabilities of security forces in Chad, Niger, Mauritania and Mali. In 2005, the effort was expanded to Algeria, Morocco, Nigeria, Senegal and Tunisia, and renamed the Trans-Saharan Counter-terrorism Initiative (TSCTI). The latter is a multi-agency effort on the part of the US government (led by the State Department, along with the Treasury, Defense, and USAID) and, beyond being a conduit for bilateral assistance, aims to improve coordination on counter-terrorism issues among participating states.[53] This route to multilateral counter-terrorism on the continent is unique to the post-9/11 period.

In the Middle East, the Gulf Cooperation Council (GCC) has consistently condemned terrorism in statements from its highest authority, the Supreme Council. However, consistent with the practice of its six member states, the GCC distinguishes terrorism from the legitimate struggle of peoples against occupation.[54] GCC states have also developed a strategy (2002), signed a declaration (2002) and an agreement (2004), established a "Permanent Anti-Terrorism Committee" (2006), and hosted international workshops on terrorism. Further, the GCC maintains an annual Joint Council and Ministerial Meeting with the EU, at which the organizations have endorsed UN counter-terrorism measures, including the Global Counter-terrorism Strategy.[55] Although the impact of GCC initiatives is difficult to evaluate, the organization has tended to emphasize the root causes of extremism and the role of the media in radicalization in its counter-terrorism diplomacy.[56]

As in other regions, efforts at multilateral counter-terrorism in South Asia are subject to the political differences among states. Notably, action against terrorism within the South Asian Association for Regional Cooperation (SAARC) remains contingent upon the contentious bilateral relations between its two biggest members—India and Pakistan.[57] Nonetheless, SAARC states adopted a Regional Convention on the Suppression of Terrorism in 1987. That convention used the 1977 European convention as a touchstone, avoiding the difficult issues of defining terrorism (but, rather, elaborating a series of offences to be covered), emphasizing extradition arrangements and identifying areas for cooperation.[58] After 9/11, acknowledging the need to update the convention, member states added a protocol (2004), drawing upon resolution 1373 and the UN Terrorist Financing Convention. However, aspects of the protocol were initially resisted by some and, as with the convention, prospects for implementation remain low.[59] SAARC has ventured some more operational measures of late (including the establishment of a Terrorist Offences Monitoring Desk in its secretariat), and a convention on mutual legal assistance was concluded in 2008.[60] Most recently, SAARC foreign ministers restated their support for the conclusion of the debate on the comprehensive convention on terrorism, while also undertaking to establish a High-Level Group of Eminent Experts, to "review and make proposals to further strengthen SAARC anti-terrorism mechanisms, including for pragmatic cooperation."[61]

Bridging South and Southeast Asia, the Bay of Bengal Initiative for Multisectoral Technical and Economic Cooperation (BIMSTEC) has taken some preliminary steps towards counter-terrorism cooperation.[62] These include an undertaking to cooperate with each other, the establishment of a group on counter-terrorism and transnational crime (led by India) and a draft convention on combating terrorism that is close to completion.[63]

Straddling Europe and Asia, the Shanghai Cooperation Organization (SCO) was formed out of the Shanghai Five in June 2001.[64] At that time, too, members agreed to a convention on "combating terrorism, separatism and extremism," elaborating broad areas and modalities for cooperation, and undertaking to establish a "regional counter-terrorist structure" in Bishkek, Kyrgyzstan. The latter was eventually established in 2004, in Tashkent, as the "Regional Anti-Terrorism Structure" (RATS), with 30 staff.[65] Cooperation through RATS has mostly involved joint exercises among military and dedicated anti-terrorism forces, for example, to protect infrastructure and rescue hostages. In 2008, the annual Heads of State Declaration affirmed the commitment of member states to the UN Global Counter-terrorism Strategy and the comprehensive convention on international terrorism. Most recently, meeting in Yekaterinburg, SCO states concluded a new convention on counter-terrorism, with the aim of shoring up the legal basis for cooperation among them.[66] There are further signs that SCO states will engage more directly in implementation of the UN Strategy, with a ministerial conference planned in 2010, in collaboration with the UN Regional Center for Central Asia in Ashgabat, Turkmenistan.[67] If this comes to fruition, it will entail a broadening of SCO's approach to counter-terrorism cooperation, beyond a focus on military tools.

Regional politics in Southeast Asia has yielded several institutions and cooperative mechanisms across a range of functional areas including security and now covering terrorism.[68] However, the traditional weakness of regional institutions—designed, as they are, to preserve the norm of non-interference and the sovereignty of their members—has often limited their ability to act beyond diplomatic statements. Synonymous with this trend is the Association of Southeast Asian Nations (ASEAN).[69] Two fora within ASEAN generally deal with terrorism: the annual Ministers' Meeting on Transnational Crime and the more frequently convened Senior Officers' Meeting on Transnational Crime. Through these gatherings, and in the Leaders' Meetings, ASEAN states have condemned terrorism and pledged joint action to suppress it.[70] In 2007, ASEAN concluded a Convention on Counter-terrorism, which enumerates terrorist offences (citing the UN terrorism conventions) and identifies areas for cooperation including, subject to the consent of the parties, the "root causes" and "conditions conducive" to terrorism.[71] For all of the norm-building, however, it is difficult to demonstrate the effect of ASEAN's pronouncements and, "rather than serving as a force multiplier ... ASEAN's response to terrorism has largely been no greater than the sum of the contributions of its individual members."[72] With that said, Ralf Emmers argues that ASEAN tends to be viewed

as an "umbrella organization" by its participants, providing a normative framework in which to pursue national counter-terrorism strategies.
In this role, ASEAN has indeed facilitated operational cooperation (e.
g. among law enforcement and intelligence officials) within the region,
while also providing a useful vehicle to engage external actors.[73] The
recent successes of ASEAN countries in reducing the number of terrorist attacks in the region can be attributed in part to the willingness
of states to engage in informal, operational forms of cooperation with
each other and those nearby.[74]

Relatedly, the ASEAN Regional Forum (ARF) was established in
1993 to foster dialogue on political and security issues, and facilitate
confidence-building and preventive diplomacy, among its diverse
membership.[75] More a "process" than an institution, the ARF established an Inter-Sessional Meeting on Counter-terrorism following 9/11.
Over time, ARF states have engaged in counter-terrorism cooperation
through thematic workshops and declaratory statements.[76] Western
members of the ARF have suggested that the body move in the direction of more operational-level cooperation and, for example, the
United States recently proposed the development of an "ARF Work-
plan on Counter-terrorism and Transnational Crime," to utilize the
Forum in a capacity-building role.[77] However, other participants
expressed some reticence about establishing a permanent mechanism.
Here, it is important to note that, despite its broader membership,
ARF functions in line with the same norms as ASEAN concerning
non-interference. As such, and with limited institutional capacity of its
own (a small staff in the ASEAN secretariat is dedicated to the Forum),
the role of the ARF is constrained.[78]

The Asia-Pacific Economic Cooperation (APEC) forum was founded in 1989 and now numbers 21 members from around the Pacific.[79]
Its mission refers to trade and investment liberalization, business facilitation, and economic and technical cooperation. Counter-terrorism
appeared on the organization's agenda only after 9/11, framed as a
necessary part of advancing the core economic goals of the organization.
According to the then Australian foreign minister, Alexander Downer,
"Security and economic prosperity in APEC cannot be separated, they
go hand in hand."[80] The extension of the organization's mandate in
this regard has not always been welcomed by other members, who have
had reservations about participating in a "global war on terror" and
who generally prefer to elaborate non-binding commitments.[81] Nonetheless, APEC has attempted, with "relative success," to pursue an
operational approach to counter-terrorism.[82] Beyond issuing forceful diplomatic statements, APEC established a Counter-terrorism Task Force

in 2003, whose mandate has recently been extended through 2010.[83] The task force is charged with overseeing capacity-building assistance through APEC and liaising with other international organizations in the field. A wide range of programs and workshops have been delivered, including on different aspects of terrorist financing and aviation security. Most prominently, since 2002, the Secure Trade in the APEC Region (STAR) initiative has involved an annual meeting on thematic issues relating to the security of airports, seaports, shipping containers, cargo and the supply chain. A further innovative tool used by APEC is the Counter-terrorism Action Plan—a template (not unlike those used by the CTC/CTED and the 1267 Committee) designed to evaluate states' implementation of relevant counter-terrorism standards. While the information contained in the plan often falls well short of being comprehensive, the mechanism was retooled in 2008 to better identify capacity-building needs. In their 2008 declaration, APEC leaders acknowledged the importance of the UN Global Counter-terrorism Strategy although, in light of the global financial crisis, terrorism was not prioritized as it had been in the past.[84]

If formal institutions in the region have yielded mixed results, since 9/11 innovative forms of multilateralism have been ventured or extended, to share best practices and train local officials, especially concerning the law enforcement aspect of counter-terrorism. Beginning in the mid-1990s, US law enforcement agencies developed "international law enforcement academies" (ILEAs) in several locations throughout the world, reflecting a concern with evolving patterns of transnational crime in the post-Cold War era.[85] An ILEA opened in Bangkok in 1998 and, despite an initial focus on drug trafficking, counter-terrorism-related courses are now offered. Although the agreement that founded ILEA-Bangkok was bilateral (between the Thai and US governments), there has been broader regional consultation (for example, on curricular issues) and courses are aimed at a regional audience (and are translated into five languages).[86] A similar path to multilateral counter-terrorism has now been taken in Malaysia and Indonesia. The Southeast Asian Regional Centre for Counter-terrorism (SEARCCT) was established in Kuala Lumpur in 2003 and falls under Malaysia's Foreign Affairs Department.[87] Since then, SEARCCT has hosted more than 1,600 officials from more than 30 countries, delivering instruction on a range of counter-terrorism priorities, including legal aspects, interdiction, maritime security, terrorist financing, crisis management, border security and the use of chemical, biological, radiological and nuclear weapons.[88] Again, multilateral collaboration here has occurred both in terms of the development of courses (which are often jointly sponsored with a wide range of donors and partners) and by serving a regional (and global) audience. In Indonesia, the Jakarta Centre for Law Enforcement Cooperation (JCLEC) opened in 2004 as a joint initiative of the Indonesian and Australian governments, but with (financial or in-kind) support from the Netherlands, Canada, the UK, Denmark, Italy, and others.[89] Courses here cover investigations, criminal intelligence, forensics, financial science and communications, and more than 840 participants from Asia, Europe, the Pacific, and the United States have participated.[90] Beyond the experience of attending classes at the three regional centers, participants benefit by developing the kinds of informal, professional networks that have long characterized law enforcement cooperation against terrorism. The three centers enjoy political support from the highest levels. For example, the foreign ministers, justice ministers and police chiefs from Australia, Indonesia, Malaysia, the Philippines, Singapore, and Thailand have met on several occasions as the "Bali Counter-terrorism Process," to build consensus and set the agenda for multilateral counter-terrorism in the subregion. The work of the three centers is endorsed in their statements.[91]

Within Oceania, the Pacific Islands Forum (PIF) has been addressing a range of transnational security threats since the pre-9/11 period.[92] Reflecting the influence of the two largest members—Australia and New Zealand—terrorism has been included on the security agenda within the region, although some observers have remained skeptical about the gravity of the threat.[93] Building on past actions in related domains, member states signed the Nasonini Declaration on Regional Security in 2002, citing resolution 1373 and undertaking to legislate and cooperate against transnational crime and terrorism.[94] However, implementing these measures proved difficult. With New Zealand in the PIF chair in 2004, a roundtable meeting was held, yielding a Counter-terrorism Working Group.[95] As a result, cooperation has been advanced, such as through the dissemination of model legislation and the convening of several workshops and training programs on terrorist financing, border security and other issues. This has involved interaction with the three UN Security Council terrorism-related committees and UNODC.[96] In sum, while "Combating terrorism has not been a number one priority for Forum island countries," multilateral counter-terrorism has been integrated into PIF, often framed as part of its response to transnational crime.[97]

Affinity-based groups

The principal contribution of the League of Arab States to multilateral counter-terrorism is the 1998 Arab Convention for the Suppression of

Terrorism. The convention has a broad scope, including measures to prevent terrorism, provisions regarding cooperation among signatories and extradition arrangements. However, the convention is more often remarked upon for its definition of terrorism which, in line with the position frequently espoused by the 22 members of the body, excludes the struggle against foreign occupation.[98] After 9/11, the Secretary-General of the League formed a team of experts to report on the impact of resolution 1373 for the League. In this regard, the League has been active in convening regional workshops on thematic counter-terrorism issues. League experts have also endorsed the UN Strategy.[99] Most recently, the definition of terrorism contained in the convention has been broadened to include incitement (covering the dissemination of printed materials and recordings), as well as the financing of terrorism. Efforts are ongoing to conclude a League convention on the latter.[100]

The 1999 Convention of the Islamic Conference on Combating Terrorism provides a similar caveat in its definition of terrorism, excluding national liberation movements. The Organization of the Islamic Conference (OIC) has been active on terrorism as far back as 1994, when it adopted a Code of Conduct for Combating International Terrorism.[101] While OIC states have often been at the center of political disputes regarding terrorism in the UN, the organization formed a ministerial-level committee on terrorism after 9/11. The OIC has also interacted with CTED officials with a view to capacity-building initiatives among members.[102] It has also collaborated with UNODC to organize workshops. The current Ten Year Program of Action, adopted in 2005, restates the commitment of members to combating terrorism, and statements out of other OIC fora, such as the foreign ministers' meetings have consistently pledged to cooperate against terrorism.[103]

A similarly strident view of international terrorism is espoused by the Non-Aligned Movement (NAM). The movement's main contribution has been at the level of norms, articulating a definition and understanding of terrorism that preserves the legitimacy of struggles by peoples under colonial or alien domination and foreign occupation. NAM's 118 members have had the issue of terrorism on their agenda since the pre-9/11 period.[104] Then, as today, statements have referred to initiatives in train in the UN General Assembly where NAM members have been able to exert most influence. (Indeed, since 1999, Assembly resolutions under the title "Measures to Eliminate International Terrorism" have devoted a preambular paragraph to recalling the relevant NAM declarations on terrorism. Recently, other bodies, including regional and subregional organizations, have also been cited en masse in a preambular paragraph—only NAM receives separate treatment).

In this regard, the most recent statement on the topic out of NAM fora takes positions on a number of issues currently before the Assembly. For example, while NAM members support the UN Global Counter-terrorism Strategy, they note the need for more interaction and transparency on the part of CTITF in implementing it.[105] Relatedly, the movement indicates its support for the Tunisian idea of an international code of conduct in combating terrorism, the Saudi proposal for an international center on the topic, the long-debated call for an international summit on terrorism under the auspices of the UN (initially suggested by Syria in the 1980s) and the conclusion of the comprehensive convention, while also calling on the Security Council to improve the integrity of the list of targets under the al Qaeda-Taliban sanctions regime. Thus, while there has been consistency in the position of NAM on terrorism over time, the movement has shown the capacity to frame current issues in terms of long-held principles.

The Commonwealth group of states has preferred an approach to multilateral counter-terrorism that emphasizes capacity-building assistance, relevant to its membership (54 states, including small jurisdictions and others in the developing world) and mission (which refers to the values of democracy and development).[106] Soon after 9/11, the Commonwealth Committee on Terrorism was formed and a Plan of Action drafted. That plan identified five main priorities: legal assistance, towards the implementation of resolution 1373; assistance in ratifying the UN terrorism conventions; a review of Commonwealth extradition arrangements; law enforcement cooperation; and measures to combat money laundering and terrorist financing.[107] Beginning in 2002, the Commonwealth Secretariat—most often acting through its Legal and Constitutional Affairs or Governance and Institutional Development divisions—began convening workshops on a range of topics. These have included legal issues (i.e. legislative drafting, prosecutions and investigations), law enforcement and policing, terrorist financing, customs issues, and assistance in reporting to UN Security Council bodies. The Secretariat has developed several tools of its own in delivering and facilitating technical assistance, including a model law on counter-terrorism (and implementation kit), a counter-terrorism training manual (enabling a "train-the-trainers" approach) and a guide to anti-money laundering and counter-terrorist financing standards.[108] The regional focus of these initiatives has been Africa, the Caribbean and the Pacific, and the Commonwealth has worked in tandem with regional and subregional bodies, as well as UN agencies.[109] Recently, the Commonwealth has expanded the scope of its counter-terrorism-related activities by studying the causes of conflict, violence and extremism, and by drawing attention to the human rights implications of counter-terrorism action.[110]

Alliances and other limited-membership groups: NATO and the G7/G8

My discussion to this point makes clear that regional and subregional organizations, and affinity-based bodies, tend to undertake certain kinds of counter-terrorism tasks, i.e. diplomatic pronouncements and the provision of capacity-building and technical assistance, toward the goal of preventing terrorist attacks. In pursuing more offensive measures, in particular those involving the use of force, states have turned to military alliances as vehicles for multilateral counter-terrorism. The most prominent example of this is the North Atlantic Treaty Organization (NATO),[111] formed in 1949 as the Western bulwark against the Soviet Union, and a defining feature of the structure of international politics for the duration of the Cold War. Since the end of the Cold War, efforts to redefine NATO's mission have attracted much debate, with some observers pointing to its irrelevance in changed circumstances, and others arguing for its ongoing utility.[112] Building on the latter argument, some within the organization have framed counter-terrorism as NATO's "new mission."[113] While there is some evidence to substantiate this claim, NATO's expansion to a counter-terrorism mission has rarely proceeded without controversy and, as such, the emergence of the "global war on terror" has rather underscored—not ameliorated—the alliance's post-Cold War dilemmas.[114]

Terrorism appeared on NATO's agenda prior to 9/11 at the urging of the United States. A working group was initially established in 1987. Later, terrorism was included in the alliance's 1999 Strategic Concept.[115] NATO's response to 9/11 was notable.[116] Within 24 hours, NATO members invoked the collective defense provision of the alliance's charter (Art. 5), thereby viewing the attacks on the United States as attacks on all alliance members. Further, NATO members offered military assistance to the United States in its invasion of Afghanistan. Subsequently, the Prague Summit in November 2002 approved a new framework (the Military Concept for Defense against Terrorism) to guide NATO's actions against terrorism, including through defensive measures, consequence management (following an attack on a member state), offensive action, and military cooperation with non-military forces.

Over time, NATO has advanced each of these goals somewhat. The most visible contribution of the alliance is of course the conflict in Afghanistan. Since 2003, NATO has commanded the International

Security Assistance Force (ISAF). Today, ISAF's mandate includes combat and non-combat roles (such as reconstruction and training Afghan forces), and covers the entire country (it was initially limited to Kabul). The authorization for ISAF derives from resolutions of the UN Security Council, and the force numbers nearly 60,000 troops from 42 countries, including all of NATO's members.[117] However, building the force to this level has proven contentious on occasions. NATO's initial offer of assistance to the United States was rebuffed in 2001, as the United States preferred to act unencumbered by its allies. The US decision to go to war with Iraq in 2003 was opposed by several alliance partners and this, in part, affected their willingness to contribute troops to Afghanistan. In committing troops, many states have imposed "national caveats," limiting the terms of their deployment. Moreover, it was only after ISAF's mandate was expanded in 2006 that it took on more combat roles.[118] Most recently, despite members coming together to celebrate the alliance's 60th anniversary, US efforts to have allies contribute more troops to the effort have yielded only modest commitments.[119]

Outside of ISAF, NATO states have pursued counter-terrorism cooperation in other domains. Since October 2001, Operation Active Endeavor (which is authorized under Art. 5) has involved allies in maritime surveillance and interdiction exercises in the Mediterranean Sea, to protect shipping and ports against terrorism. Under this initiative, more than 100,000 merchant vessels have been hailed and more than 148 suspect ships have been boarded.[120] Other counter-terrorism actions have included limited roles in intelligence sharing, technological development and consequence management (in post-attack scenarios). In addition, from 2004, NATO has been engaged in training Iraqi security forces.[121] Still, de Nevers concludes that, by virtue of enduring gaps in capabilities and perceptions among member states, NATO plays a "largely supportive" role in counter-terrorism.[122] As with others, she questions the suitability of NATO to the diverse tasks of counter-terrorism cooperation. Further, there is a sense in which the limitations of the alliance reflect the limitations of multilateralism per se, given that "Many of the tasks of counter-terrorism alliances are better done in a bilateral setting."[123] Recent efforts by states to develop innovative forms of security-related counter-terrorism cooperation (such as US efforts in Africa, the counter-terrorism centers in Southeast Asia, and the SCO) can also be viewed in this light.

Just as NATO has been pressed into service to advance certain "hard power" aspects of counter-terrorism, states sometimes prefer more flexible cooperative arrangements to advance non-military, operational-level tasks. The archetypical example here is the G7—subsequently G8 (after Russia joined in 1997)—group of states. The G8 offers several advantages to its members. Its limited membership means that consensus can be easier to achieve. Also, given that its members include several of the leading counter-terrorism assistance donors in the world, the G8 has the potential to wield significant influence. However, the G8 states have not always achieved consensus and influence through collective action. States within the group sometimes have different priorities and the system of a rotating presidency means that issues may not receive consistent attention or adequate follow-up. These dilemmas are borne out in the history of G7/G8 diplomacy on counter-terrorism, as in the post-9/11 period.[124]

The G7 first addressed the topic of terrorism in 1978 with the Bonn statement on air hijacking. Over time, the group issued several more statements, sometimes with specific undertakings to act, and on both general and specific issues.[125] Indeed, the group evolved several tools in its pre-9/11 efforts to suppress terrorism. At the broadest level, summit statements and declarations lent political weight to counter-terrorism issues, while also generating publicity for the cause. At the ministerial level, the G7/G8 provided a forum for foreign, justice, interior and finance officials to convene. This aided the harmonization of national counter-terrorism legislation, providing a bridge between the more technical aspects of counter-terrorism and the political function of the summits themselves. Finally, beginning with the 1986 Tokyo Summit, the G7/G8 has maintained a schedule of expert-level meetings. This mechanism was renewed in 1996, when the G8 adopted the "Agreement on 25 Measures for Combating Terrorism" and created a "Counter-terrorist Directory of Skills and Competencies." Between 1996 and 9/11, four such G8 Counter-terrorism Expert Meetings were held. According to Andre Belelieu, the multilayered structure "allowed the G8 to evolve into a forum producing ambitious, comprehensive and detailed counter-terrorism agreements that ... produced effective results, such as the [1995] Ottawa and [1996] ministerial declarations on terrorism."[126] However, despite this upbeat assessment, he also reflects that, "if the G8 ... failed in one major respect, this would be its tendency to follow up years of impressive results with complete inactivity on this issue."[127] As such, an inconsistent political focus on terrorism undermined the ability of the G8 to achieve the goals it had once set for itself.

G8 states have somewhat replicated this record in the post-9/11 period, although there are now signs of a break with the past. Again, the G8 has defined a broad counter-terrorism agenda. The first opportunity to do so came with the June 2002 summit in Kananaskis,

Canada.[128] The group duly established priorities for counter-terrorism (e.g. terrorist financing, removing terrorists' sanctuary in Afghanistan, and border controls), while also endorsing resolution 1373 and the UN terrorism-related conventions.[129] A separate statement on transport security listed a series of areas for action, including on the movement of people (e.g. systems for states to exchange data on passengers), shipping containers, aviation and maritime security, and land transportation.[130] These measures were complemented by action in 2003 to create a "Counter-terrorism Action Group" (CTAG) to build political will and coordinate capacity-building assistance among donors. In doing so, the G8 again referred to the role of the CTC in this regard and undertook to work closely with it.[131] Indeed, the CTC is a standing member of CTAG, as is the European Commission, while several non-G8 states (donors, such as Australia, Switzerland and Spain) and international organizations (e.g. UNODC, OSCE, ICAO, IMO and the World Bank) have attended meetings.[132]

Also in 2003, the G8 extended the transportation security initiative to cover the use of Man-Portable Air Defense Systems (MANPADS) by terrorists.[133] A further statement elaborated an Action Plan to counter the spread of WMD.[134] As these developments suggest, the G8's counter-terrorism agenda tended to broaden over time. For example, in 2004, the "G8 Secure and Facilitated International Travel Initiative (SAFTI)" was agreed, with 28 individual items for action, restating and extending existing measures.[135] Further, the 2005 summit at Gleneagles in Scotland—which was interrupted by the London bombings on 7 July that year—introduced a concern for the prevention of radicalization and recruitment to terrorism.[136] However, just as the substantive focus of the G8's counter-terrorism pronouncements became broader, the capacity-building mission of the CTAG began to wane. Eric Rosand cites several reasons for this.[137] Recall that the CTC was experiencing a period of relative weakness around this time, reducing its input into CTAG's decision-making on capacity-building assistance. Group members found that their initial success (which focused on terrorist financing, where institutional partners were relatively effective) could not be replicated in other domains. In turn, they devoted less time to CTAG meetings and downgraded their status relative to other G8 fora.

But even if CTAG has not always met the expectations of its founders, there are signs of a renewal. In recent years, the G8 has made a point of indicating support for the UN's counter-terrorism work (including endorsement of the Global Counter-terrorism Strategy).[138] More substantively, beginning under the Japanese presidency of the G8 in 2008, there has been an effort to capitalize on the newfound momentum within CTED. Meetings are better coordinated, information is exchanged in advance and CTED utilizes the forum to identify capacity-building priorities. As a result, there are numerous examples of assistance having been provided pursuant to this approach.[139] Further, there is reason to think that the work of the Japanese will be consolidated under the Italian and Canadian presidencies of the G8.

Multilateral counter-terrorism in practice: towards regime complexity

In the Introduction, I cited Raustiala and Victor's idea of a "regime complex" (that is, "an array of partially overlapping and nonhierarchical institutions governing a particular issue area") to suggest that multilateral counter-terrorism today can be usefully understood in this way.[140] To illustrate this claim, this section briefly surveys three key areas of counter-terrorism cooperation—law enforcement and intelligence, terrorist financing, and maritime security. In each of these domains, multiple national, regional and international actors are involved in counter-terrorism activities, elaborating new norms and rules, and implementing diverse programs. Beyond this similarity, the form and content of cooperation varies across these three areas. Different political dynamics and interests yield different cooperative outcomes and varying degrees of institutionalization, both within and across issue areas. These kinds of dynamics also characterize other aspects of multilateral counter-terrorism, and domains such as migration control and non-proliferation could also be raised in this context.[141] For present purposes, the examples given here reveal both the diversity and limits of multilateralism, which is sometimes declined in favor of unilateral or bilateral action.

Law enforcement and intelligence cooperation

As noted in the preceding chapter, since 9/11 Interpol has experienced both functional and organizational expansion in the area of counter-terrorism.[142] Over this period, Interpol's approach has emphasized communications, including, most notably, the "I-24/7" system (a secure, internet-based mechanism to facilitate the exchange of and access to information). Other projects—whether on lost and stolen travel documents, theft of radiological materials, tracing small arms and light weapons, or money laundering—aim to leverage the institutional advantages of Interpol while being sensitive to the inherent dilemmas of law enforcement cooperation among 187 member states.[143] As Mathieu Deflem argues, "The diversity among Interpol's member agencies ... has ... hindered the organization's effectiveness in its missions, as members do not always trust one another. Therefore, unilaterally executed transnational police operations may be preferred instead of participation in the multilateral structures of Interpol."[144] Such reticence towards cooperation may be particularly acute on matters relating to terrorism.

As a consequence of this, states have developed other, smaller fora for law enforcement cooperation against terrorism. In many parts of the world, law enforcement and police cooperation are organized at the regional level. In some cases, these bodies have both assisted in and benefited from regional capacity-building efforts. For example, the East African Police Chiefs' Cooperation Organization (EAPCCO) is housed in the Interpol subregional bureau in Nairobi and facilitates its members' access to Interpol resources.[145] In Southeast Asia, regional police cooperation has taken the form of a discussion forum, with a few operational initiatives. The peak body in the region, ASEANAPOL, has only recently announced its intention to establish a headquarters in Kuala Lumpur.[146] In that region, training activities for law enforcement officials have been advanced through innovative mechanisms, such as ILEA-Bangkok, SEARCCT and JCLEC. In Europe, efforts to develop a regional law enforcement body have been constrained by the same kinds of obstacles that manifest at the global level—relatively weak institutions and a lack of trust among members.[147] To date, cooperation has produced some institutional and programmatic innovations, including threat assessments and other analytical products pitched at the regional level.

Beneath regional arrangements such as these are the ad hoc or less formal mechanisms that law enforcement officials have long utilized to facilitate cooperation. Many such contacts occur bilaterally, but have nonetheless yielded novel forms of exchange. One such example concerns the New York City Police Department (NYPD). The NYPD was the first police department in the United States to develop a dedicated counter-terrorism bureau (in 2002) and has worked over time to improve relationships with partner agencies in the United States, especially those at the federal level. More notably for present purposes, the NYPD is now an international actor in its own right, with liaison officers stationed in several cities in key regions, such as Europe and the Middle East. In turn, the NYPD has used these relationships in post-attack situations (including in London, Madrid and Mumbai), to channel information in real time to analysts in New York, enabling up-to-date assessments of the threat to New York.[148]

There are of course other examples of close bilateral ties among law enforcement officers.[149] The point of raising them here is to note the range of approaches to counter-terrorism cooperation that law enforcement officials have forged over time. These include, but are by no means limited to, multilateralism at the global and regional levels. Indeed, as in earlier periods of history, practitioners are apt to note that, of all the options for cooperation, bilateral ties have the most utility. The law enforcement aspects of multilateral counter-terrorism ought to be viewed in this light.

Formal institutions are even less likely to figure prominently in intelligence cooperation. It is no accident that, in a book about *multilateral* counter-terrorism, relatively little has been said about perhaps the most important counter-terrorism tool—intelligence and covert action—which states most often pursue either unilaterally or bilaterally.[150] Put simply, sharing sources, raw data or analytical products in multilateral fora entails risks: "intelligence costs tend to rise and benefits decline as the number of parties increases because the importance of ensuring competitive advantage ... biases most intelligence services against sharing sensitive sources in multiparty arrangements."[151] But this should not be interpreted to mean that intelligence cooperation is a complete non-starter. Far from it—the nature of intelligence cooperation on counter-terrorism has changed over time and, on the whole, there has been an uptick in cooperation since 9/11. Three developments are of note here.

First, driving the increase in cooperation, new bilateral relationships have emerged among states that did not cooperate in the past. According to Chris Clough, "the most unlikely alliances have arisen: the United States and European intelligence agencies working with those of Russia and China; Iran and India; Pakistan and Israel; and all of the Middle East and Far Eastern nations, bar the inevitable rogue few."[152] This development is interpreted as a straightforward, pragmatic response by clandestine agencies faced with a threat that no single service can contain.[153] With that said, such collaborations leave states open to criticism for cooperating with unsavory partners. Viewed alongside recent high-profile intelligence controversies (such as rendition and Iraqi WMD), some have wondered whether current accountability mechanisms at the national level ought to be revised.[154]

Second, pre-existing intelligence groupings have been utilized as part of the counter-terrorism effort after 9/11. These groups include the UK/USA Agreement (which also includes Australia, Canada and New Zealand), the Club of Berne (comprising EU member states, as well as Norway and Switzerland) and the NATO Special Committee.[155]

However, these groups are assessed to have had a "minimal" impact at best and, in describing their role, Stéphane Lefebvre restates the importance of bilateral relationships.[156]

Third, in one case at least, a new mechanism has emerged since 9/11 to facilitate dialogue and collaboration among intelligence services. The seventh "Meeting of Heads of Special Services, Security Agencies and Law Enforcement Organizations" was hosted by Russia's Federal Security Service in Khanty-Mansiysk in March 2008. It was attended by 76 delegates from 54 countries, as well as representatives from the UN CTC and from regional bodies. The forum has grown since 37 states attended the initial meeting in 2002. This group has made a point of endorsing UN counter-terrorism measures and provides an annual briefing on its meetings to the Security Council.[157] Beyond declaratory statements, the size and longevity of the meeting sets it apart from other intelligence-related groupings. But this also infers that cooperation is likely to remain more normative than operational.

These developments rather underscore the functional origins of intelligence cooperation—"Collaboration is not an end in itself. It is utility that drives collaboration."[158] To put the point in comparative perspective, whereas states have been happy to disagree on terrorism in certain UN fora, intelligence cooperation only proceeds on the basis of shared interests. As a consequence, to draw on international relations theory, "Perhaps clandestine agencies and their intelligence alliances should be viewed less as exponents of realism and more as smooth and experienced exemplars of liberal institutionalism."[159] Indeed, the fact that patterns of intelligence cooperation have changed subsequent to 9/11 perhaps reflects a degree of convergence among states' perceptions of the threat from terrorism today.

Cooperation to suppress the financing of terrorism

If institutions have played a secondary role in law enforcement and intelligence cooperation, multilateralism has been central to the effort to suppress terrorist financing. Assessments of the financial aspects of the "global war on terror" make the point that cooperation has advanced both quickly and broadly.[160] This outcome reflects the unique attributes of existing institutions in this domain, which were designed by strong states to set and enforce anti-money-laundering standards. Their adaptation to the task of countering terrorist financing attests to the ability of strong states to influence patterns of cooperation, while also illustrating the diverse forms of multilateral counter-terrorism today.

In the years prior to 9/11, several states pursued terrorists' finances without significant efforts at coordination and cooperation. Although the Security Council had imposed financial sanctions three times for reasons related to terrorism in the 1990s, these measures were not robustly implemented by states at that time. Similarly, the 1999 UN Convention for the Suppression of the Financing of Terrorism attracted scant support, and only four states took the opportunity to join it before 9/11. Only after 9/11 did counter-terrorist financing initiatives become institutionalized, on the back of the anti-money-laundering initiatives of the 1980s and 1990s. The key multilateral mechanism here has been the Financial Action Task Force (FATF). The rise of the FATF and the anti-money-laundering regime is described in greater depth elsewhere,[161] but four of its pre-9/11 features are relevant here. First, the FATF is a limited-membership body comprising mostly industrialized states.[162] The FATF had been initiated in 1989 by the G7 and initially included 15 states. For this reason, Dan Drezner characterizes the FATF as a "club," enabling it to develop rules that reflect consensus among strong states but involve high adjustment costs for others.[163] Although membership of the FATF grew over time, pre-9/11 accounts of the emergence of the anti-money-laundering regime emphasize the role of powerful states.[164]

Second, the FATF member states exercised influence by developing standards. The "40 Recommendations" against money laundering were first issued in 1990 and include measures concerning customer identification, record-keeping practices and suspicious transaction reporting. While the initial focus of the anti-money-laundering effort was drug money, the recommendations provide scope for implementing states to legislate on other so-called predicate offences (the proceeds of which would be covered by laundering laws). Moreover, despite the limited membership of the FATF, it established an active external relations effort and the recommendations urge banks to exercise special caution regarding transactions involving countries that do not conform to the standard. They call upon members to ensure that subsidiaries of home financial institutions registered aboard adhere to the recommendations. Subsequently, the G7 invited non-members to implement the recommendations.[165] In doing so, the FATF extended to itself a global mandate.

Third, the FATF disseminated its standards through a growing network of anti-money-laundering officials and experts. Under the aegis of FATF member states, so-called FATF-style regional bodies (FSRBs) emerged in the Caribbean (in 1990), the Asia-Pacific (1997), within the Council of Europe (1997), in Eastern and Southern Africa (1999) and South America (2000).[166] Over the course of the 1990s, anti-money-laundering standards were increasingly discussed among officials from national financial intelligence units (FIUs), who initiated the Egmont Group of FIUs in 1995. In 2000, a group of private sector banks—the "Wolfsberg Group"—developed a series of principles for banks to adopt in order to comply with anti-money-laundering standards. More generally, FATF influence was extended through its interactions with a host of international and regional organizations, including the IMF, the World Bank, regional development banks, the Commonwealth, the Offshore Group of Banking Supervisors, the World Customs Organization, Interpol, the International Organization of Securities Commissions, and the (precursor to) UNODC.[167] As each body endorsed the "40 Recommendations," rules authored by the FATF "club" gained authority for all.

Fourth, the FATF utilized several mechanisms to enforce the recommendations, including a graduated series of self-assessments and peer review evaluations, with the possibility of sanctions for non-compliance against both members and non-members. Most prominently, the Non-Cooperative Countries and Territories (NCCT) initiative, launched in 2000, provided a mechanism to "name and shame" non-compliant states, requiring that members subject transactions to additional scrutiny. While considered discriminatory and overtly political by some,[168] it is credited with inducing compliance with global standards.[169]

There are important differences between money laundering and terrorist financing. Whereas the former seeks to cleanse monies gained through past criminal activity, the latter includes the detection and apprehension of resources (both licit and illicit) that may be used for future terrorist acts. Despite these differences, the FATF has been adapted to the "global war on terror," as counter-terrorist financing measures have been framed by the United States and others as complementary to the nascent anti-money-laundering regime.[170] In October 2001, FATF members convened an extraordinary session to consider "necessary steps for preventing and combating terrorist financing activity."[171] At this meeting the mandate of the FATF was formally extended and "8 Special Recommendations on Terrorist Financing" (SRs) were elaborated. A ninth SR was added in October 2004. The nine SRs include recommendations to criminalize terrorist financing (i.e. the provision of funds for the purpose of terrorism, or for the benefit of terrorists), to require suspicious transactions reports related to terrorism, and to better regulate charities and wire transfer services.[172] They are widely acknowledged to set the global standard for counter-terrorist financing and have been adopted as such by the global anti-money-laundering network. That network continues to grow. FSRBs now cover each continent and the Egmont Group has added more than 40 new FIUs as members since 9/11.[173] Importantly, in mid-2002 the boards of both the World Bank and the IMF recognized the (then) "40+8 Recommendations" as the relevant international standard in the area, as they developed action plans to enhance their efforts to counter money laundering and terrorist financing. On the ground, this meant that the Bank and the Fund collaborated with the FATF and FSRBs in developing a common methodology for peer reviews to assess state compliance with the recommendations. Following a successful pilot program, the Bank and the Fund made anti-money-laundering and counter-terrorist financing activities part of their permanent reporting activities in March 2004. Since then, some 118 jurisdictions globally have been reviewed utilizing this methodology.[174]

The nine SRs now also have the explicit endorsement of the UN Security Council, following the passage of resolution 1617 (2005). As a result, FATF rules have the force of international law by fiat. A wide range of other international and regional organizations have also endorsed the SRs, including the CTC/CTED (where they are included in the *Directory of International Best Practices*), CTAG and UNODC. Further, professional organizations, other than those concerned with money laundering alone, have also certified FATF and UN counter-terrorist financing measures as key global standards. For example, each of the peak organizations for regulators in the banking, insurance and securities sectors has taken steps in this direction.[175] In the offshore financial sector, FATF recommendations have been "welcomed" by the Offshore Group of Banking Supervisors, with a renewed commitment to implementing global standards.[176] Among private sector banks, the Wolfsberg Group adopted a statement supporting FATF recommendations and elaborating principles for their implementation by the financial sector.[177] Once again, rules developed within a "club" have achieved global prominence.

The nine SRs are enforced in a number of ways, principally using self-assessment questionnaires, and peer and external reviews in line with the FATF/World Bank/IMF common methodology. For much of the post-9/11 period, the means for encouraging convergence with the nine SRs has been more likely to involve carrots—in the form of technical assistance from the sources recounted above—than sticks. In fact, in announcing the collaboration between the FATF and the Bank and Fund, the FATF also indicated that it would not add any new jurisdictions to the NCCT list, effectively removing the "name and shame" mechanism as a means for coercing compliance for states not already on that list.[178] However, the FATF has recently moved to replace that tool, initiating an "International Cooperation Review Group" process, that enables it to at least name those jurisdictions that present a money laundering or terrorist financing risk (states are then urged to take measures to protect themselves). At present, Iran has been named in this way.[179]

The mandate of the FATF has continued to evolve over time. For example, subsequent to Security Council resolution 1540 (2004), the FATF has acted to suppress the financial aspects of WMD proliferation. Of course, the work of the FATF, and the broader effort to regulate the financial sector to suppress terrorist financing, attracts a range of critics. These include human rights and development advocates, as well as private sector bankers who have experienced increasing levels of government intervention over time.[180] The ability to assess these claims is beyond the scope of this chapter—suffice it to note the importance of developing robust measures of effectiveness in this area. Rather, my point here is to demonstrate the extent of cooperation to suppress terrorist financing, which is unique in both a historical sense (i.e. the reach of multilateralism has not been achieved on this issue in the past) and a contemporary sense (in that few areas of multilateral counterterrorism are so broad and deep). In other words, measures to counter terrorist financing now resemble a "regime complex."

Responding to the threat of maritime terrorism

Prior to 9/11, maritime counter-terrorism was not central to the mission of the International Maritime Organization (IMO), and multilateral action had evolved only in response to events. For example, after the hijacking of the *Achille Lauro* in 1985, IMO took several steps to secure ships and ports. These measures included adopting the Convention for the Suppression of Unlawful Acts against the Safety of Maritime Navigation (the "SUA Convention," which entered into force in 1992) and developing a circular on the adoption of security plans for ships and ports.[181] Subsequently, IMO participated in training and capacity-building programs on maritime security. But the response to 9/11 brought more far-reaching change. Since then, the maritime security agenda has broadened, several institutions (beyond IMO alone) have been engaged and multilateral outcomes have emerged via multiple paths, with strong states (especially the United States) leading from the front.

In November 2001 IMO's highest governing body, the Assembly, passed a resolution to review existing measures to prevent and suppress terrorist acts.[182] Responding to a petition by the United States, the resolution also decided that an inter-sessional working group (ISWG) should be established to undertake the review, in order to prepare recommendations for the next round of the Maritime Safety Committee (MSC) the following year. US action in IMO was prompted by new domestic legislation—the Maritime Transportation Security Act 2002 (MTSA), passed in November of that year. The MTSA manifests a multi-tiered approach to security, outlining standards to secure ports, the ships that pass through them, the cargo they carry and the seafarers and port workers employed along the way. Among other measures, the Act requires the Secretary of Homeland Security to conduct safety audits of local and foreign ports, to assess their anti-terrorism measures and, where necessary, prescribe sanctions. The Act requires "standards and procedures for screening and evaluating cargo prior to loading in a foreign port for shipment to the United States either directly or via a foreign port," as well as "standards and procedures for allowing the United States government to ensure and validate compliance with this program."[183]

The United States sought to advance all of these measures through IMO. However, once meetings of the ISWG commenced, these proposals received a mixed reception.[184] While the United States requested that these measures be implemented through amendments to the 1974 Safety of Life at Sea Convention (SOLAS) (which attracted high levels of compliance), others doubted whether such a range of actions was within the remit of that convention. As a result, some proposals were rejected outright and others were delegated to other organizations or deferred for later consideration. But some issues—specifically, port vulnerability plans, ship security plans, and ship and company security officers—were accepted by the ISWG. Following the introduction of the term "port facility" to ensure the applicability of SOLAS (which is limited to the ship-port interface),[185] the group added port security plans to this bundle of measures. Together, they went on to comprise the International Ship and Port Facility Security Code (ISPS Code) which was passed as a new chapter of SOLAS in December 2002. The code commits SOLAS-contracting governments to a range of risk-assessment, inspection and certification measures pertaining to ships and ports. Regarding the enforcement of the code, port authorities have the right to exercise control and compliance measures regarding visiting ships. Importantly, where a port state perceives that the security of the port facility may be compromised, ships may be denied entry. Entry may also be denied on the grounds that ports visited earlier in a ship's journey, or other ships with which it has interfaced, represent a breach of security standards. The deadline for implementing the code was set for 1 July 2004.[186] In the lead-up to the deadline, industry critics expressed concern that compliance levels would be low and that ship and port operators would incur high costs.[187] As it turned out, levels of compliance were soon above 90 percent for ports and ships.[188] Since that time, the ISPS Code has been embraced as the global standard for securing ships and ports, and is included in the CTC/CTED *Directory of International Best Practices*. IMO, in collaboration with other international and regional organizations, has developed guidance on the code and delivered or facilitated capacity-building assistance towards its implementation, across the world.[189] IMO is also an active member of CTITF.

The route to a multilateral agreement on the security of shipping containers was rather different. In passing the ISPS Code, the issue (which had been put on the agenda by the United States) was delegated to the World Customs Organization (WCO). At about the same time, US officials began talking about a "Container Security Initiative" (CSI). Such an initiative would establish a series of bilateral agreements with foreign ports to identify and prescreen high-risk containers, expanding the use of scanning technology. By the end of March 2002, three Canadian ports had signed on to the measures and, reciprocally, Canadian customs officials were stationed in certain US ports. Since that time, some 60 ports on all continents have concluded bilateral agreements with the US Customs and Border Protection agency (CBP), including the world's 20 largest ports, which were targeted for membership first.[190]

Under these agreements, CBP officers are posted in foreign ports to undertake risk assessments of US-bound cargo. Containers deemed risky are screened using "non-intrusive inspectional" (NII) equipment. Host countries are responsible for the acquisition and operation of NII equipment. Formally, the United States offers no sanctions or incentives to states for joining, or failing to join, CSI. Rather, the benefits are indirect as CSI sends a positive signal about security standards at a port. As CSI gained signatories, measures concerning container security were advanced through more traditional multilateral fora. The United States won support for CSI principles from the G8.[191] Subsequently, the "Framework of Standards to Secure and Facilitate Global Trade" ("SAFE Framework") was negotiated through the WCO. Similar to the ISPS Code, the development of the Framework occurred through a special working group—this time a High-Level Strategic Group—in which the United States was "in the thick of the process."[192] Adopted by the WCO's Council in June 2005, the Framework bears a resemblance to CSI. It implements four principles: harmonization of electronic advance cargo information requirements; a consistent risk-management approach to assess threats to cargo security; offshore screening using NII equipment; and partnerships with business to provide incentives for improved security.[193] The Framework has attracted criticism from some in the industry that US-derived standards will impose undue costs for other states and the private sector.[194] But implementation of the Framework remains a decision for member states and by June 2009, 157 countries had expressed their intention to implement it.[195] The Framework is included in the CTC/CTED *Directory of International Best Practices*, and the WCO is a member of CTITF.

Also derivative of the ISPS Code negotiations, states have rewritten rules for identifying seafarers, through the International Labour Organization (ILO). The 2003 Seafarers' Identity Document Convention (Revised) was the first international agreement to utilize new technologies for storing biometric data (in this case, using a globally interoperable barcode) for the purpose of individual identification, preceding the development of biometric passport standards within ICAO.[196] The convention entered into force in February 2005.

A non-traditional path to multilateralism also characterizes measures to ensure against WMD proliferation on the high seas. Here, the United States again acted outside of international institutions—by striking multiple bilateral agreements and engaging in "quiet cooperation"—but a broad "coalition of the willing" has emerged over time.[197] In May 2003, President George W. Bush announced the "Proliferation Security Initiative" (PSI) in a speech in Krakow, Poland. The initial 11 participants signed a "Statement of Interdiction Principles" in Paris in September of that year.[198] The principles commit signatories to act against proliferation in a number of ways. For example, they are urged to adopt streamlined procedures for exchanging information about suspected proliferation activity. In a more interventionist vein, signatories undertake to bolster the ability of national authorities to police their own waters and ships in light of proliferation risks, and "To seriously consider providing consent under the appropriate circumstances to the boarding and searching of its own flag vessels by other states, and to the seizure of such WMD-related cargoes in such vessels that may be identified by such states."[199] With South Korea having joined in May 2009, 95 states now participate in PSI, which is frequently characterized as "an activity, not an organization." Here, participation means engaging in interdiction exercises and undertaking other cooperative maritime counter-proliferation efforts, such as joint training, the conclusion of mutual boarding agreements and information exchange.[200]

PSI has not been without controversy and has been criticized for "lack of transparency, stretching if not violating the principles of international law, weakening the UN system, being ineffective and politically divisive, and diluting other non-proliferation efforts."[201] Drew Winner points out that the principles were drafted to be consistent with existing international law, especially regarding freedom of navigation on the high seas, where action requires the permission of the flag state.[202] The United States argues that the "foundation of [each participant's] ability to act in support of PSI activities is [their] respective national legal authorities and relevant international law and frameworks. There is ample authority to support interdiction actions at sea."[203] The United States has taken a number of measures to bolster PSI's multilateral bona fides, such as securing support from its G8 partners.[204] Further support came from the then UN Secretary-General, Kofi Annan (who cited it in his *In Larger Freedom* Report).[205] However, the United States was unable to have language supporting PSI included in resolution 1540 (2004). Similarly, the 2005 Protocol to the SUA Convention is complementary to PSI, without endorsing it directly. The United States signed the protocol in February 2006.[206] In recommending it to the Senate, President Bush summarized its impact: "The 2005 SUA Protocol also provides for a ship-boarding regime based on flag state consent that will provide an international legal basis for interdiction at sea of weapons of mass destruction, their delivery systems and related materials."[207] In spite of these developments, critics argue that ongoing disagreements—especially concerning the legality of interdictions—undermine the strength of emerging norms and rules.[208]

The maritime security agenda has continued to evolve since 9/11. For example, IMO has maintained a focus on implementing standards regarding communications systems for ships, while also becoming involved in measures to secure maritime "chokepoints," such as the Malacca Straits in Southeast Asia.[209] Threat perceptions—often a point of contention among states—have also changed over time, not least as a result of the recent concern about piracy in and around the Horn of Africa. In the future, it is likely that maritime security will continue to involve a range of actors, carving out different roles (operations, standard-setting, technical assistance provision, etc.), across the several parts of the maritime supply chain. Clearly, not all of these activities are motivated by terrorism alone. But the clustering of such measures in the post-9/11 period reflects the fact that many states have come to view cooperation as integral to their own security against maritime threats.

Conclusion

This overview of multilateral counter-terrorism beyond the UN reveals that a wide range of bodies has engaged in some form of action against terrorism, both before and after 9/11. Amid this record of activity, we can begin to see the emergence of "regime complexes," as multiple actors are involved, elaborating multiple and overlapping sets of rules and norms. As these developments have evolved, five trends can be discerned.

First, as Eric Rosand and Sebastian von Einsiedel note, few new institutions have been created to address the threat of terrorism over time.[210] Rather, as within the UN, existing institutional arrangements have been adapted to new tasks related to counter-terrorism. This observation underscores the view that institutions are easier to maintain than to create.[211]

Second, the involvement of institutions has been centered on certain activities, namely norm-building and the provision of capacity-building and technical assistance. The volume of activity here is unique to the post-9/11 period, but the tendency for institutions to focus on these tasks is consistent over time. Third, it follows from this that institutions have had most impact on the "preventive" aspects of counter-terrorism. Multilateralism, it seems, is more often suited to developing and implementing standards for border controls, banks and biometric passports, rather than for apprehending bad guys. In turn, fourth, the core tasks of counter-terrorism—especially law enforcement and intelligence operations—have not witnessed similar upswings in multilateral activity. Here, the break with the past is less stark and states have generally continued to prefer bilateral action.

Finally, multilateral counter-terrorism beyond the UN is anything but an apolitical exercise. Of course, some examples of consensual cooperation are forthcoming, and sometimes these emerge in surprising places (such as recent intelligence collaborations). However, more often than not, multilateralism is used as a political tool by states to advance preferred forms of cooperation, or to resist such advances from others. Here, the breadth of institutions engaged on the issue reflects that states have sought to utilize fora that are likely to yield desired outcomes.

5 Multilateral counter-terrorism
Today and tomorrow

Terrorism today, as for the last century or more, is an internationalized, globalized threat. As such, we might expect that states would pursue counter-terrorism measures on a cooperative, multilateral basis. This intuition is partially borne out in the modern history of counter-terrorism cooperation. On the one hand, it seems, international cooperation against terrorism today is perhaps stronger than it has ever been. The number and variety of institutions involved and the depth of their interaction with states are without precedent in the modern era. On the other hand, however, most cooperation has focused on preventive counter-terrorism measures, where existing institutions have been more readily adapted to tasks of counter-terrorism. As this suggests, counter-terrorism cooperation varies across the tools of counter-terrorism policy, across time and across institutional fora. In interpreting these developments, I have leant towards a realist account of international cooperation, which emphasizes the competitive nature of state interactions. Although there are examples of consensus, and although we often observe the influence of shared ideas (e.g. through professional or expert networks in certain areas), multilateral counter-terrorism remains intensely political and this, in turn, impedes the ability of states to establish broad-based cooperation. In concluding, I pose two key questions concerning the effectiveness of multilateral counter-terrorism as well as prospects for the future.

Does multilateral counter-terrorism work?

Especially in the post-9/11 era, states have gone to a lot of trouble to construct and implement multilateral mechanisms to suppress terrorism. They have incurred significant financial burdens and have set aside other fundamental priorities. Having done so, it is important to ask: has it been worth it? What is the contribution of multilateralism to counter-terrorism more generally? Most pointedly, how many terrorist attacks have multilateral measures averted? How many would-be terrorists have chosen a non-violent path as a result of initiatives advanced multilaterally? Are we safer because of multilateral counter-terrorism?

These are not easy questions to answer, not least because it is difficult to measure the effect of particular policies when events (terrorist attacks) *don't* happen. With that said, these are among the most important questions facing multilateralists as they seek to advance cooperation among states, while justifying their actions to national constituencies. Put simply, the legitimacy and utility of the multilateral effort would be enhanced if we could clearly demonstrate its effectiveness. There are several possible methods for doing so. A comprehensive approach would develop indicators for the specific rules elaborated. This is easier to do in some areas than in others. For example, as the reports of the 1267 Monitoring Team make clear, the various impacts of the financial sanctions can be quantified in terms of funds frozen, prosecutions secured, suspicious transaction reports filed, and so on. One can imagine quantifiable data in maritime security (containers inspected, ships boarded, etc.) and in other domains, too. It is beyond the scope of this chapter to compile a range of comprehensive measures for this purposes and I am not aware of any such effort to do so across the breadth of multilateral counter-terrorism today.

Suffice it to note that several obstacles emerge here. There is always a question as to what, exactly, such quantifiable indicators are measuring, i.e. are they really evidence of effective counter-terrorism, or merely a proxy that reveals effort expended more than tangible results? Further, many multilateral initiatives do not yield reliable, consistent and quantifiable data (e.g. how to measure the effectiveness of measures to stem incitement to terrorism, or to address "conditions conducive"?). Beyond that, analysts would face a dilemma in balancing the costs of implementing multilateral rules (which would present a measurement challenge in itself) against the benefits.

An alternative approach is to think counter-factually about multilateral counter-terrorism. How would the broader counter-terrorism effort be different if multilateralism had not been pursued with such vigor since 9/11? Here, we might speculate, the value-added of international cooperation is easier to identify. For example, it is difficult to imagine that so many states would have enacted counter-terrorism legislation in recent years without it being required under resolution 1373. From this we can surmise that if multilateral counter-terrorism did not exist, it would be useful to invent it. But again, that is an inaccurate way of gauging the contribution of multilateralism to counter-terrorism generally, such that we might advise policy-makers on how best to pursue specific counter-terrorism tasks.

My point in raising these issues here is not to provide conclusive answers which, again, would require further, careful study. Rather, I simply wish to note that, for all of the institutions, initiatives and mechanisms mobilized around multilateral counter-terrorism, the debate on effectiveness is underdeveloped. In the absence of a willingness to have a frank discussion about the effectiveness of counter-terrorism policies—and in the absence of the kind of "cost/benefit" analysis suggested here—we do not know how much attention to counter-terrorism is too much. In turn, debates are prone to politicization as counter-terrorism action is justified by varying perceptions of the terrorist threat. If terrorism has achieved prominence on the international agenda in the wake of the 9/11 attacks, it behooves us to ask how we should balance it with other priorities over time. In the rush to action, and in the cut and thrust of international politics, there ought to be space for consideration of the comparative advantages of multilateral institutions in the counter-terrorism effort, to inform future developments.

What are the future prospects for multilateral counter-terrorism?

My realist interpretation of patterns of multilateral counter-terrorism is broadly consistent with those offered in the past (by Crenshaw, Wilkinson, and Pillar, respectively, cited in Chapter 2), although I acknowledge significant developments in the empirical record, especially in the post-9/11 period in domains of preventive counter-terrorism. In light of this, one might infer that the constraints on counter-terrorism cooperation are somewhat timeless and that, in turn, they are unlikely to be overcome any time soon. Indeed, thinking intuitively, it is difficult to imagine a situation in which broad-based cooperation against terrorism (that is, cooperation on each of the aspects of counter-terrorism policy) might emerge in the future. Such sustained periods of "extraordinary politics" are rare in international relations. Rather, as the descriptive account of multilateral counter-terrorism in this book confirms, cooperation more often emerges out of contestation among states than out of a broad and lasting consensus about the threat of terrorism and appropriate responses to it. But this should not be read to mean that the metaphorical glass is half empty. Such a pessimistic conclusion may be misplaced. The fact that there is some semblance of continuity in terms of counter-terrorism cooperation over time (i.e. that competitive political dynamics tend to determine cooperative outcomes) hints that states have fairly consistently revealed preferences in terms of counter-terrorism cooperation. In other words, we now have a good sense of what kinds of cooperative arrangements will "work" and what won't. In turn, that knowledge can be applied to improve the efficiency of existing measures and to venture new approaches on a selective basis. Thus, while I am skeptical about the prospects for some contemporary initiatives (such as the comprehensive convention on international terrorism, which rather plays to the weaknesses of multilateralism in this field), I am more optimistic that multilateral activity will become an increasingly important part of states' counter-terrorism agendas over time. A glass half empty, viewed from a different perspective, is a glass half full.

In the short term, as discussed in the conclusion of Chapter 3, patterns of multilateral counter-terrorism will be contingent on developments among the UN's terrorism-related bodies in New York. But the fate of multilateral counter-terrorism today will not be determined in New York alone. Multilateral counter-terrorism is now institutionalized outside of the UN, and states have shown the capacity to innovate in developing cooperative arrangements to advance their objectives. Rather, what is at stake in New York is whether and how much the UN is central to processes of multilateral counter-terrorism. Some eight years after the world's most deadly terrorist attack on the world's most powerful state, those processes exhibit more vitality than ever.

Appendix A
International legal instruments related to terrorism

(NB: For more information, including brief narrative summaries, see www.un.org/terrorism/instruments.shtml)

1963   Convention on Offences and Certain Other Acts Committed On Board Aircraft

1970   Convention for the Suppression of Unlawful Seizure of Aircraft

1971   Convention for the Suppression of Unlawful Acts against the Safety of Civil Aviation

          1988   Protocol for the Suppression of Unlawful Acts of Violence at Airports Serving International Civil Aviation, supplementary to the Convention for the Suppression of Unlawful Acts against the Safety of Civil Aviation

1973   Convention on the Prevention and Punishment of Crimes Against Internationally Protected Persons

1979   International Convention against the Taking of Hostages

1980   Convention on the Physical Protection of Nuclear Material

1988   Convention for the Suppression of Unlawful Acts against the Safety of Maritime Navigation

          1988   Protocol for the Suppression of Unlawful Acts Against the Safety of Fixed Platforms Located on the Continental Shelf

          2005   Protocol to the Convention for the Suppression of Unlawful Acts against the Safety of Maritime Navigation

2005   Protocol to the Protocol for the Suppression of
         Unlawful Acts against the Safety of Fixed
         Platforms Located on the Continental Shelf

1991   Convention on the Marking of Plastic Explosives for the
         Purpose of Detection
1997   International Convention for the Suppression of
         Terrorist Bombings
1999   International Convention for the Suppression of the
         Financing of Terrorism
2005   International Convention for the Suppression of Acts of
         Nuclear Terrorism

Appendix B
UN Security Council resolution 1373

United Nations

Security Council

Resolution 1373 (2001)

ADOPTED BY THE SECURITY COUNCIL AT ITS 4385TH MEETING,
ON 28 SEPTEMBER 2001

The Security Council,

Reaffirming its resolutions 1269 (1999) of 19 October 1999 and 1368 (2001) of 12 September 2001,

Reaffirming also its unequivocal condemnation of the terrorist attacks which took place in New York, Washington, D.C. and Pennsylvania on 11 September 2001, and expressing its determination to prevent all such acts,

Reaffirming further that such acts, like any act of international terrorism, constitute a threat to international peace and security,

Reaffirming the inherent right of individual or collective self-defence as recognized by the Charter of the United Nations as reiterated in resolution 1368 (2001),

Reaffirming the need to combat by all means, in accordance with the Charter of the United Nations, threats to international peace and security caused by terrorist acts,

Deeply concerned by the increase, in various regions of the world, of acts of terrorism motivated by intolerance or extremism,

Calling on States to work together urgently to prevent and suppress terrorist acts, including through increased cooperation and full implementation of the relevant international conventions relating to terrorism,

Recognizing the need for States to complement international cooperation by taking additional measures to prevent and suppress, in their territories through all lawful means, the financing and preparation of any acts of terrorism,

Reaffirming the principle established by the General Assembly in its declaration of October 1970 (resolution 2625 (XXV)) and reiterated by the Security Council in its resolution 1189 (1998) of 13 August 1998, namely that every State has the duty to refrain from organizing, instigating, assisting or participating in terrorist acts in another State or acquiescing in organized activities within its territory directed towards the commission of such acts,

Acting under Chapter VII of the Charter of the United Nations,

1. *Decides* that all States shall:
   (a) Prevent and suppress the financing of terrorist acts;
   (b) Criminalize the wilful provision or collection, by any means, directly or indirectly, of funds by their nationals or in their territories with the intention that the funds should be used, or in the knowledge that they are to be used, in order to carry out terrorist acts;
   (c) Freeze without delay funds and other financial assets or economic resources of persons who commit, or attempt to commit, terrorist acts or participate in or facilitate the commission of terrorist acts; of entities owned or controlled directly or indirectly by such persons; and of persons and entities acting on behalf of, or at the direction of such persons and entities, including funds derived or generated from property owned or controlled directly or indirectly by such persons and associated persons and entities;
   (d) Prohibit their nationals or any persons and entities within their territories from making any funds, financial assets or economic resources or financial or other related services available, directly or indirectly, for the benefit of persons who commit or attempt to commit or facilitate or participate in the commission of

terrorist acts, of entities owned or controlled, directly or indirectly, by such persons and of persons and entities acting on behalf of or at the direction of such persons;

2. *Decides also* that all States shall:
   (a) Refrain from providing any form of support, active or passive, to entities or persons involved in terrorist acts, including by suppressing recruitment of members of terrorist groups and eliminating the supply of weapons to terrorists;
   (b) Take the necessary steps to prevent the commission of terrorist acts, including by provision of early warning to other States by exchange of information;
   (c) Deny safe haven to those who finance, plan, support, or commit terrorist acts, or provide safe havens;
   (d) Prevent those who finance, plan, facilitate or commit terrorist acts from using their respective territories for those purposes against other States or their citizens;
   (e) Ensure that any person who participates in the financing, planning, preparation or perpetration of terrorist acts or in supporting terrorist acts is brought to justice and ensure that, in addition to any other measures against them, such terrorist acts are established as serious criminal offences in domestic laws and regulations and that the punishment duly reflects the seriousness of such terrorist acts;
   (f) Afford one another the greatest measure of assistance in connection with criminal investigations or criminal proceedings relating to the financing or support of terrorist acts, including assistance in obtaining evidence in their possession necessary for the proceedings;
   (g) Prevent the movement of terrorists or terrorist groups by effective border controls and controls on issuance of identity papers and travel documents, and through measures for preventing counterfeiting, forgery or fraudulent use of identity papers and travel documents;

3. *Calls* upon all States to:
   (a) Find ways of intensifying and accelerating the exchange of operational information, especially regarding actions or movements of terrorist persons or networks; forged or falsified travel documents; traffic in arms, explosives or sensitive materials; use of communications technologies by terrorist groups; and the threat posed by the possession of weapons of mass destruction by terrorist groups;

(b) Exchange information in accordance with international and domestic law and cooperate on administrative and judicial matters to prevent the commission of terrorist acts;

(c) Cooperate, particularly through bilateral and multilateral arrangements and agreements, to prevent and suppress terrorist attacks and take action against perpetrators of such acts;

(d) Become parties as soon as possible to the relevant international conventions and protocols relating to terrorism, including the International Convention for the Suppression of the Financing of Terrorism of 9 December 1999;

(e) Increase cooperation and fully implement the relevant international conventions and protocols relating to terrorism and Security Council resolutions 1269 (1999) and 1368 (2001);

(f) Take appropriate measures in conformity with the relevant provisions of national and international law, including international standards of human rights, before granting refugee status, for the purpose of ensuring that the asylum-seeker has not planned, facilitated or participated in the commission of terrorist acts;

(g) Ensure, in conformity with international law, that refugee status is not abused by the perpetrators, organizers or facilitators of terrorist acts, and that claims of political motivation are not recognized as grounds for refusing requests for the extradition of alleged terrorists;

4. *Notes* with concern the close connection between international terrorism and transnational organized crime, illicit drugs, money-laundering, illegal arms-trafficking, and illegal movement of nuclear, chemical, biological and other potentially deadly materials, and in this regard *emphasizes* the need to enhance coordination of efforts on national, subregional, regional and international levels in order to strengthen a global response to this serious challenge and threat to international security;

5. *Declares* that acts, methods, and practices of terrorism are contrary to the purposes and principles of the United Nations and that knowingly financing, planning and inciting terrorist acts are also contrary to the purposes and principles of the United Nations;

6. *Decides* to establish, in accordance with rule 28 of its provisional rules of procedure, a Committee of the Security Council, consisting of all the members of the Council, to monitor implementation of

this resolution, with the assistance of appropriate expertise, and *calls upon* all States to report to the Committee, no later than 90 days from the date of adoption of this resolution and thereafter according to a timetable to be proposed by the Committee, on the steps they have taken to implement this resolution;

7. *Directs* the Committee to delineate its tasks, submit a work programme within 30 days of the adoption of this resolution, and to consider the support it requires, in consultation with the Secretary-General;

8. *Expresses* its determination to take all necessary steps in order to ensure the full implementation of this resolution, in accordance with its responsibilities under the Charter;

9. *Decides* to remain seized of this matter.

Appendix C
The United Nations Global Counter-terrorism Strategy

United Nations
20 September 2006
Sixtieth session
Agenda items 46 and 120
Resolution adopted by the General Assembly
[*without reference to a Main Committee (A/60/L.62)*]

60/288. The United Nations Global Counter-Terrorism Strategy

The General Assembly,

Guided by the purposes and principles of the Charter of the United Nations, and reaffirming its role under the Charter, including on questions related to international peace and security,

Reiterating its strong condemnation of terrorism in all its forms and manifestations, committed by whomever, wherever and for whatever purposes, as it constitutes one of the most serious threats to international peace and security,

Reaffirming the Declaration on Measures to Eliminate International Terrorism, contained in the annex to General Assembly resolution 49/60 of 9 December 1994, the Declaration to Supplement the 1994 Declaration on Measures to Eliminate International Terrorism, contained in the annex to General Assembly resolution 51/210 of 17 December 1996, and the 2005 World Summit Outcome,[1] in particular its section on terrorism,

Recalling all General Assembly resolutions on measures to eliminate international terrorism, including resolution 46/51 of 9 December 1991, and Security Council resolutions on threats to international peace and security caused by terrorist acts, as well as relevant resolutions of the General Assembly on the protection of human rights and fundamental freedoms while countering terrorism,

Recalling also that, in the 2005 World Summit Outcome, world leaders rededicated themselves to support all efforts to uphold the sovereign equality of all States, respect their territorial integrity and political independence, to refrain in their international relations from the threat or use of force in any manner inconsistent with the purposes and principles of the United Nations, to uphold the resolution of disputes by peaceful means and in conformity with the principles of justice and international law, the right to self-determination of peoples which remain under colonial domination or foreign occupation, non-interference in the internal affairs of States, respect for human rights and fundamental freedoms, respect for the equal rights of all without distinction as to race, sex, language or religion, international cooperation in solving international problems of an economic, social, cultural or humanitarian character, and the fulfilment in good faith of the obligations assumed in accordance with the Charter,

Recalling further the mandate contained in the 2005 World Summit Outcome that the General Assembly should develop without delay the elements identified by the Secretary-General for a counter-terrorism strategy, with a view to adopting and implementing a strategy to promote comprehensive, coordinated and consistent responses, at the national, regional and international levels, to counter terrorism, which also takes into account the conditions conducive to the spread of terrorism,

Reaffirming that acts, methods and practices of terrorism in all its forms and manifestations are activities aimed at the destruction of human rights, fundamental freedoms and democracy, threatening territorial integrity, security of States and destabilizing legitimately constituted Governments, and that the international community should take the necessary steps to enhance cooperation to prevent and combat terrorism,

Reaffirming also that terrorism cannot and should not be associated with any religion, nationality, civilization or ethnic group,

Reaffirming further Member States' determination to make every effort to reach an agreement on and conclude a comprehensive convention on international terrorism, including by resolving the outstanding issues related to the legal definition and scope of the acts covered by the convention, so that it can serve as an effective instrument to counter terrorism,

Continuing to acknowledge that the question of convening a high-level conference under the auspices of the United Nations to formulate an international response to terrorism in all its forms and manifestations could be considered,

Recognizing that development, peace and security, and human rights are interlinked and mutually reinforcing,

Bearing in mind the need to address the conditions conducive to the spread of terrorism,

Affirming Member States' determination to continue to do all they can to resolve conflict, end foreign occupation, confront oppression, eradicate poverty, promote sustained economic growth, sustainable development, global prosperity, good governance, human rights for all and rule of law, improve intercultural understanding and ensure respect for all religions, religious values, beliefs or cultures,

1. *Expresses its appreciation* for the report entitled "Uniting against terrorism: recommendations for a global counter-terrorism strategy" submitted by the Secretary-General to the General Assembly;[2]

2. *Adopts* the present resolution and its annex as the United Nations Global Counter-Terrorism Strategy ("the Strategy");

3. *Decides*, without prejudice to the continuation of the discussion in its relevant committees of all their agenda items related to terrorism and counter-terrorism, to undertake the following steps for the effective follow-up of the Strategy:

   (*a*) To launch the Strategy at a high-level segment of its sixty-first session;

   (*b*) To examine in two years progress made in the implementation of the Strategy, and to consider updating it to respond to changes, recognizing that many of the measures contained in the Strategy can be achieved immediately, some will require sustained work through the coming few years and some should be treated as long-term objectives;

   (*c*) To invite the Secretary-General to contribute to the future deliberations of the General Assembly on the review of the implementation and updating of the Strategy;

(*d*) To encourage Member States, the United Nations and other appropriate international, regional and subregional organizations to support the implementation of the Strategy, including through mobilizing resources and expertise;

(*e*) To further encourage non-governmental organizations and civil society to engage, as appropriate, on how to enhance efforts to implement the Strategy;

4. *Decides* to include in the provisional agenda of its sixty-second session an item entitled "The United Nations Global Counter-Terrorism Strategy".

99th plenary meeting
8 September 2006

Annex

Plan of action

We, the States Members of the United Nations, resolve:

1. To consistently, unequivocally and strongly condemn terrorism in all its forms and manifestations, committed by whomever, wherever and for whatever purposes, as it constitutes one of the most serious threats to international peace and security;

2. To take urgent action to prevent and combat terrorism in all its forms and manifestations and, in particular:

(*a*) To consider becoming parties without delay to the existing international conventions and protocols against terrorism, and implementing them, and to make every effort to reach an agreement on and conclude a comprehensive convention on international terrorism;

(*b*) To implement all General Assembly resolutions on measures to eliminate international terrorism and relevant General Assembly resolutions on the protection of human rights and fundamental freedoms while countering terrorism;

(*c*) To implement all Security Council resolutions related to international terrorism and to cooperate fully with the counter-terrorism subsidiary bodies of the Security Council in the fulfilment of their tasks, recognizing that many States continue to require assistance in implementing these resolutions;

3. To recognize that international cooperation and any measures that we undertake to prevent and combat terrorism must comply with our obligations under international law, including the Charter of the United Nations and relevant international conventions and protocols, in particular human rights law, refugee law and international humanitarian law.

I. Measures to address the conditions conducive to the spread of terrorism

We resolve to undertake the following measures aimed at addressing the conditions conducive to the spread of terrorism, including but not limited to prolonged unresolved conflicts, dehumanization of victims of terrorism in all its forms and manifestations, lack of the rule of law and violations of human rights, ethnic, national and religious discrimination, political exclusion, socio-economic marginalization and lack of good governance, while recognizing that none of these conditions can excuse or justify acts of terrorism:

1. To continue to strengthen and make best possible use of the capacities of the United Nations in areas such as conflict prevention, negotiation, mediation, conciliation, judicial settlement, rule of law, peacekeeping and peacebuilding, in order to contribute to the successful prevention and peaceful resolution of prolonged unresolved conflicts. We recognize that the peaceful resolution of such conflicts would contribute to strengthening the global fight against terrorism;

2. To continue to arrange under the auspices of the United Nations initiatives and programmes to promote dialogue, tolerance and understanding among civilizations, cultures, peoples and religions, and to promote mutual respect for and prevent the defamation of religions, religious values, beliefs and cultures. In this regard, we welcome the launching by the Secretary-General of the initiative on the Alliance of Civilizations. We also welcome similar initiatives that have been taken in other parts of the world;

3. To promote a culture of peace, justice and human development, ethnic, national and religious tolerance and respect for all religions, religious values, beliefs or cultures by establishing and encouraging, as appropriate, education and public awareness programmes involving all sectors of society. In this regard, we encourage the United Nations Educational, Scientific and Cultural Organization to play a key role,

including through inter-faith and intra-faith dialogue and dialogue among civilizations;

4. To continue to work to adopt such measures as may be necessary and appropriate and in accordance with our respective obligations under international law to prohibit by law incitement to commit a terrorist act or acts and prevent such conduct;

5. To reiterate our determination to ensure the timely and full realization of the development goals and objectives agreed at the major United Nations conferences and summits, including the Millennium Development Goals. We reaffirm our commitment to eradicate poverty and promote sustained economic growth, sustainable development and global prosperity for all;

6. To pursue and reinforce development and social inclusion agendas at every level as goals in themselves, recognizing that success in this area, especially on youth unemployment, could reduce marginalization and the subsequent sense of victimization that propels extremism and the recruitment of terrorists;

7. To encourage the United Nations system as a whole to scale up the cooperation and assistance it is already conducting in the fields of rule of law, human rights and good governance to support sustained economic and social development;

8. To consider putting in place, on a voluntary basis, national systems of assistance that would promote the needs of victims of terrorism and their families and facilitate the normalization of their lives. In this regard, we encourage States to request the relevant United Nations entities to help them to develop such national systems. We will also strive to promote international solidarity in support of victims and foster the involvement of civil society in a global campaign against terrorism and for its condemnation. This could include exploring at the General Assembly the possibility of developing practical mechanisms to provide assistance to victims.

II. Measures to prevent and combat terrorism

We resolve to undertake the following measures to prevent and combat terrorism, in particular by denying terrorists access to the means to carry out their attacks, to their targets and to the desired impact of their attacks:

1. To refrain from organizing, instigating, facilitating, participating in, financing, encouraging or tolerating terrorist activities and to take appropriate practical measures to ensure that our respective territories are not used for terrorist installations or training camps, or for the preparation or organization of terrorist acts intended to be committed against other States or their citizens;

2. To cooperate fully in the fight against terrorism, in accordance with our obligations under international law, in order to find, deny safe haven and bring to justice, on the basis of the principle of extradite or prosecute, any person who supports, facilitates, participates or attempts to participate in the financing, planning, preparation or perpetration of terrorist acts or provides safe havens;

3. To ensure the apprehension and prosecution or extradition of per-petrators of terrorist acts, in accordance with the relevant provi-sions of national and international law, in particular human rights law, refugee law and international humanitarian law. We will endea-vour to conclude and implement to that effect mutual judicial assis-tance and extradition agreements and to strengthen cooperation between law enforcement agencies;

4. To intensify cooperation, as appropriate, in exchanging timely and accurate information concerning the prevention and combating of terrorism;

5. To strengthen coordination and cooperation among States in com-bating crimes that might be connected with terrorism, including drug trafficking in all its aspects, illicit arms trade, in particular of small arms and light weapons, including man-portable air defence systems, money-laundering and smuggling of nuclear, chemical, biological, radiological and other potentially deadly materials;

6. To consider becoming parties without delay to the United Nations Convention against Transnational Organized Crime [3] and to the three protocols supplementing it,[4] and implementing them;

7. To take appropriate measures, before granting asylum, for the pur-pose of ensuring that the asylum-seeker has not engaged in terrorist

activities and, after granting asylum, for the purpose of ensuring that the refugee status is not used in a manner contrary to the provisions set out in section II, paragraph 1, above;

8. To encourage relevant regional and subregional organizations to create or strengthen counter-terrorism mechanisms or centres. Should they require cooperation and assistance to this end, we encourage the Counter-Terrorism Committee and its Executive Directorate and, where consistent with their existing mandates, the United Nations Office on Drugs and Crime and the International Criminal Police Organization, to facilitate its provision;

9. To acknowledge that the question of creating an international centre to fight terrorism could be considered, as part of international efforts to enhance the fight against terrorism;

10. To encourage States to implement the comprehensive international standards embodied in the Forty Recommendations on Money-Laundering and Nine Special Recommendations on Terrorist Financing of the Financial Action Task Force, recognizing that States may require assistance in implementing them;

11. To invite the United Nations system to develop, together with Member States, a single comprehensive database on biological incidents, ensuring that it is complementary to the biocrimes database contemplated by the International Criminal Police Organization. We also encourage the Secretary-General to update the roster of experts and laboratories, as well as the technical guidelines and procedures, available to him for the timely and efficient investigation of alleged use. In addition, we note the importance of the proposal of the Secretary-General to bring together, within the framework of the United Nations, the major biotechnology stakeholders, including industry, the scientific community, civil society and Governments, into a common programme aimed at ensuring that biotechnology advances are not used for terrorist or other criminal purposes but for the public good, with due respect for the basic international norms on intellectual property rights;

12. To work with the United Nations with due regard to confidentiality, respecting human rights and in compliance with other obligations under international law, to explore ways and means to:

    (a) Coordinate efforts at the international and regional levels to counter terrorism in all its forms and manifestations on the Internet;

    (b) Use the Internet as a tool for countering the spread of terrorism, while recognizing that States may require assistance in this regard;

13. To step up national efforts and bilateral, subregional, regional and international cooperation, as appropriate, to improve border and customs controls in order to prevent and detect the movement of terrorists and prevent and detect the illicit traffic in, inter alia, small arms and light weapons, conventional ammunition and explosives, and nuclear, chemical, biological or radiological weapons and materials, while recognizing that States may require assistance to that effect;

14. To encourage the Counter-Terrorism Committee and its Executive Directorate to continue to work with States, at their request, to facilitate the adoption of legislation and administrative measures to implement the terrorist travel-related obligations and to identify best practices in this area, drawing whenever possible on those developed by technical international organizations, such as the International Civil Aviation Organization, the World Customs Organization and the International Criminal Police Organization;

15. To encourage the Committee established pursuant to Security Council resolution 1267 (1999) to continue to work to strengthen the effectiveness of the travel ban under the United Nations sanctions regime against Al-Qaida and the Taliban and associated individuals and entities, as well as to ensure, as a matter of priority, that fair and transparent procedures exist for placing individuals and entities on its lists, for removing them and for granting humanitarian exceptions. In this regard, we encourage States to share information, including by widely distributing the International Criminal Police Organization/United Nations special notices concerning people subject to this sanctions regime;

16. To step up efforts and cooperation at every level, as appropriate, to improve the security of manufacturing and issuing identity and travel documents and to prevent and detect their alteration or fraudulent use, while recognizing that States may require assistance in doing so. In this regard, we invite the International Criminal

Police Organization to enhance its database on stolen and lost travel documents, and we will endeavour to make full use of this tool, as appropriate, in particular by sharing relevant information;

17. To invite the United Nations to improve coordination in planning a response to a terrorist attack using nuclear, chemical, biological or radiological weapons or materials, in particular by reviewing and improving the effectiveness of the existing inter-agency coordination mechanisms for assistance delivery, relief operations and victim support, so that all States can receive adequate assistance. In this regard, we invite the General Assembly and the Security Council to develop guidelines for the necessary cooperation and assistance in the event of a terrorist attack using weapons of mass destruction;

18. To step up all efforts to improve the security and protection of particularly vulnerable targets, such as infrastructure and public places, as well as the response to terrorist attacks and other disasters, in particular in the area of civil protection, while recognizing that States may require assistance to this effect.

III. Measures to build States' capacity to prevent and combat terrorism and to strengthen the role of the United Nations system in this regard

We recognize that capacity-building in all States is a core element of the global counter-terrorism effort, and resolve to undertake the following measures to develop State capacity to prevent and combat terrorism and enhance coordination and coherence within the United Nations system in promoting international cooperation in countering terrorism:

1. To encourage Member States to consider making voluntary contributions to United Nations counter-terrorism cooperation and technical assistance projects, and to explore additional sources of funding in this regard. We also encourage the United Nations to consider reaching out to the private sector for contributions to capacity-building programmes, in particular in the areas of port, maritime and civil aviation security;

2. To take advantage of the framework provided by relevant international, regional and subregional organizations to share best practices in counter-terrorism capacity-building, and to facilitate their contributions to the international community's efforts in this area;

3. To consider establishing appropriate mechanisms to rationalize States' reporting requirements in the field of counter-terrorism and eliminate duplication of reporting requests, taking into account and respecting the different mandates of the General Assembly, the Security Council and its subsidiary bodies that deal with counter-terrorism;

4. To encourage measures, including regular informal meetings, to enhance, as appropriate, more frequent exchanges of information on cooperation and technical assistance among Member States, United Nations bodies dealing with counter-terrorism, relevant specialized agencies, relevant international, regional and subregional organizations and the donor community, to develop States' capacities to implement relevant United Nations resolutions;

5. To welcome the intention of the Secretary-General to institutionalize, within existing resources, the Counter-Terrorism Implementation Task Force within the Secretariat in order to ensure overall coordination and coherence in the counter-terrorism efforts of the United Nations system;

6. To encourage the Counter-Terrorism Committee and its Executive Directorate to continue to improve the coherence and efficiency of technical assistance delivery in the field of counter-terrorism, in particular by strengthening its dialogue with States and relevant international, regional and subregional organizations and working closely, including by sharing information, with all bilateral and multilateral technical assistance providers;

7. To encourage the United Nations Office on Drugs and Crime, including its Terrorism Prevention Branch, to enhance, in close consultation with the Counter-Terrorism Committee and its Executive Directorate, its provision of technical assistance to States, upon request, to facilitate the implementation of the international conventions and protocols related to the prevention and suppression of terrorism and relevant United Nations resolutions;

8. To encourage the International Monetary Fund, the World Bank, the United Nations Office on Drugs and Crime and the International Criminal Police Organization to enhance cooperation with States to help them to comply fully with international norms and obligations to combat money-laundering and the financing of terrorism;

9. To encourage the International Atomic Energy Agency and the Organization for the Prohibition of Chemical Weapons to continue their efforts, within their respective mandates, in helping States to build capacity to prevent terrorists from accessing nuclear, chemical or radiological materials, to ensure security at related facilities and to respond effectively in the event of an attack using such materials;

10. To encourage the World Health Organization to step up its technical assistance to help States to improve their public health systems to prevent and prepare for biological attacks by terrorists;

11. To continue to work within the United Nations system to support the reform and modernization of border management systems, facilities and institutions at the national, regional and international levels;

12. To encourage the International Maritime Organization, the World Customs Organization and the International Civil Aviation Organization to strengthen their cooperation, work with States to identify any national shortfalls in areas of transport security and provide assistance, upon request, to address them;

13. To encourage the United Nations to work with Member States and relevant international, regional and subregional organizations to identify and share best practices to prevent terrorist attacks on particularly vulnerable targets. We invite the International Criminal Police Organization to work with the Secretary- General so that he can submit proposals to this effect. We also recognize the importance of developing public-private partnerships in this area.

IV. Measures to ensure respect for human rights for all and the rule of law as the fundamental basis of the fight against terrorism

We resolve to undertake the following measures, reaffirming that the promotion and protection of human rights for all and the rule of law is essential to all components of the Strategy, recognizing that effective counter-terrorism measures and the protection of human rights are not conflicting goals, but complementary and mutually reinforcing, and stressing the need to promote and protect the rights of victims of terrorism:

1. To reaffirm that General Assembly resolution 60/158 of 16 December 2005 provides the fundamental framework for the "Protection of human rights and fundamental freedoms while countering terrorism";

2. To reaffirm that States must ensure that any measures taken to combat terrorism comply with their obligations under international law, in particular human rights law, refugee law and international humanitarian law;

3. To consider becoming parties without delay to the core international instruments on human rights law, refugee law and international humanitarian law, and implementing them, as well as to consider accepting the competence of international and relevant regional human rights monitoring bodies;

4. To make every effort to develop and maintain an effective and rule-of-law-based national criminal justice system that can ensure, in accordance with our obligations under international law, that any person who participates in the financing, planning, preparation or perpetration of terrorist acts or in support of terrorist acts is brought to justice, on the basis of the principle to extradite or prosecute, with due respect for human rights and fundamental freedoms, and that such terrorist acts are established as serious criminal offences in domestic laws and regulations. We recognize that States may require assistance in developing and maintaining such effective and rule-of-law-based criminal justice systems, and we encourage them to resort to the technical assistance delivered, inter alia, by the United Nations Office on Drugs and Crime;

5. To reaffirm the important role of the United Nations system in strengthening the international legal architecture by promoting the rule of law, respect for human rights and effective criminal justice systems, which constitute the fundamental basis of our common fight against terrorism;

6. To support the Human Rights Council and to contribute, as it takes shape, to its work on the question of the promotion and protection of human rights for all in the fight against terrorism;

7. To support the strengthening of the operational capacity of the Office of the United Nations High Commissioner for Human Rights, with a particular emphasis on increasing field operations and presences. The Office should continue to play a lead role in examining the question of protecting human rights while countering terrorism, by making general recommendations on the human rights obligations of States and providing them with assistance and

advice, in particular in the area of raising awareness of international human rights law among national law enforcement agencies, at the request of States;

8. To support the role of the Special Rapporteur on the promotion and protection of human rights and fundamental freedoms while countering terrorism. The Special Rapporteur should continue to support the efforts of States and offer concrete advice by corresponding with Governments, making country visits, liaising with the United Nations and regional organizations and reporting on these issues.

Notes

1 See resolution 60/1.
2 A/60/825.
3 Resolution 55/25, annex I.
4 Resolution 55/25, annexes II and III; and resolution 55/255, annex.

Appendix D

Main actors of the United Nations system in counter-terrorism efforts

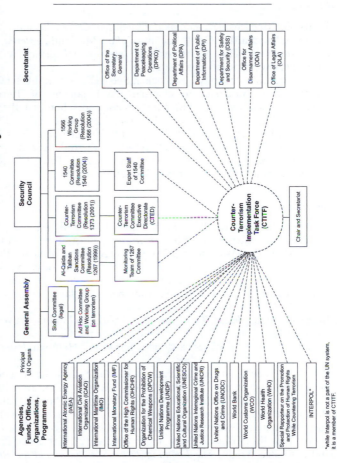

Source: www.un.org/terrorism/pdfs/CT_organogram_Feb2009-3.pdf

Notes

Foreword

1 Frank G. Madsen, *Transnational Organized Crime* (London: Routledge, 2009); and Richard J. Goldstone and Adam M. Smith, *International Judicial Institutions: The Architecture of International Justice at Home and Abroad* (London: Routledge, 2009).

2 See, for example, Thomas J. Biersteker, Sue E. Eckert, and Peter Romaniuk, "International Initiatives to Combat the Financing of Terrorism," in *Countering the Financing of Global Terrorism*, ed. Thomas J. Biersteker and Sue E. Eckert (New York and London: Routledge, 2007), 234–59; and Thomas J. Biersteker, Sue E. Eckert, Aaron Halegua, and Peter Romaniuk, "Consensus From the Bottom Up? Assessing the Influence of the Sanctions Reform Processes," in *International Sanctions*, ed. Peter Wallensteen and Carina Staibano (London: Frank Cass, 2005), 15–30.

Introduction

1 See David C. Rapoport, "The Four Waves of Modern Terrorism," in *Attacking Terrorism: Elements of a Grand Strategy*, ed. Audrey Kurth Cronin and James M. Ludes (Washington, D.C.: Georgetown University Press, 2004), 46–73; and David C. Rapoport, "The International World as Some Terrorists Have Seen It: A Look at a Century of Memoirs," in *Inside Terrorist Organizations*, 2nd edition, ed. David C. Rapoport (Portland, Oreg.: Frank Cass, 2001), 32–57.

2 Bruce Hoffman, *Inside Terrorism* (New York: Columbia University Press, 2006), ch. 3.

3 Rapoport, "The Four Waves of Modern Terrorism"; Hoffman, *Inside Terrorism*, ch. 4.

4 Recall bin Laden's fatwa, "Declaration of War against the Americans Occupying the Land of the Two Holy Places," August 1996, available at www.pbs.org/newshour/terrorism/international/fatwa_1996.html. On the rise of al Qaeda, see: Marc Sageman, *Understanding Terror Networks* (Philadelphia, Pa.: University of Pennsylvania Press, 2004); Fawaz Gerges, *The Far Enemy: Why Jihad Went Global* (New York: Cambridge University Press, 2005); and Lawrence Wright, *The Looming Tower: Al-Qaeda and the Road to 9/11* (New York: Vintage Books, 2006).

5 World Islamic Front Statement, "Jihad Against Jews and Crusaders," 23 February 1998, available at www.fas.org/irp/world/para/docs/980223-fatwa.htm

6 For a comprehensive account of the 9/11 plot, see National Commission on Terrorist Attacks against the United States, *The 9/11 Commission Report*, 2004, www.9-11commission.gov. In addition, note the two staff monographs released by the 9/11 Commission—on terrorist financing and terrorist travel—also available at www.9-11commission.gov

7 Robert O. Keohane, "The Globalization of Informal Violence, Theories of World Politics, and the 'Liberalism of Fear,'" *Dialog-IO* (Spring 2002): 41.

8 Marc Sageman, *Leaderless Jihad* (Philadelphia, Pa.: University of Pennsylvania Press, 2008), 48.

9 Sageman, *Leaderless Jihad*, 49.

10 Sageman, *Leaderless Jihad*, chs. 6 and 7.

11 These include the 2004 Madrid train bombings, the murder of Dutch film maker Theo van Gogh in 2005, the Sharm el-Sheikh bombings that year, and plots in Melbourne and Sydney (2005), Toronto (2006), Koblenz (2006), and London and Glasgow (2007): Sageman, *Leaderless Jihad*, 139.

12 Sageman, *Leaderless Jihad*, vii–viii.

13 On the global reach of jihadi ideas, see: Olivier Roy, *Globalized Islam: The Search for a New Ummah* (New York: Columbia University Press, 2004); and Faisal Devji, *Landscapes of the Jihad: Militancy, Morality and Modernity* (Ithaca, N.Y.: Cornell University Press, 2005).

14 Bruce Hoffman, "Global Terrorist Threat: Is al Qaeda on the March, or on the Run?", *Middle East Policy* 14, no. 2 (2007): 44–58. Note Hoffman's review of Sageman's *Leaderless Jihad*, and the subsequent exchange: Bruce Hoffman, "The Myth of Grass-Roots Terrorism: Why Osama bin Laden Still Matters," *Foreign Affairs* 87, no. 3 (2008): 133–38; Marc Sageman and Bruce Hoffman, "Does Osama Still Call the Shots? Debating the Containment of al Qaeda's Leadership," *Foreign Affairs* 87, no. 4 (2008): 163–66.

15 National Intelligence Council, *National Intelligence Estimate: The Terrorist Threat to the US Homeland*, July 2007. Available at www.dni.gov/press_releases/20070717_release.pdf.

16 For a summary of terrorist groups, see the US Department of State's annual *Country Reports on Terrorism* (formerly *Patterns of Global Terrorism*), available at www.state.gov/s/ct/rls/crt/

17 Charles W. Kegley, Jr., *The New Global Terrorism: Characteristics, Causes, Controls* (Upper Saddle River, N.J.: Prentice Hall, 2007), 9.

18 For example, see Jane Boulden and Thomas G. Weiss, eds., *Terrorism and the UN: Before and After September 11* (Bloomington: Indiana University Press, 2004); Edward C. Luck "The Uninvited Challenge: Terrorism Targets the United Nations," in *Multilateralism Under Challenge: Power, International Order and Structural Change*, ed. Edward Newman, Ramesh Thakur, and John Tirman (Tokyo: United Nations University Press, 2006), 336–55; Edward Newman, *A Crisis of Global Institutions? Multilateralism and International Security* (New York: Routledge, 2007), ch. 7; David Cortright and George A. Lopez, eds., *Uniting Against Terror: Cooperative Nonmilitary Responses to the Global Terrorist Threat* (Cambridge, Mass.: MIT Press, 2007); Peter Romaniuk, "Institutions as Swords and Shields: Multilateral Counter-terrorism Since 9/11," *Review of International Studies*, forthcoming. Note also the articles and reports of the Center on Global

Counter-terrorism Cooperation, which provide ample evidence of this trend (www.globalct.org).

19 For a recent summary, see Newman, *A Crisis of Global Institutions?* ch. 1.

20 Peter J. Katzenstein and Nobuo Okawara, "Japan, Asia-Pacific Security and the Case for Analytical Eclecticism," *International Security* 26, no. 3 (2001/02): 177.

21 For critical perspectives on "terrorism studies," see: Magnus Ranstorp, ed., *Mapping Terrorism Research: State of the Art, Gaps and Future Direction* (London: Routledge, 2007); Jeroen Gunning, "A Case for Critical Terrorism Studies?", *Government and Opposition* 42, no. 3 (2007): 363–93; Andrew Silke, ed., *Research on Terrorism: Trends, Achievements and Failures* (London: Frank Cass, 2004).

22 John Gerard Ruggie, "Multilateralism: The Anatomy of an Institution," in *Multilateralism Matters: The Theory and Praxis of an Institutional Form*, ed. John Gerard Ruggie (New York: Columbia University Press, 1993), 11.

23 Peter Haas, "Introduction: Epistemic Communities and International Policy Coordination," *International Organization* 46, no. 1 (1992): 3.

24 Robert O. Keohane, "Multilateralism: An Agenda for Research," *International Journal* 45, no. 4 (1990): 731.

25 "Regimes" are defined by Stephen Krasner as "sets of implicit and explicit principles, norms, rules and decision-making procedures around which actors' expectations converge in a given area of international relations." See Stephen D. Krasner, "Structural Causes and Regime Consequences: Regimes as Intervening Variables," in *International Regimes*, ed. Stephen D. Krasner (Ithaca, N.Y.: Cornell University Press, 1983), 2. More generally, see Robert O. Keohane, *After Hegemony: Cooperation and Discord in the World Political Economy* (Princeton, N.J.: Princeton University Press, 1984).

26 Keohane, *After Hegemony*; Kenneth A. Oye, ed., *Cooperation Under Anarchy* (Princeton, N.J.: Princeton University Press, 1986).

27 Keohane, "The Globalization of Informal Violence," 37.

28 Keohane, "The Globalization of Informal Violence," 37.

29 Randall L. Schweller and David Priess, "A Tale of Two Realisms: Expanding the Institutions Debate," *Mershon International Studies Review* 41, no. 1 (1997): 1–32.

30 See John J. Mearsheimer, "The False Promise of International Institutions," *International Security* 19, no. 3 (1994/95): 5–49.

31 Joseph Grieco, "Anarchy and the Limits of Cooperation: A Realist Critique of the Newest Liberal Institutionalism," *International Organization* 42, no. 3 (1988): 485–508.

32 Stephen D. Krasner, "Global Communications and National Power: Life on the Pareto Frontier," *World Politics* 43, no. 3 (1991): 336–66.

33 Some recent examples include: Lloyd Gruber, *Ruling the World: Power Politics and the Rise of Supranational Institutions* (Princeton, N.J.: Princeton University Press, 2000); and Daniel W. Drezner, *All Politics is Global: Explaining International Regulatory Regimes* (Princeton, N.J.: Princeton University Press, 2007).

34 Elsewhere, I have described this dynamic by using the metaphor of "swords" and "shields," i.e. institutions may provide a way for powerful states to exert influence, but may also offer opportunities for weaker states

to resist (Romaniuk, "Institutions as Swords and Shields"). On "forum shopping" see Drezner, *All Politics is Global.*

35 Michael Mastanduno and Ethan Kapstein, "Realism and State Strategies After the Cold War," in *Unipolar Politics: Realism and State Strategies After the Cold War*, ed. Ethan Kapstein and Michael Mastanduno (New York: Columbia University Press, 1999), 1–27.

36 Jane Boulden and Thomas G. Weiss, "Tactical Multilateralism: Coaxing America Back to the UN," *Survival* 46, no. 3 (2004): 103–14. See also Rosemary Foot, S. Neil MacFarlane, and Michael Mastanduno, eds., *US Hegemony and International Organizations: The United States and Multilateral Institutions* (New York: Oxford University Press, 2003).

37 Shepard Forman and Derk Segaar, "New Coalitions for Global Governance: The Changing Dynamics of Multilateralism," *Global Governance* 12, no. 2 (2006): 207.

38 Kal Raustiala and David Victor, "The Regime Complex for Plant Genetic Resources," *International Organization* 58, no. 2 (2004): 279.

39 Anne-Marie Slaughter, *A New World Order* (Princeton, N.J.: Princeton University Press, 2004), 14.

40 Oran R. Young, "Regime Dynamics: The Rise and Fall of International Regimes," in *International Regimes*, ed. Krasner, 93–113.

41 Keohane, "Multilateralism: An Agenda for Research," 731.

42 Forman and Segaar, "New Coalitions for Global Governance"; Newman, *A Crisis of Global Institutions?*

43 Magnus Ranstorp, "Introduction: Mapping Terrorism Research—Challenges and Priorities," in *Mapping Terrorism Research*, ed. Ranstorp, 15.

44 Paul R. Pillar, *Terrorism and US Foreign Policy* (Washington, D.C.: Brookings Institution Press, 2003), 29–40.

45 Pillar, *Terrorism and US Foreign Policy*, ch. 4.

46 Pillar, *Terrorism and US Foreign Policy*, 77.

47 Audrey Kurth Cronin, "Introduction: Meeting and Managing the Threat," in *Attacking Terrorism: Elements of a Grand Strategy*, ed. Audrey Kurth Cronin and James M. Ludes (Washington, D.C.: Georgetown University Press, 2004), 1–16.

48 Nora Bensahel, "A Coalition of Coalitions: International Cooperation Against Terrorism," *Studies in Conflict and Terrorism* 29, no. 1 (2006): 35–49.

49 Robert J. Art and Louise Richardson, "Introduction," in *Democracy and Counter-terrorism: Lessons from the Past*, ed. Louise Richardson and Robert J. Art (Washington, D.C.: United States Institute of Peace Press, 2007), 1–24.

50 David Cortright and George A. Lopez, "Strategies and Policy Challenges for Winning the Fight Against Terrorism," in *Uniting Against Terror*, ed. Cortright and Lopez, ch. 8.

51 Alexander T. J. Lennon, "Introduction: The Battle for Hearts and Minds," in *The Battle for Hearts and Minds: Using Soft Power to Undermine Terrorist Networks*, ed. Alexander T. J. Lennon (Cambridge, Mass.: MIT Press, 2003), vii–xii.

52 Boaz Ganor, *The Counter-terrorism Puzzle: A Guide for Decisionmakers* (New Brunswick, N.J.: Transaction Publishers, 2005).

53 For example, see Barry Buzan, "Will the 'Global War on Terrorism' be the new Cold War?" *International Affairs* 82, no. 6 (2006): 1101–18.

54 For example, Amnesty International and Human Rights Watch maintain websites that monitor counter-terrorism practices. See www.amnesty.org/en/counter-terror-with-justice and www.hrw.org/en/category/topic/counterterrorism

55 Tore Bjørgo and John Horgan, "Introduction," in *Leaving Terrorism Behind: Individual and Collective Disengagement*, ed. Tore Bjørgo and John Horgan (New York: Routledge, 2008), 1–13.

56 United States, *National Strategy for Combating Terrorism* (2003). Available at www.globalsecurity.org/security/library/policy/national/counter_terrorism_strategy.pdf

57 United States, *National Strategy for Combating Terrorism* (2006), 1. Available at www.globalsecurity.org/security/library/policy/national/nsct_sep2006.pdf

58 *The European Union Counter-terrorism Strategy* (2005). Available at http://register.consilium.europa.eu/pdf/en/05/st14/st14469-re04.en05.pdf

59 "Uniting Against Terrorism: Recommendations for a Global Counter-terrorism Strategy (Report of the Secretary-General)," General Assembly, A/60/825, 27 April 2006.

60 "The United Nations Global Counter-terrorism Strategy," General Assembly resolution, A/RES/60/288, 20 September 2006.

61 Martha Crenshaw, "Counter-terrorism Policy and the Political Process," *Studies in Conflict and Terrorism* 24, no. 5 (2001): 329–37; Peter J. Katzenstein "Same War, Different Views: Germany, Japan and Counter-terrorism," *International Organization* 57, no. 4 (2002): 731–60; Pillar, *Terrorism and US Foreign Policy*, 123–29.

62 See Ranstorp, "Introduction," and Berto Jongman, "Research Desiderata in the Field of Terrorism" (ch. 12) in *Mapping Terrorism Research*, ed. Ranstorp.

63 Jon B. Alterman, Sara Simon, Martha Crenshaw, and Paul Wilkinson, "How Terrorism Ends," ed. Richard H. Solomon, United States Institute of Peace, Special Report no. 48 (1999), available at: www.usip.org/pubs/specialreports/sr990525.html; Audrey Kurth Cronin, "How al Qaida Ends," *International Security* 31, no. 1 (2006): 7–48; Louise Richardson and Robert J. Art, eds., *Democracy and Counter-terrorism*; Seth G. Jones and Martin C. Libicki, *How Terrorist Groups End: Lessons for Countering al Qa'ida* (Santa Monica, Calif.: RAND, 2008).

64 Tore Bjørgo and John Horgan, eds., *Leaving Terrorism Behind*; Anne Aldis and Graeme P. Herd, eds., *The Ideological War on Terror: Worldwide Strategies for Counter-terrorism* (New York: Routledge, 2007).

65 Yonah Alexander, ed., *Combating Terrorism: Strategies of Ten Countries* (Ann Arbor: University of Michigan Press, 2002); Wyn Rees, *Transatlantic Counter-terrorism Cooperation: The New Imperative* (New York: Routledge, 2006); Doron Zimmerman and Andreas Wenger, eds., *How States Fight Terrorism: Policy Dynamics in the West* (Boulder, Colo.: Lynne Rienner, 2007).

66 Boulden and Weiss, eds., *Terrorism and the UN*; Victor V. Ramraj, Michael Hor, and Kent Roach, eds., *Global Antiterrorism Law and Policy* (New York: Cambridge University Press, 2005); Cortright and Lopez, eds., *Uniting Against Terror*; Luck "The Uninvited Challenge"; Romaniuk, "Institutions as Swords and Shields"; Romaniuk, "International Organizations and Terrorism," *International Studies Association Compendium Project* (forthcoming).

67 David Cortright and George A. Lopez, "Strategic Counter-terrorism," in *Uniting Against Terror*, ed. Cortright and Lopez, 3; Ronald D. Crelinsten,

"Counter-terrorism as Global Governance: A Research Inventory," in *Mapping Terrorism Research*, ed. Ranstorp, ch. 10.

68 Martha Crenshaw, *Terrorism and International Cooperation*, Occasional Paper no. 11, Institute for East-West Studies (New York: Westview Press, 1989).

1 Historical precedents for multilateral counter-terrorism

1 Richard Bach Jensen, "The International Campaign Against Anarchist Terrorism, 1880–1930s," *Terrorism and Political Violence* 21, no. 1 (2009): 92.

2 Thomas M. Franck and Bert B. Lockwood, "Preliminary Thoughts Towards an International Convention on Terrorism," *American Journal of International Law* 68, no. 1 (1974): 70.

3 Marie Fleming, "Propaganda by the Deed: Terrorism and Anarchist Theory in the Late Nineteenth Century," *Studies in Conflict and Terrorism* 4, nos. 1–4 (1980): 1–23.

4 Richard Bach Jensen, "The International Campaign Against Anarchist Terrorism, 1880–1930s," 89–91. In light of its history, Jensen treats the Russian case as unique and cites Anna Griefman's (*Thou Shalt Kill: Revolutionary Terrorism in Russia, 1894–1917* (Princeton, N.J.: Princeton University Press, 1995), 125) estimate that, between 1901 and 1916, "the majority of the 17,000 wounded or killed ... by terrorists suffered their fate at the hands of anarchists" (Jensen, "The International Campaign Against Anarchist Terrorism," 90).

5 Jensen, "The International Campaign Against Anarchist Terrorism," 89–91. See also Richard Bach Jensen, "Daggers, Rifles and Dynamite: Anarchism Terrorism in 19th Century Europe," *Terrorism and Political Violence* 16, no. 1 (2004): 116–53.

6 Rick Coolsaet, *Al Qaeda the Myth: The Root Causes of Terrorism and How to Tackle Them* (Ghent, Belgium: Academia Press, 2005), 27.

7 This paragraph draws on Jensen, "The International Campaign Against Anarchist Terrorism," 91–93.

8 Richard Bach Jensen, "The International Anti-Anarchist Conference of 1898 and the Origins of Interpol," *Journal of Contemporary History* 16, no. 2 (1981): 323–47.

9 Hsi-Huey Liang, *The Rise of the Modern Police and the European State System from Metternich to the Second World War* (New York: Cambridge University Press, 1992), 161–62; Jensen, "The International Anti-Anarchist Conference of 1898," 327.

10 Liang, *The Rise of the Modern Police*, 163.

11 Jensen, "The International Anti-Anarchist Conference of 1898," 327.

12 Mathieu Deflem, "'Beasts Without Nationality': The Uncertain Origins of Interpol, 1898–1910," in *Handbook of Transnational Crime and Justice*, ed. Philip Reichel (Thousand Oaks, Calif.: Sage, 2005), 279; Liang, *The Rise of the Modern Police*, 163–65.

13 Jensen, "The International Anti-Anarchist Conference of 1898," 328.

14 Jensen, "The International Anti-Anarchist Conference of 1898," 328–29.

15 Jensen, "The International Anti-Anarchist Conference of 1898," 330.

16 Jensen, "The International Campaign Against Anarchist Terrorism," 94–95; Jensen, "The International Anti-Anarchist Conference of 1898," 330–35.

17 Message to the Senate and House of Representatives, 57th Congress, 3 December 1901, as cited in Richard Bach Jensen, "The United States, International Policing and the War Against Anarchist Terrorism, 1900–1914," *Terrorism and Political Violence* 13, no. 1 (2001): 19. This paragraph draws upon this article.

18 Jensen, "The United States, International Policing and the War Against Anarchist Terrorism," 19.

19 Jensen, "The United States, International Policing and the War Against Anarchist Terrorism."

20 Jensen, "The International Campaign Against Anarchist Terrorism," 97.

21 Jensen, "The International Campaign Against Anarchist Terrorism," 98.

22 This term was used by the Austrian ambassador to London, who responded cynically to the British failure to sign the protocol: Liang, *The Rise of the Modern Police*, 173.

23 Liang, *The Rise of the Modern Police*, 173–74.

24 Jensen, "The International Campaign Against Anarchist Terrorism," 98–99.

25 Deflem, "'Beasts Without Nationality.'"

26 Jensen, "The International Campaign Against Anarchist Terrorism," 98–101.

27 Jensen, "The International Campaign Against Anarchist Terrorism," 101–3.

28 This passage draws on: Bogdan Zlataric, "History of International Terrorism and its Legal Control," in *International Terrorism and Political Crimes*, ed. M. Cherif Bassiouni (Springfield, Ill.: Charles Thomas, 1975), 474–84; Ben Saul, "Attempts to Define 'Terrorism' in International Law," *Netherlands International Law Review* 52, no. 1 (2005): 57–83; Ben Saul, *Defining Terrorism in International Law* (New York: Oxford University Press, 2006); and, Ben Saul, "The Legal Response of the League of Nations to Terrorism," *Journal of International Criminal Justice* 4, no. 1 (2006): 78–102.

29 The relevant text is excerpted in M. Cherif Bassiouni, ed., *International Terrorism and Political Crimes*, 472–73.

30 For a detailed account, in addition to the sources cited above, see Geoffrey Marston, "Early Attempts to Suppress Terrorism: The Terrorism and International Criminal Court Conventions of 1937," *British Year Book of International Law* 73 (2002): 293–313.

31 That ratifying state was India, which took the rare step of acting separately from the British Commonwealth to do so. See J. G. Starke, "Note: The Convention for the Prevention and Punishment of Terrorism," *British Year Book of International Law* 19 (1938): 215. The text of the convention is available in M. Cherif Bassiouni, *International Terrorism: Multilateral Conventions (1937–2001)* (Ardley, N.Y.: Transnational Publishers, 2001).

32 Saul, "Attempts to Define 'Terrorism' in International Law," 64–65; Saul, "The Legal Response of the League of Nations to Terrorism," 89–97.

33 Saul, "The Legal Response of the League of Nations to Terrorism," 82–83, 87–88.

34 Saul, "Attempts to Define 'Terrorism' in International Law," 65–66; Saul, "The Legal Response of the League of Nations to Terrorism," 89–97. See also John Dugard, "International Terrorism: Problems of Definition," *International Affairs* 50, no. 1 (1974): 69–70.

35 Geoffrey Marston, "Early Attempts to Suppress Terrorism," 312–13.

36 Rick Coolsaet, "Anarchist Outrages," *Le Monde Diplomatique* (English edition), September 2004, available at http://mondediplo.com/2004/09/

03anarchists; note also Jensen's discussion, "The International Campaign Against Anarchist Terrorism," 104–7.

37 Jensen, "The International Campaign Against Anarchist Terrorism," 104–7. On the distinction between al Qaeda as an organization ("al Qaeda Central") and al Qaeda as a social movement, see Marc Sageman, *Leaderless Jihad: Terror Network in the Twenty-First Century* (Philadelphia: University of Pennsylvania Press, 2008). Note also Sageman's discussion of the role of the internet in contemporary terrorism (ch. 6).

38 Mathieu Deflem, "'Beasts Without Nationality': The Uncertain Origins of Interpol, 1898–1910," 279.

39 Jensen, "The International Anti-Anarchist Conference of 1898," 340.

40 Jensen, "The International Anti-Anarchist Conference of 1898," 341.

41 Starke, "Note: The Convention for the Prevention and Punishment of Terrorism," 215.

42 Mathieu Deflem, *Policing World Society: Historical Foundations of International Police Cooperation* (New York: Oxford University Press, 2002), 73. See also Liang, *The Rise of the Modern Police*, and Andreas and Nadelmann, *Policing the Globe*.

43 Jensen, "The International Anti-Anarchist Conference of 1898."

44 Ben Saul, "The Legal Response of the League of Nations to Terrorism," 79.

45 Harold D. Lasswell, "The Garrison State," *American Journal of Sociology* 46, no. 4 (1941): 455–68.

2 Multilateral counter-terrorism and the United Nations, 1945–2001

1 Seymour Maxwell Finger, "International Terrorism and the United Nations," in *International Terrorism: National, Regional and Global Perspectives*, ed. Yonah Alexander (New York: Praeger, 1976), 323–26.

2 I arrived at this figure by adding the total number of incidents recorded in the two "Global Terrorism Database" (GTD) datasets (available at www.start.umd.edu/start/data/gtd) for the relevant time period. GTD 1 records 61,637 incidents for the period 1970–97. GTD 2 utilizes a broader approach to defining terrorism, but includes a total of 41,399 incidents between 1 January 1998 and 10 September 2001.

3 David C. Rapoport, "The Four Waves of Modern Terrorism," in *Attacking Terrorism: Elements of a Grand Strategy*, ed. Audrey Kurth Cronin and James M. Ludes (Washington, D.C.: Georgetown University Press, 2004), 46–73.

4 On the concept of "path dependence," see James Mahoney, "Path Dependence in Historical Sociology," *Theory and Society* 29, no. 4 (2000): 507–48.

5 Data on hijackings in this period vary across the available sources. However, for the period 1948–67 there were less than seven such incidents only. By contrast, there were some 350 incidents in the following five years. See: Paul Sheppard and Eugene Sochor, "Setting International Aviation Security Standards," in *Aerial Piracy and Aviation Security*, ed. Yonah Alexander and Eugene Sochor (Dordrecht, Netherlands: Martinus Nijhoff, 1990), 3–19; CIA, *Research Study: International and Transnational Terrorism—Diagnosis and Prognosis*, PR 76 10030 (April 1976) (available at www.terrorisminfo.mipt.org/Patterns-of-Global-Terrorism.asp); Alona E. Evans, "Aircraft Highjacking: Its Cause and Cure," *American Journal of International Law* 63, no. 4 (1969): 695–710.

6 See Gerald F. FitzGerald, "Toward Legal Suppression of Acts Against Civil Aviation," *International Conciliation*, no. 585 (November 1971): 42–82.

7 FitzGerald, "Toward Legal Suppression of Acts Against Civil Aviation," 51.

8 FitzGerald, "Toward Legal Suppression of Acts Against Civil Aviation," 56.

9 See General Assembly resolutions 2551 (XXIV) (12 December 1969) and 2645 (XXV) (25 November 1970), and Security Council resolution 286 (9 September 1970).

10 Gerald FitzGerald, "Aviation Terrorism and the International Civil Aviation Organization," *Canadian Yearbook of International Law* 25 (1987): 219–41; Rodney Wallis, *Combating Air Terrorism* (Maclean, Va.: Brassey's, 1993), ch. 4.

11 Wallis, *Combating Air Terrorism*, 101.

12 Finger, "International Terrorism and the United Nations," 328–29.

13 Thomas M. Franck and Bert B. Lockwood, Jr., "Preliminary Thoughts Towards an International Convention on Terrorism," *American Journal of International Law* 68, no. 1 (1974): 70–71, n. 13.

14 FitzGerald, "Aviation Terrorism and the International Civil Aviation Organization," 224.

15 Bruce Hoffman, *Inside Terrorism* (New York: Columbia University Press, 2006), ch. 3.

16 For a detailed account of the Council's action on terrorism over time, see Edward C. Luck, "Tackling Terrorism," in *The UN Security Council: From the Cold War to the 21st Century*, ed. David M. Malone (Boulder, Colo.: Lynne Rienner, 2004), 85–100.

17 On these developments, see M. J. Peterson, "Using the General Assembly," in *Terrorism and the UN: Before and After September 11*, ed. Jane Boulden and Thomas G. Weiss (Bloomington: Indiana University Press, 2004), 178–81; and Finger, "International Terrorism and the United Nations," 329–37. The quotation is from Finger, "International Terrorism and the United Nations," 329.

18 Address by Yasser Arafat to the General Assembly of the United Nations, 13 November 1974. Available at www.monde-diplomatique.fr/cahier/proche-orient/arafat74-en

19 "Measures to prevent terrorism and other forms of violence which endanger or take human lives or jeopardize fundamental freedoms, and study of the underlying causes of those forms of terrorism and acts of violence which lie in misery, frustration, grievance, and despair and which cause some people to sacrifice human lives, including their own, in an attempt to effect radical changes," study prepared by the Secretariat in accordance with the decision taken by the Sixth Committee at its 1314th meeting on 27 September 1972 (General Assembly document A/C.6/418), 2 November 1972, para. 66.

20 Fereydoun Hoveyda, "The Problem of Terrorism at the United Nations," *Terrorism: An International Journal* 1, no. 1 (1977): 77.

21 John Dugard, "International Terrorism: Problems of Definition," *International Affairs* 50, no. 1 (1974): 78–81. See also Finger, "International Terrorism and the United Nations," 332–33.

22 On the Soviet position, see Robert O. Freedman, "Soviet Policy Toward International Terrorism," in *International Terrorism: National, Regional and Global Perspectives*, ed. Yonah Alexander (New York: Praeger, 1976), 115–47.

23 Thomas M. Franck and Bert B. Lockwood, Jr., "Preliminary Thoughts Towards an International Convention on Terrorism," *American Journal of International Law* 68, no. 1 (1974): 72–75.

24 *Report of the Ad Hoc Committee on International Terrorism* A/32/37 (28 April 1977) and A/34/37 (17 April 1979).

25 General Assembly resolutions 32/147 (16 December 1977); 34/145 (17 December 1979); 36/109 (10 December 1981); 38/130 (19 December 1983); 40/61 (9 December 1985); 42/159 (7 December 1987); and 44/29 (4 December 1989).

26 Peterson, "Using the General Assembly," 177.

27 *Report of the Ad Hoc Committee on International Terrorism,* A/34/37 (17 April 1979), para. 23.

28 *Report of the Ad Hoc Committee,* A/34/37, para. 118.

29 Finger, "International Terrorism and the United Nations," 335.

30 Franck and Lockwood, "Preliminary Thoughts Towards an International Convention on Terrorism," 89.

31 Finger, "International Terrorism and the United Nations," 337–39.

32 Luck, "Tackling Terrorism," 88–93; Sydney D. Bailey, "The UN Security Council and Terrorism," *International Relations* 11, no. 6 (1993), 533–53.

33 Security Council resolution 337, 15 August 1973.

34 The origins and impact of the convention are discussed by: Robert Rosenstock, "International Convention Against the Taking of Hostages: Another International Community Step Against Terrorism," *Denver Journal of International Law and Policy* 9, no. 1 (1980): 169–95; Clive C. Aston, "The United Nations Convention Against the Taking of Hostages: Realistic or Rhetoric?" *Studies in Conflict and Terrorism* 5, nos. 1 & 2 (1981): 139–60; Wil D. Verwey, "The International Hostages Convention and National Liberation Movements," *American Journal of International Law* 75, no. 1 (1981): 69–92; John W. McDonald, Jr., "The United Nations Convention against the Taking of Hostages: The Inside Story," *Terrorism: An International Journal* 6, no. 4 (1983): 545–60; and Joseph J. Lambert, *Terrorism and Hostages in International Law: A Commentary on the Hostages Convention 1979* (Cambridge: Grotius Publications, 1990).

35 General Assembly resolution 31/106 (15 December 1976).

36 This quotation is from a document submitted by Libya, cited by Verwey, "The International Hostages Convention," 70 (fn. 4).

37 On the importance of the working groups, see McDonald, Jr., "The United Nations Convention against the Taking of Hostages."

38 General Assembly resolution 3101 (XXVIII) (12 December 1973).

39 For example, Aston, "The United Nations Convention against the Taking of Hostages."

40 Lambert, *Terrorism and Hostages in International Law,* 263–98.

41 Brian M. Jenkins, "International Cooperation in Locating and Recovering Stolen Nuclear Materials," *Terrorism: An International Journal* 6, no. 4 (1983): 561–75.

42 George Bunn, "International Arrangements against Nuclear Terrorism," in *Preventing Nuclear Terrorism,* ed. Paul Leventhal and Yonah Alexander (Lexington, Mass.: Lexington Books, 1987), 339–59.

43 In this regard, see Hans Blix, "The Role of the IAEA in the Development of International Law," *Nordic Journal of International Law* 58, nos. 3 & 4

(1989): 231–42; George Bunn, "Physical Protection of Nuclear Materials: Strengthening Global Norms," *IAEA Bulletin* 39, no. 4 (1997): 4–8; and George Bunn, "Raising International Standards to Protect Nuclear Materials from Theft or Sabotage," *Nonproliferation Review* (Summer 2000): 146–56.

44 Oldrich Bures, "EU Counter-terrorism Policy: A Paper Tiger?" *Terrorism and Political Violence* 18, no. 1 (2006): 58–59.

45 General Assembly resolutions A/RES/36/109 (10 December 1981) and A/RES/38/130 (19 December 1983).

46 Until 1993, these reports utilized variations on the long title, *Measures to prevent terrorism and other forms of violence which endanger or take human lives or jeopardize fundamental freedoms, and study of the underlying causes of those forms of terrorism and acts of violence which lie in misery, frustration, grievance, and despair and which cause some people to sacrifice human lives, including their own, in an attempt to effect radical changes.* From this period, see General Assembly documents: A/36/425 (21 September 1981); A/38/355 (21 September 1983); A/40/445 (20 August 1985); A/42/519 (8 September 1987) and A/44/456 (25 August 1989). Hereafter, the long title is shortened to *Measures to Prevent Terrorism ...*

47 General Assembly resolution A/RES/39/159 (23 January 1985).

48 Peterson, "Using the General Assembly," 179–81.

49 US Department of State, *Patterns of Global Terrorism: 1985* (October 1986).

50 *Measures to Prevent Terrorism ...* , Report of the Sixth Committee. (General Assembly document A/40/1003), 7 December 1985.

51 The former is quoted in Robert D. McFadden, "Terror in 1985: Brutal Attacks, Tough Response," *New York Times*, 30 December 1985, 1. The latter is quoted by John F. Murphy, "The Future of Multilateralism and Efforts to Combat Terrorism," *Columbia Journal of Transnational Law* 25 (1986–87): 56.

52 Security Council resolution S/RES/579 (18 December 1985), para. 1.

53 FitzGerald, "Aviation Terrorism and the International Civil Aviation Organization," 232–35. These developments are also summarized in ICAO's report to the Secretary-General pursuant to General Assembly resolution 40/61. See *Measures to Prevent Terrorism ...* , Report of the Secretary-General. General Assembly document A/42/519 (8 September 1987), 11–13.

54 FitzGerald, "Aviation Terrorism and the International Civil Aviation Organization," 235–37.

55 See Philippe Kirsch, "The 1988 ICAO and IMO Conferences: An International Consensus against Terrorism," *Dalhousie Law Journal* 12, no. 1 (1989): 5–33.

56 *Measures to Prevent Terrorism ...* , Report of the Secretary-General. General Assembly document A/42/519 (8 September 1987), 11.

57 These developments are summarized in Hartmut G. Hesse, "Maritime Security in a Multilateral Context: IMO Activities to Enhance Maritime Security," *Journal of Marine and Coastal Law* 18, no. 3 (2003): 327–40. See also *Measures to Prevent Terrorism ...* , Report of the Secretary-General. General Assembly document A/46/346 (30 August 1991), 25–32.

58 Kirsch, "The 1988 ICAO and IMO Conferences," 9, 13–15; Tullio Treves, "The Rome Convention for the Suppression of Unlawful Acts Against the Safety of Maritime Navigation," in *Maritime Terrorism and International Law*, ed. Natalino Ronzitti (Dordrecht, Netherlands: Kluwer, 1990), 69–90.

59 See General Assembly resolutions 42/159 (7 December 1987), para. 11, and 44/29 (4 December 1989), para. 13.
60 For example, *Measures to Prevent Terrorism ...* , Report of the Secretary-General. General Assembly document A/44/456 (25 August 1989).
61 Security Council resolutions 618 (29 July 1988) and 638 (31 July 1989).
62 General Assembly resolution 44/29 (4 December 1989), para. 12; Security Council resolution 635 (14 June 1989).
63 See *Measures to Prevent Terrorism ...* , Report of the Sixth Committee. General Assembly document A/42/832 (3 December 1987) and US Department of State, *Patterns of Global Terrorism: 1987* (August 1988).
64 On these incidents, see Luck, "Tackling Terrorism," 88–93.
65 For example, Murphy, "The Future of Multilateralism," and "The Need for International Cooperation in Combating Terrorism," *Terrorism: An International Journal* 13, no. 6 (1990): 381–96.
66 Peterson, "Using the General Assembly," 184.
67 Martha Crenshaw, *Terrorism and International Cooperation* (Boulder, Colo.: Westview Press, 1989).
68 Crenshaw, *Terrorism and International Cooperation*, ch. 3.
69 Crenshaw, *Terrorism and International Cooperation*, ch. 4.
70 See Igor Beliaev and John Marks, eds., *Common Ground on Terrorism: Soviet-American Cooperation against the Politics of Terror* (New York: W. W. Norton, 1991).
71 The role of the Council in this period is also summarized by: Ed Luck, "Tackling Terrorism"; Ed Luck, *UN Security Council: Practice and Promise* (London: Routledge, 2006), ch. 9; Ed Luck, "The Uninvited Challenge: Terrorism Targets the United Nations," in *Multilateralism Under Challenge: Power, International Order and Structural Change*, ed. Edward Newman and Ramesh Thakur (Tokyo: United Nations University Press, 2006), 336–55; Chantal de Jonge Oudraat, "The Role of the Security Council," in *Terrorism and the UN: Before and After September 11*, ed. Jane Boulden and Thomas G. Weiss (Bloomington: Indiana University Press, 2004), 151–72; and Ben Saul, "Definition of 'Terrorism' in the UN Security Council: 1985–2004," *Chinese Journal of International Law* 4, no. 1 (2005): 141–66.
72 For an overview, see David Cortright and George A. Lopez, *The Sanctions Decade: Assessing UN Strategies in the 1990s* (Boulder, Colo.: Lynne Rienner, 2000), ch. 6.
73 *Note by the President of the Security Council*, Security Council document S/23500 (31 January 1992).
74 Linda Hossie, "Old Problems Cloud UN's New World: Security Council Summit Marked by Discord Among Members," *Globe and Mail* (Canada), 1 February 1992.
75 This passage draws on Cortright and Lopez, *The Sanctions Decade*, 107–21.
76 This passage draws on Cortright and Lopez, *The Sanctions Decade*, 121–26.
77 *Report of the Secretary-General Pursuant to Security Council Resolution 1070 (1996)*. Security Council document S/1996/940 (14 November 1996), paras. 13–14.
78 For example, see Lawrence Wright, *The Looming Tower: Al Qaeda and the Road to 9/11* (Vintage Books: New York, 2006), ch. 12.
79 Recall Security Council resolutions S/RES/1189 (13 August 1998), S/RES/1193 (28 August 1998) and S/RES/1214 (8 December 1998).

80 On the "sanctions debate" see David A. Baldwin, "The Sanctions Debate and the Logic of Choice," *International Security* 24, no. 3 (Winter 1999/2000): 80–107.

81 Cortright and Lopez, *The Sanctions Decade*, 120–21; Luck, "Tackling Terrorism," 94–95; de Jonge Oudraat, "The Role of the Security Council," 154–55.

82 de Jonge Oudraat, "The Role of the Security Council," 155–56.

83 Cortright and Lopez, *The Sanctions Decade*.

84 I am referring here to the three "sanctions reform processes": the Bonn-Berlin Process on Travel Bans and Arms Embargoes; the Interlaken Process on Targeted Financial Sanctions; and the Stockholm Process on Implementing Targeted Sanctions. For a summary of these, see Thomas J. Biersteker, Sue E. Eckert, Aaron Halegua, and Peter Romaniuk, "Consensus from the Bottom Up? Assessing the Influence of the Sanctions Reform Processes," in *International Sanctions: Between Words and Wars in the Global System*, ed. Peter Wallensteen and Carina Staibano (Portland, Oreg.: Frank Cass, 2005), 15–30.

85 Recall the comments of the Malaysian (on national liberation movements) and Bahraini (on state terrorism) delegates in *Record of the 4053rd Meeting of the Security Council*. Security Council document S/PV.4053 (19 October 1999).

86 Luck, "Tackling Terrorism," 93.

87 Virginia Morris and M.-Christiane Bourloyannis-Vrailas, "The Work of the Sixth Committee at the Forty Eighth Session of the UN General Assembly," *American Journal of International Law* 88, no. 2 (1994): 347–48.

88 *Measures to Eliminate International Terrorism*, Report of the Secretary-General. General Assembly document A/49/257 (25 July 1994).

89 General Assembly document A/C.6/51/6 (11 November 1996).

90 See the "Agreement on 25 Measures," issued by the Ministerial Conference on Terrorism, Paris, France, 30 July 1996.

91 *Measures to Eliminate International Terrorism*, Report of the Secretary-General. General Assembly document A/51/336 (6 September 1996).

92 *Measures to Eliminate International Terrorism*, General Assembly document A/51/336 (6 September 1996), para. 35.

93 Virginia Morris and M.-Christiane Bourloyannis-Vrailas, "The Work of the Sixth Committee at the Fifty-First Session of the UN General Assembly," *American Journal of International Law* 91, no. 3 (1997): 545–46.

94 See Virginia Morris and M.-Christiane Bourloyannis-Vrailas, "The Work of the Sixth Committee at the Fifty-Second Session of the UN General Assembly," *American Journal of International Law* 92, no. 3 (1998): 574–75; Samuel M. Witten, "The International Convention for the Suppression of Terrorist Bombings," *American Journal of International Law* 92, no. 4 (1998): 774–81.

95 The negotiations are summarized in *Report of the Ad Hoc Committee Established by General Assembly resolution 51/210 of 17 December 1996*, General Assembly document A/54/37 (5 May 1999); and *Measures to Eliminate International Terrorism*, Report of the Working Group, General Assembly document A/C.6/54/L.2 (26 October 1999).

96 *Report of the Ad Hoc Committee Established by General Assembly resolution 51/210 of 17 December 1996*. General Assembly document A/53/37 (23 July 1998).

97 For a useful overview of the negotiations, see Center for Nonproliferation Studies, "International Convention for the Suppression of Acts of Nuclear Terrorism," *Inventory of International Nonproliferation Organizations and Regimes* (updated 25 February 2009). Available at http://cns.miis.edu/inventory/index.htm

98 *Report of the Ad Hoc Committee Established by General Assembly resolution 51/210 of 17 December 1996*, General Assembly document A/54/37 (5 May 1999).

99 Recall that several regional and other organizations—including the NAM and the G7—were cited in the preamble of resolution 51/210 (17 December 1996). Only the NAM was noted in the resolutions 53/108 (8 December 1998), 54/110 (9 December 1999) and 55/158 (12 December 2000).

100 *Report of the Ad Hoc Committee Established by General Assembly resolution 51/210 of 17 December 1996*, General Assembly document A/55/37 (8 March 2000), para. 23.

101 *Measures to Eliminate International Terrorism*, General Assembly resolution A/RES/55/158 (12 December 2000), paras. 13–14.

102 *Summary Record of the 36th Meeting of the Sixth Committee*, General Assembly document A/C.6/55/SR.36 (22 November 2000), para. 4.

103 *Measures to Eliminate International Terrorism*, Report of the Working Group, General Assembly document A/C.6/55/L.2 (19 October 2000).

104 *Report of the Ad Hoc Committee Established by General Assembly resolution 51/210 of 17 December 1996*, General Assembly document A/55/37 (8 March 2000), para. 17.

105 See Mahmoud Hmoud, "Negotiating the Draft Comprehensive Convention on International Terrorism," *Journal of International Criminal Justice* 4, no. 5 (2006): 1031–43.

106 These reports are archived at www.un.org/terrorism/sg-reports.shtml. See *Measures to Eliminate International Terrorism*, Report of the Secretary-General, General Assembly documents A/52/304 (28 August 1997), A/53/314 (31 August 1998), A/54/301 (3 September 1999), A/55/179 (26 July 2000) and A/56/160 (3 July 2001).

107 Note in particular the 1985 Milan Plan of Action, adopted by the Seventh Crime Congress, 26 August–2 September, and endorsed by General Assembly resolution 40/32 (29 November 1985). For a brief history of the Terrorism Prevention Branch, see *Strengthening the Terrorism Prevention Branch*, Report of the Secretary-General. General Assembly document A/57/152 (2 July 2002).

108 *Vienna Declaration and Program of Action*, Note by the Secretariat, General Assembly document A/CONF.157/23 (12 July 1993), Part I, para. 17.

109 General Assembly resolution A/RES/48/122 (30 December 1993).

110 General Assembly resolutions A/RES/49/185 (23 December 1994) and 50/186 (22 December 1995).

111 General Assembly resolutions A/RES/52/133 (12 December 1997) and 54/164 (17 December 1999).

112 Michael J. Dennis, "The Fifty-Second Session of the UN Commission on Human Rights," *American Journal of International Law* 91, no. 1 (1997): 169–70.

113 Michael J. Dennis, "The Fifty-Third Session of the UN Commission on Human Rights," *American Journal of International Law* 92, no. 1 (1998): 115–16.
114 Michael J. Dennis, "The Fifty-Sixth Session of the UN Commission on Human Rights," *American Journal of International Law* 95, no. 1 (2001): 214–15.
115 Commission on Human Rights document E/CN.4/RES/1994/46 (4 March 1994), para. 5.
116 The reports are archived at http://www2.ohchr.org/english/issues/terrorism/rapporteur/index.htm. Note also the discussion by Peter van Krieken, *Terrorism and the International Legal Order* (The Hague, Netherlands: T. M. C. Asser Press, 2002), ch. 4.
117 Paul Pillar, *Terrorism and US Foreign Policy* (Washington, D.C.: Brookings Institution Press, 2003), 77.
118 Pillar, *Terrorism and US Foreign Policy*, 73–79.
119 Paul Wilkinson, *Terrorism Versus Democracy: The Liberal State Response* (Portland, Oreg.: Frank Cass, 2001), 200.
120 Luck, "Tackling Terrorism"; de Jonge Oudraat, "The Role of the Security Council."

3 Multilateral counter-terrorism and the United Nations after 9/11

1 With General Assembly resolution A/RES/55/282 (7 September 2001) the International Day of Peace was assigned a permanent date and is now celebrated on 21 September each year.
 2 "Postponed by Terrorist Attack, 'Peace Bell' Ceremony Held at UN Headquarters," UN News Centre, 14 September 2001.
 3 "Opening Annual Session, General Assembly Condemns Terror Attacks Against US," UN News Centre, 12 September 2001. See also, "UN Staff from Across Globe Join in One Voice of Solidarity with Terror Victims," UN News Centre, 14 September 2001.
 4 Leszek Balcerowicz introduces this concept to describe political developments after the collapse of communism: "Understanding Post-communist Transitions," *Journal of Democracy* 5, no. 4 (1994): 85.
 5 Balcerowicz, "Understanding Post-communist Transitions," 85.
 6 The Strategy is annexed to General Assembly resolution A/RES/60/288 (8 September 2008).
 7 I thank Eric Rosand for the characterization of the UN system as nimble. Scholarly arguments utilizing the concepts of learning and adaptation are referred to in the conclusion of the chapter.
 8 Chantal de Jonge Oudraat, "The Role of the Security Council," in *Terrorism and the UN: Before and After September 11*, ed. Jane Boulden and Thomas G. Weiss (Bloomington: Indiana University Press, 2004): 160–61.
 9 "Letter dated 7 October 2001 from the Permanent Representative of the United States of America to the United Nations addressed to the President of the Security Council," Security Council document S/2001/946 (7 October 2001).
10 de Jonge Oudraat gives the example of Russia: "The Role of the Security Council," 161.

11 For example, resolution 1368 was not mentioned by US Secretary of State Colin Powell in his address to the Security Council on 5 February 2003, where he laid out the case for war against Iraq. See Security Council document S/PV.4701 (5 February 2003).

12 Edward C. Luck, "Tackling Terrorism," in *The UN Security Council: From the Cold War to the 21st Century*, ed. David M. Malone (Boulder, Colo.: Lynne Rienner, 2004), 93.

13 For example, General Assembly resolution A/RES/51/210 (17 December 1996), para. 3(a). The asset freeze called for in S/RES/1373, para. 1(c) and (d) effectively broadens the scope of the measures imposed by S/RES/1267 (15 October 1999) and S/RES/1333 (19 December 2000).

14 In addition to those resolutions cited in the preceding note, recall General Assembly resolutions titled "Measures to Eliminate International Terrorism," especially Assembly resolution A/RES/49/60 (9 December 1994) and the "Declaration on Measures to Eliminate International Terrorism" annexed to it. Security Council resolution S/RES/1269 (19 October 1999) also includes similar provisions.

15 The reports are available at www.un.org/terrorism/sg-reports.shtml

16 Thomas J. Biersteker, Sue E. Eckert, and Peter Romaniuk, *Targeted Financial Sanctions: A Manual for Design and Implementation (Contributions from the Interlaken Process)* (Providence, R.I.: Watson Institute for International Studies, 2001), 30–32.

17 George J. Andreopoulos, "The Challenges and Perils of Normative Overstretch," in *The UN Security Council and the Politics of International Authority*, ed. Bruce Cronin and Ian Hurd (New York: Routledge, 2008), 113–18. Note that the term "human rights" appears once in resolution 1373, in the context of ensuring that asylum procedures should not be abused by terrorists, though they ought to conform to human rights law.

18 de Jonge Oudraat, "The Role of the Security Council," 161.

19 See Kendall W. Stiles, "The Power of Procedure and the Procedures of the Powerful: Anti-Terror Law in the United Nations," *Journal of Peace Research* 43, no. 1 (2006): 48–50.

20 "Letter dated 19 October 2001 from the Chairman of the Counter-Terrorism Committee addressed to the President of the Security Council," Security Council document S/2001/986 (19 October 2001).

21 Counter-Terrorism Committee, *Guidelines for the Committee in the Conduct of Its Work* (16 October 2001), available at www.un.org/sc/ctc/documents/guidelines.htm

22 Security Council resolution S/RES/1377 (12 November 2001).

23 Greenstock's position is set out in his address briefing to the Council contained in Security Council document S/2002/PV.4453 (18 January 2002).

24 Office of the High Commissioner for Human Rights, *Proposals for "Further Guidance" for the Submission of Reports Pursuant to Paragraph 6 of Security Council resolution 1373 (2001) (Intended to Supplement the Guidance of 26 October 2001)—Compliance with International Human Rights Standards* (23 September 2002), available at www.un.org/sc/ctc/documents/ohchr2.htm

25 Address by High Commissioner for Human Rights, Sergio Vieira de Mello, to the Counter-Terrorism Committee of the UN Security Council (21 October 2002), available at www.un.org/sc/ctc/documents/HC.htm

26 See Curtis A. Ward, "Building Capacity to Combat International Terrorism: The Role of the United Nations Security Council," *Journal of Conflict and Security Law* 8, no. 2 (2003): 296–98.
27 Security Council resolution S/RES/1456 (20 January 2003), para. 6 of the declaration attached to the resolution.
28 For an upbeat assessment of the early record of the CTC, see Ward, "Building Capacity to Combat International Terrorism," on which this passage draws.
29 Of the 159 states mentioned here, 80 had requested assistance through the CTC, while the others utilized other mechanisms. Further details are provided by Ward, "Building Capacity to Combat International Terrorism," 302.
30 "Outcome Document of the Special Meeting of the Counter-Terrorism Committee with International, Regional and Subregional Organizations," Security Council document S/AC.40/2003/SM.1/4 (31 March 2003).
31 The Inter-American Committee is generally known by its Spanish acronym, CICTE (Comité Interamericano Contra el Terrorismo).
32 Ward, "Building Capacity to Combat International Terrorism," 289.
33 Security Council resolution S/RES/1452 (20 December 2002).
34 Security Council resolution S/RES/1455 (17 January 2003).
35 Peter Wallensteen, Carina Staibano, and Mikael Eriksson, eds., *Making Targeted Sanctions Effective: Guidelines for UN Policy Options (Results from the Stockholm Process on Implementing Targeted Sanctions)* (Uppsala, Sweden: Uppsala University, 2003); Peter Wallensteen and Carina Staibano, eds., *International Sanctions: Between Words and Wars in the Global System* (New York: Frank Cass, 2005).
36 The reports of the Monitoring Group are available at www.un.org/sc/commit tees/1267/monitoringgroup.shtml
37 *Report of the monitoring group Established Pursuant to Security Council Resolution 1363 (2001) and Extended by Resolutions 1390 (2002) and 1455 (2003)*, Security Council document S/2003/669 (8 July 2003), para. 146.
38 For example, the United States was displeased with the group's interventions on the question of a link between al Qaeda and Saddam Hussein (see Eric Rosand and Sebastian von Einsiedel, "9/11, the War on Terror and the Evolution of Multilateral Institutions," in *Cooperating for Peace and Security: Evolving Institutions and Arrangements in a Context of Changing US Security Policy* (New York: Cambridge University Press, forthcoming)). Further, the group issued—but later withdrew—a chart of Southeast Asian group, Jemaah Islamiah, alleging links between extremists and established political parties and civil society organizations in the region. See *Second report of the monitoring group established Pursuant to Security Council Resolution 1363 (2001) and Extended by Resolution 1390 (2002)*, Security Council document S/2002/1050 (20 September 2002), annex IV. The excision of the offending annex was requested in "Letter dated 26 December 2002 from the Chairman of the Security Council Committee Established Pursuant to Resolution 1267 (1999) to the President of the Council," Security Council document S/2002/1427 (2 January 2003), but is available on the 1267 Committee's website.
39 Paul C. Szasz, "The Security Council Starts Legislating," *American Journal of International Law* 96, no. 4 (2002): 901–5; Eric Rosand, "The Security

Council as 'Global Legislator': Ultra Vires or Ultra Innovative?" *Fordham International Law Journal* 28, no. 3 (2005): 542–90; Stefan Talmon, "The Security Council as World Legislature," *American Journal of International Law* 99, no. 1 (2005): 175–93.

40 *Report by the Chair of the Counter-Terrorism Committee on the Problems Encountered in the Implementation of Security Council Resolution 1373 (2001)*, Security Council document S/2004/70 (26 January 2004).

41 *Report by the Chair of the Counter-Terrorism Committee*, Security Council document S/2004/70 (26 January 2004), 15.

42 *Second Report of the monitoring group Established Pursuant to Resolution 1363 (2001) and Extended by Resolutions 1390 (2002) and 1455 (2003), on Sanctions against Al-Qaida, the Taliban and Individuals and Entities Associated with Them*, Security Council document S/2003/1070 (2 December 2003).

43 *Second report of the monitoring group*, Security Council document S/2003/ 1070 (2 December 2003), 5.

44 These dilemmas are discussed in Alistair Millar and Eric Rosand, *Allied against Terrorism: What's Needed to Strengthen the Worldwide Commitment* (New York: The Century Foundation, 2006), chs. 2–3.

45 Gabriel H. Oosthuizen and Elizabeth Wilmshurst, "Terrorism and Weapons of Mass Destruction: United Nations Security Council Resolution 1540," Briefing Paper 04/01, Chatham House (September 2004).

46 Peter van Ham and Olivia Bosch, "Global Non-Proliferation and Counter-terrorism: The Role of Resolution 1540 and Its Implications," in *Global Non-Proliferation and Counter-terrorism: The Impact of UNSCR 1540*, ed. O. Bosch and P. van Ham (Washington, D.C.: Brookings Institution Press, 2007), 3–23.

47 Millar and Rosand, *Allied against Terrorism*, 21–22.

48 *Proposal for the Revitalisation of the Counter-Terrorism Committee*, Security Council document S/2004/124 (19 February 2004).

49 *Organizational plan for the Counter-Terrorism Committee Executive Directorate*, Security Council document S/2004/624 (12 August 2004).

50 In addition, as Rosand and von Einsiedel recount, the Secretariat resisted the establishment of CTED under the direct authority of the Council ("9/ 11, the War on Terror and the Evolution of Multilateral Institutions").

51 On budget and personnel issues, see Millar and Rosand, *Allied against Terrorism*, 16–18, 29–34.

52 Security Council resolution S/RES/1624 (14 September 2005).

53 Security Council resolution S/RES/1631 (17 October 2005).

54 The reports of the Monitoring Team are archived at www.un.org/sc/commit tees/1267/monitoringteam.shtml. The first and second reports are Security Council documents S/2004/679 (25 August 2004) and S/2005/83 (15 February 2005).

55 The Council adopted a relatively broad definition, including "acts or activities" that indicate that an individual, group or entity is "supporting acts or activities of ... Al-Qaida, Usama bin Laden or the Taliban, or any cell, affiliate, splinter group or derivative thereof" (Security Council resolution S/RES/1617 (29 July 2005), para. 2).

56 These developments are described by Millar and Rosand, *Allied against Terrorism*, 18–19.

57 Eric Rosand, Alistair Millar, and Jason Ipe, *The UN Security Council's Counter-terrorism Program: What Lies Ahead?* Occasional paper, International Peace Academy, October 2007, 4–6.
58 In contrast to the upbeat appraisal given by Ward ("Building Capacity to Combat International Terrorism"), Luck writes that the response to 9/11, "reflected an escalation of … well-established patterns more than … a radical departure." Edward C. Luck, "The Uninvited Challenge: Terrorism Targets the United Nations," in *Multilateralism Under Challenge? Power, International Order and Structural Change*, ed. Edward Newman, Ramesh Thakur, and John Tirman (Tokyo: United Nations University Press, 2006), 342.
59 General Assembly resolution A/RES/56/1 (18 September 2001).
60 Stiles, "The Power of Procedure and the Procedures of the Powerful"; Mahmoud Hmoud, "Neogtiating the Draft Comprehensive Convention on International Terrorism," *Journal of International Criminal Justice* 4, no. 5 (2006): 1031–43.
61 General Assembly resolution A/RES/56/88 (12 December 2001).
62 General Assembly resolution A/RES/56/160 (19 December 2001).
63 General Assembly resolution A/RES/56/253 (24 December 2001), para. 103.
64 General Assembly resolution A/RES/57/219 (18 December 2002).
65 "Summary Record of the 57th Meeting of the Third Committee," General Assembly document A/C.3/57/SR.57 (16 December 2002).
66 General Assembly resolution A/RES/57/220 (18 December 2002).
67 General Assembly resolution A/RES/57/83 (22 November 2002).
68 General Assembly resolution A/RES/57/27 (19 November 2002); *Strengthening the Terrorism Prevention Branch of the Secretariat*, Report of the Secretary-General, General Assembly document A/57/152 (2 July 2002).
69 General Assembly resolution A/RES/57/292 (20 December 2002), part IV.
70 *Measures to Eliminate International Terrorism*, Report of the Secretary-General, A/57/183 (2 July 2002).
71 General Assembly resolution A/RES/58/136 (22 December 2003).
72 *Protection of Human Rights and Fundamental Freedoms while Countering Terrorism*, Report of the Secretary-General, General Assembly document A/58/266 (8 August 2003).
73 See UN Commission on Human Rights resolutions 2002/35 (22 April 2002), 2003/37 (23 April 2003) and 2003/68 (25 April 2003).
74 Human Rights Watch, "Briefing to the 59th Session of the UN Commission on Human Rights," 1 February 2003. Available at www.hrw.org/en/reports/2003/02/01/human-rights-and-counter-terrorism. The work of Human Rights Watch on this issue is archived at www.hrw.org/en/category/topic/counterterrorism. Amnesty International is also active on the issue, see www.amnesty.org/en/counter-terror-with-justice
75 General Assembly resolution A/RES/58/187 (22 December 2003). India alone abstained from the vote on the resolution citing, among other things, the role given to the High Commissioner.
76 *Protection of Human Rights and Fundamental Freedoms while Countering Terrorism*, Study of the United Nations High Commissioner for Human Rights, General Assembly document A/59/428 (8 October 2004), para. 47. This report provides a detailed summary of the work of the UN human rights bodies on the issue of counter-terrorism, as well as specifying the gaps in coverage. See also *Protection of Human Rights and Fundamental*

Freedoms while Countering Terrorism, Report of the Secretary-General, General Assembly document A/59/404 (1 October 2004).

77 United Nations High Commission for Human Rights resolution 2004/87 (21 April 2004).

78 See General Assembly resolution A/RES/59/191 (20 December 2004).

79 See General Assembly resolutions A/RES/59/80 (3 December 2004) and A/RES/59/153 (20 December 2004).

80 *Measures to Prevent Terrorists from Acquiring Weapons of Mass Destruction*, Report of the Secretary-General, A/59/156 (14 July 2004); *Strengthening International Cooperation and Technical Assistance in Preventing and Combating Terrorism*, Report of the Secretary-General, A/59/187 (30 July 2004).

81 The negotiations leading to the convention are summarized in Center for Nonproliferation Studies, *Inventory of International Nonproliferation Organizations and Regimes: International Convention for the Suppression of Acts of Nuclear Terrorism* (updated to 25 February 2009), available at www.nti.org/e_research/official_docs/inventory/pdfs/nucterr.pdf

82 *International Convention for the Suppression of Acts of Nuclear Terrorism*, arts. 1–2.

83 General Assembly resolution A/RES/60/1 (24 October 2005).

84 See General Assembly resolutions A/RES/60/43 (8 December 2005) and A/RES/60/78 (8 December 2005), respectively.

85 General Assembly resolution A/RES/60/73 (8 December 2005).

86 "Promotion and Protection of Human Rights: Protection of Human Rights and Fundamental Freedoms while Countering Terrorism," Note by the United Nations High Commissioner for Human Rights, Economic and Social Council document E/CN.4/2005/103 (7 February 2005), para. 91.

87 United Nations High Commission for Human Rights resolution 2005/80 (21 April 2005). Note that the mandate of the Special Rapporteur that had been appointed by the Sub-Commission on the Promotion and Protection of Human Rights in the mid-1990s was not renewed beyond 2004. Those reports are archived at http://www2.ohchr.org/english/issues/terrorism/rapporteur/index.htm

88 "Protection of Human Rights and Fundamental Freedoms while Countering Terrorism," Note by the Secretary-General, General Assembly document A/60/370 (21 September 2005).

89 General Assembly resolution A/RES/60/158 (14 December 2005).

90 Luck, "The Uninvited Challenge," 346. Luck notes the danger for the Secretary-General of being associated too closely with the United States, especially in light of the unpopular decision to go to war in Iraq.

91 *Report of the Policy Working Group on the United Nations and Terrorism*, Released as a document of both the General Assembly and the Security Council, A/57/273-S/2002/875 (6 August 2002), para. 2.

92 I thank Eric Rosand for this observation. To measure the actual impact of the report is of course difficult. Suffice it to note that it was cited at least once in introducing a new resolution to the General Assembly (by the Indians in the First Committee, yielding the resolution on "Measures to Prevent Terrorists from Acquiring Weapons of Mass Destruction," A/RES/57/83 (22 November 2002)).

93 *Report of the Policy Working Group*, para. 10.

94 *Report of the Policy Working Group*, paras. 9–10.

95 *Report of the Policy Working Group*, para. 14.
96 Secretary-General's address to the UN General Assembly, 23 September 2003.
97 *A More Secure World: Our Shared Responsibility*, Report of the High-level Panel on Threats, Challenges and Change, General Assembly document A/59/565 (2 December 2004).
98 *A More Secure World*, para. 148.
99 "Secretary-General Offers Global Strategy for Fighting Terrorism in Address to Madrid Summit," UN Press release SG/SM/9757 (10 March 2005).
100 *In Larger Freedom: Towards Development, Security and Human Rights for All*, Report of the Secretary-General, A/59/2005 (21 March 2005), paras. 87–94.
101 "Secretary-General Offers Global Strategy for Fighting Terrorism in Address to Madrid Summit."
102 *In Larger Freedom*, para. 91.
103 General Assembly resolution A/60/1 (24 October 2005).
104 *Uniting against Terrorism: Recommendations for a Global Counter-terrorism Strategy*, Report of the Secretary-General, General Assembly document A/60/825 (27 April 2006).
105 General Assembly resolution A/RES/60/288 (8 September 2006).
106 On the negotiations, see Eric Rosand and Sebastian von Einsiedel, "9/11, the War on Terror and the Evolution of Multilateral Institutions"; "UN Adopts Global Counter-terrorism Strategy," Voice of America News (www.voanews.com), 8 September 2006.
107 General Assembly document A/60/PV.99 (8 September 2006). Note in particular the statements by the delegates from Syria, Cuba, Venezuela, Pakistan, Iran, Sudan, and Lebanon.
108 See Eric Rosand, "From Adoption to Action: The UN's Role in Implementing its Global Counter-terrorism Strategy," Policy Brief, Center on Global Counter-terrorism Cooperation, April 2009.
109 *Report of the Counter-Terrorism Committee to the Security Council for Its Consideration as Part of Its Comprehensive Review of the Counter-Terrorism Committee Executive Directorate*, Security Council document S/2005/800 (16 December 2005).
110 *Report of the Counter-Terrorism Committee to the Security Council for Its Consideration as Part of Its Comprehensive Review of the Counter-Terrorism Committee Executive Directorate*, Security Council document S/2006/989 (18 December 2006).
111 See www.un.org/sc/ctc/bestpractices/best_prac.html. Note also Alistair Millar et al., *Report on Standards and Practices for Improving States' Implementation of UN Security Council Counter-terrorism Mandates (Prepared for the Netherlands Ministry of Foreign Affairs)* (Center on Global Counter-terrorism Cooperation, 2006), available at www.globalct.org/images/content/pdf/reports/best_pratices.pdf
112 Briefing by Prof. Martin Scheinin, UN Special Rapporteur on the Promotion and Protection of Human Rights and Fundamental Freedoms while Countering Terrorism, to the Counter-Terrorism Committee, 26 October 2006.
113 *Report of the Counter-Terrorism Committee to the Security Council*, Security Council document S/2006/989 (18 December 2006), para. 31.

114 For summaries of CTC and CTED activity in 2007, see the briefings by the chairman of the CTC to the Security Council (22 May and 14 November), available at www.un.org/sc/ctc/resources.html.

115 *Organizational plan for the Counter-Terrorism Committee Executive Directorate*, Security Council document S/2008/80 (8 February 2008).

116 Briefing by the H. E. Mr. Jean-Maurice Ripert, acting chairman of the Security Council Committee established pursuant to resolution 1373 (2001) concerning counter-terrorism, to the Security Council (26 May 2009).

117 *Survey of the Implementation of Security Council Resolution 1373 (2001)*, Report of the Counter-Terrorism Committee, Security Council document S/2008/379 (10 June 2008).

118 Statement by Prof. Martin Scheinin, UN Special Rapporteur on the Promotion and Protection of Human Rights and Fundamental Freedoms while Countering Terrorism, to the Counter-Terrorism Committee, 20 October 2008.

119 Security Council resolution S/RES/1730 (19 December 2006). This mechanism operates across all of the sanctions regimes imposed by the Council, not only the al Qaeda-Taliban sanctions. Resolution 1730 was preceded by a detailed report into the procedures for listing and delisting, prepared by the Watson Institute for International Studies at Brown University. The Watson report described the creation of a focal point as one of several options that the Council might pursue. Among the others was the establishment of a review mechanism, independent of the Council but with power to reconsider its decisions. Although the Council declined to take that approach, as I describe below, that option remains preferred by human rights advocates. See Thomas J. Biersteker and Sue E. Eckert, *Strengthening Targeted Sanctions through Fair and Clear Procedures* (Providence, R.I.: Watson Institute for International Studies, 2006).

120 See www.un.org/sc/committees/1267/narrative.shtml

121 Available at www.un.org/sc/committees/1267/monitoringteam.shtml

122 On this point, see Security Council resolution S/RES/1732 (21 December 2006), endorsing the *Report of the Informal Working Group of the Security Council on General Issues of Sanctions*, Security Council document S/2006/997 (22 December 2006).

123 Joined cases C-402/05P and C-415/05P, *Yassin Abdullah Kadi and Al Barakaat International Foundation v. Council of the European Union and the Commission of the European Communities*, Judgment of the Court (Grand Chamber), 3 September 2008. Available at curia.europa.eu

124 *Ninth Report of the Analytical Support and Sanctions Monitoring Team, Submitted Pursuant to Resolution 1822 (2008) Concerning Al-Qaida and the Taliban and Associated Individuals and Entities*, Security Council document S/2009/245 (13 May 2009), paras. 19–25.

125 These scenarios are considered by the Monitoring Team: *Ninth Report of the Analytical Support and Sanctions Monitoring Team*, paras. 21–23.

126 Richard Barrett, "Sanctions and the Battle for Legitimacy: Terrorism and Counter-terrorism," *International Herald Tribune*, 10 September 2008, 12.

127 "Press Conference by Special Rapporteur on Human Rights and Countering Terrorism," Department of Public Information, United Nations, 22 October 2008; *Report of the Special Rapporteur on the Promotion and Protection of*

Human Rights and Fundamental Freedoms while Countering Terrorism, General Assembly document A/63/223 (6 August 2008).

128 *Ninth Report of the Analytical Support and Sanctions Monitoring Team,* paras. 27–30.
129 *Ninth Report of the Analytical Support and Sanctions Monitoring Team,* para. 25.
130 *Ninth Report of the Analytical Support and Sanctions Monitoring Team,* paras. 35–37.
131 See Security Council resolutions S/RES/1617 (29 July 2005), S/RES/1699 (8 August 2006) and S/RES/1735 (22 December 2006).
132 See www.interpol.int/Public/NoticesUN/Default.asp
133 *Ninth Report of the Analytical Support and Sanctions Monitoring Team,* paras. 106–11.
134 *Report of the Committee Established Pursuant to Security Council Resolution 1540 (2004),* Security Council document S/2008/493 (30 July 2008).
135 See the Committee's reports, Security Council documents S/2006/257 (25 April 2006), annex X, and S/2008/493 (30 July 2008), annex XVIII.
136 Peter Crail, "Implementing UN Security Council Resolution 1540: A Risk-Based Approach," *Nonproliferation Review* 13, no. 2 (2006): 356–99; Monika Heupel, "Surmounting the Obstacles to Implementing UN Security Council Resolution 1540," *Nonproliferation Review* 15, no. 1 (2008): 95–102.
137 *Report of the Committee Established Pursuant to Security Council Resolution 1540 (2004),* Security Council document S/2008/493 (30 July 2008), para. 139.
138 Security Council resolutions S/RES/1673 (27 April 2006) and S/RES/1810 (25 April 2008).
139 "Consideration of Options for Funding Mechanisms for the Implementation of Security Council Resolution 1540 (2004)," Paper prepared by the Chairman of the Security Council Committee established pursuant to resolution 1540 (2004), S/2009/171 (1 April 2009).
140 See "Joint Statement on Behalf of the Committees Established Pursuant to Resolutions 1267 (1999), 1373 (2001) and 1540 (2004)," Address to the Security Council by Ambassador Mayr-Harting (chairman of the 1267 Committee), 26 May 2009.
141 See www.un.org/sc/ctc/pdf/comparativetable.pdf
142 "Heads of Security Council Counter-terrorism Bodies Stress Need for Stock-taking," UN News Centre, 26 May 2009.
143 General Assembly resolutions A/RES/61/40 (18 December 2006), A/RES/62/71 (6 December 2007) and A/RES/63/129 (11 December 2008).
144 In debates in the Sixth Committee, Algeria, Cuba, Egypt, Iran, Sudan, Syria and Venezuela have objected to the reference to NATO: General Assembly documents A/C.6/61/SR.23 (29 November 2006), A/C.6/62/SR.28 (31 December 2007) and A/C.6/63/SR.26 (1 December 2008).
145 Note the remarks by the Tunisian delegate in Sixth Committee debates: General Assembly documents A/C.6/61/SR.23 (29 November 2006), A/C.6/62/SR.28 (31 December 2007) and A/C.6/63/SR.26 (1 December 2008).
146 For example, see *Report of the Ad Hoc Committee Established by General Assembly Resolution 51/210 of 17 December 1996: Eleventh Session (5, 6 and 15 February 2007),* General Assembly document A/62/37 (2007), paras. 24–25.

147 On WMD and terrorism, see General Assembly resolutions A/RES/61/86 (18 December 2006), A/RES/62/33 (5 December 2007) and A/RES/63/60 (2 December 2008). On radioactive materials, see General Assembly resolution A/RES/62/391 (5 December 2007).
148 General Assembly resolution A/RES/61/172 (19 December 2006).
149 General Assembly resolution A/RES/62/172 (18 December 2007).
150 General Assembly resolutions A/RES/61/171 (19 December 2006), A/ RES/62/159 (18 December 2007), and A/RES/63/185 (18 December 2008).
151 Reports of the Special Rapporteur on the promotion and protection of human rights and fundamental freedoms while countering terrorism, General Assembly documents A/61/267 (16 August 2006), A/62/263 (15 August 2007) and A/63/223 (6 August 2008). The Special Rapporteur also reports to the Human Rights Council, archived at: http://www2.ohchr.org/english/issues/terrorism/rapporteur/reports.htm
152 Amnesty International, *Security and Human Rights: Counter-terrorism and the United Nations* (London: Amnesty International, 2008).
153 Human Rights Council resolution 6/28 (14 December 2007).
154 *United Nations Global Counter-terrorism Strategy: Activities of the United Nations System in Implementing the Strategy*, Report of the Secretary-General, General Assembly document A/62/898 (7 July 2008), para. 5. See also the CTITF website: www.un.org/terrorism/cttaskforce.shtml
155 Available at www.un.org/terrorism/cthandbook/index.html
156 *United Nations Global Counter-terrorism Strategy: Activities of the United Nations System*, annex.
157 The World Bank, the International Monetary Fund and the UN Office on Drugs and Crime (with the support of CTED, the al Qaeda-Taliban Monitoring Team and Interpol), *Final Report: Counter-Terrorism Implementation Task Force Working Group on Tackling the Financing of Terrorism*, January 2009. Available at www.un.org/terrorism/workgroup5.shtml
158 Counter-Terrorism Implementation Task Force, *Report of the Working Group on Countering the Use of the Internet for Terrorist Purposes*, February 2009. Available at www.un.org/terrorism/workgroup6.shtml
159 Counter-Terrorism Implementation Task Force, *First Report of the Working Group on Radicalization and Extremism that Lead to Terrorism: Inventory of State Programmes*, n.d. Available at www.un.org/terrorism/pdfs/radicalization.pdf
160 The symposium yielded a report: *Supporting Victims of Terrorism* (New York; United Nations, 2008), available at www.un.org/terrorism/pdfs/UN%20Report%20on%20Supporting%20Victims%20of%20Terrorism.pdf
161 *United Nations Global Counter-terrorism Strategy: Activities of the United Nations System.*
162 *United Nations Global Counter-terrorism Strategy: Activities of the United Nations System*, para. 88.
163 *United Nations Global Counter-terrorism Strategy: Activities of the United Nations System*, para. 92.
164 Center on Global Counter-terrorism Cooperation, *International Process on Global Counter-terrorism Cooperation* (September 2008). This document and other information on the process are available at www.globalct.org/ourWork_projects_international_process.php

165 The relevant debates are from the General Assembly, Sixty-second session: 117th Plenary Meeting, A/62/PV.117 (4 September 2008), 118th Plenary Meeting A/62/PV.118 (4 September 2008) and 119th Plenary Meeting A/62/PV.119 (4 September 2008).

166 General Assembly resolution A/RES/62/272 (5 September 2008).

167 "UN Counter-terrorism Task Force Shifts into New Operational Phase," UN News Centre, 4 March 2009.

168 Unless otherwise noted, in this section I draw on the following sources: the CTC *Directory of International Best Practices, Codes and Standards* (www.un.org/sc/ctc/bestpractices/best_prac.html); the CTITF *UN Counter-Terrorism Online Handbook* (www.un.org/terrorism/cthandbook/index.html); the Secretary-General's reports to the General Assembly under the titles *Measures to Eliminate International Terrorism* and *Measures to Prevent Terrorists from Acquiring Weapons of Mass Destruction* (www.un.org/terrorism/sg-reports.shtml); *United Nations Global Counter-terrorism Strategy: Activities of the United Nations System*; and Alistair Millar et al. *Report on Standards and Practices* (www.globalct.org/images/content/pdf/reports/best_practices.pdf)

169 In Chapter 5, these developments are discussed in the broader context of post-9/11 actions on maritime security.

170 *Nuclear Security—Measures to Protect Against Nuclear Terrorism: Progress Report and Nuclear Security Plan for 2006–2009*, Report by the director general, IAEA General Conference document GC(49)/17 (23 September 2005).

171 *Assistance in Implementing the Universal Conventions and Protocols Related to Terrorism*, Report of the Secretary-General, General Assembly document A/63/89 (24 June 2008). More recently, see UNODC/TPB, *Delivering Counter-terrorism Assistance* (March 2009), available at www.unodc.org

172 Thomas J. Biersteker, Sue E. Eckert, and Peter Romaniuk, "International Initiatives to Suppress Terrorist Financing," in *Countering the Financing of Terrorism*, ed. T. J. Biersteker and S. E. Eckert (London: Routledge, 2007), 234–59.

173 The WCO's SAFE Framework is discussed in the broader context of post-9/11 maritime security initiatives in Chapter 5.

174 World Customs Organization, *WCO SAFE Framework of Standards* (2007). Available at www.wcoomd.org/files/1.%20Public%20files/PDFand-Documents/SAFE%20Framework_EN_2007_for_publication.pdf; "Members Who Have Expressed Their Intention to Implement the WCO Framework of Standards to Secure and Facilitate Global Trade," World Customs Organization, 2 June 2009.

175 Article 3 states that "It is strictly forbidden for the Organization to undertake any intervention or activities of a political, military, religious or racial character."

176 Interpol, "Best Practices in Combating Terrorism" (n.d.), available at www.un.org/sc/ctc/pdf/bestprac-interpol.pdf; Mathieu Deflem, "Global Rule of Law or Global Rule of Law Enforcement? International Police Cooperation and Counter-Terrorism," *Annals of the American Academy of Political and Social Science* 603 (2006), 240–52. More generally, see Frank Madsen, *Transnational Organized Crime* (London: Routledge, 2009).

177 Peter Romaniuk, "International Organizations and Terrorism," *International Studies Association Compendium Project*, forthcoming; David Cortright and George A. Lopez, eds., *Uniting Against Terror: Cooperative Non-military Responses to the Global Terrorist Threat* (Cambridge, Mass.: MIT Press, 2007); Ronald D. Crelinsten, " Counter-terrorism as Global Governance: A Research Inventory," in *Mapping Terrorism Research: State of the Art, Gaps and Future Direction*, ed. Magnus Ranstorp (London: Routledge, 2007), 210–35; Victor V. Ramraj, Michael Hor, and Ken Roach, eds., *Global Anti-terrorism Law and Policy* (New York: Cambridge University Press, 2005); Jane Boulden and Thomas G. Weiss, eds., *Terrorism and the UN: Before and After September 11* (Bloomington: Indiana University Press, 2004).

178 Peter Romaniuk, "Institutions as Swords and Shields: Multilateral Counter-terrorism since 9/11," *Review of International Studies*, forthcoming; Luck, "The Uninvited Challenge."

179 Kendall W. Stiles, "The Power of Procedure and the Procedures of the Powerful: Anti-Terror Law in the United Nations," *Journal of Peace Research* 43, no. 1 (2006): 37–54.

180 See Rosemary Foot, "The United Nations, Counter-terrorism and Human Rights: Institutional Adaptation and Embedded Ideas," *Human Rights Quarterly* 29, no. 2 (2007): 489–514; as well as Monika Heupel, "Combining Hierarchical and Soft Modes of Governance: The UN Security Council's Approach to Terrorism and Weapons of Mass Destruction After 9/11," *Conflict and Cooperation* 43, no. 1 (2008): 7–29; Monika Heupel, "Adapting to Transnational Terrorism: The UN Security Council's Evolving Approach to Terrorism," *Security Dialogue* 38, no. 4 (2007): 477–99; Thomas J. Biersteker, "The UN's Counter-terrorism Efforts: Lessons for UNSCR 1540, " in *Global Non-Proliferation and Counter-terrorism*, ed. Olivia Bosch and Peter van Ham, 24–40.

181 Again, I thank Eric Rosand for this characterization. Note also Rosand and von Einsiedel, "9/11, the War on Terror and the Evolution of Multilateral Institutions."

182 See also, Edward C. Luck, *UN Security Council: Practice and Promise* (London: Routledge, 2006), ch. 9.

183 Eric Rosand, "From Adoption to Action," 4.

184 Center on Global Counter-terrorism Cooperation, *International Process on Global Counter-terrorism Cooperation*, 1–7.

4 Multilateral counter-terrorism beyond the UN

1 Shepard Forman and Derk Segaar, "New Coalitions for Global Governance: The Changing Dynamics of Multilateralism," *Global Governance* 12, no. 2 (2006): 205–25; Edward Newman, *A Crisis of Global Institutions? Multilateralism and International Security* (New York: Routledge, 2007), ch. 7.

2 For example, the full list of bodies that have collaborated in some form with CTC/CTED numbers 90, of which 62 are not part of the UN system. See the "List of Organizations, Entities and Offices" (n.d.) provided on the CTC website (www.un.org/sc/ctc/pdf/IROEO.pdf).

3 See Eric Rosand, Alistair Millar, Jason Ipe, and Michael Healey, *The UN Global Counter-terrorism Strategy and Regional and Subregional Bodies: Strengthening a Critical Partnership* (Washington, D.C. and New York: Center for Global Counter-terrorism Cooperation, 2008), 4.

4 For further discussion, see Rosand et al., *The UN Global Counter-terrorism Strategy and Regional and Subregional Bodies*; and *Index of International, Regional and Subregional Organizations*, Security Council document S/AC.40/2003/SM.1/2 (26 February 2003).

5 Geoffrey M. Levitt, "The International Legal Response to Terrorism: A Reevaluation," *University of Colorado Law Review* 60, no. 3 (1989): 543–44.

6 John Cope and Janie Hulse, "Hemispheric Response to Terrorism: A Call to Action," in *Caribbean Security in the Age of Terror: Challenge and Change*, ed. Ivelaw L. Griffith (Kingston, Jamaica: Ian Randle Publishers, 2004), 426–32.

7 Enrique Lagos and Timothy D. Rudy, "Preventing, Punishing and Eliminating Terrorism in the Western Hemisphere: A Post-9/11 Inter-American Treaty," *Fordham International Law Journal* 26, no. 6 (2003), 1619–48.

8 The text of the convention is available on the CICTE website: www.cicte.oas.org/Rev/En/. For background on the development of the conventions, see Lagos and Rudy, "Preventing, Punishing and Eliminating Terrorism."

9 Eric Rosand, Alistair Millar, and Jason Ipe, *Implementing the UN Global Counter-terrorism Strategy in the Latin America and Caribbean Region* (Washington, D.C. and New York: Center on Global Counter-terrorism Cooperation, 2008).

10 Rosand et al. *The UN Global Counter-terrorism Strategy and Regional and Subregional Bodies*, 20.

11 Rosand et al., *Implementing the UN Global Counter-terrorism Strategy in the Latin America and Caribbean Region*, 13–23.

12 The 15 members of CARICOM are: Antigua and Barbuda, the Bahamas, Barbados, Belize, Dominica, Grenada, Guyana, Haiti, Jamaica, Montserrat, Saint Lucia, St. Kitts and Nevis, St. Vincent and the Grenadines, Suriname, and Trinidad and Tobago. See www.caricom.org

13 The seven members of SICA are Belize, Costa Rica, El Salvador, Guatemala, Honduras, Nicaragua, and Panama. See www.sica.int/index_en.aspx.

14 Rosand et al., *Implementing the UN Global Counter-terrorism Strategy in the Latin America and Caribbean Region*, 32–34.

15 For a fuller account of the Council's work on terrorism, see www.coe.int/t/e/legal_affairs/legal_co-operation/fight_against_terrorism

16 For background on the Convention, see Council of Europe, "Explanatory Report: European Convention on the Suppression of Terrorism (ETS no. 090)" (n.d.), available at http://conventions.coe.int/Treaty/en/Reports/Html/090.htm

17 See www.coe.int/t/e/legal_affairs/legal_co-operation/fight_against_terrorism/3_CODEXTER/

18 For more information, including the text of the conventions, see http://conventions.coe.int/Treaty/Commun/ListeTraites.asp?MA=50&CM=7&CL=ENG

19 There is a growing literature on the EU's counter-terrorism policy. In addition to the sources cited below, see: *Journal of Common Market Studies* 46, no. 1 (2008), special issue on the EU and counter-terrorism; Victor Mauer, "The European Union and Counter-Terrorism," in *Securing Europe?*

Implementing the European Security Strategy, ed. A. Deighton and V. Mauer (Zurich, Switzerland: Centre for Security Studies, 2006), 89–97; Karin von Hippel, ed., *Europe Confronts Terrorism* (Basingstoke, UK: Palgrave, 2005); Daniel Keohane, "The EU and Counter-terrorism," (London: CER Working Paper, 2005); Monica den Boer, "The EU Counter-terrorism Wave: Window of Opportunity or Profound Policy Transformation?" in *Confronting Terrorism: European Experiences, Threat Perceptions and Policies*, ed. M. van Leeuwen (The Hague, Netherlands: Kluwer, 2003), 185–206; Fernando Reinares, ed., *European Democracies against Terrorism: Governmental Policies and Intergovernmental Cooperation* (Burlington, Vt.: Ashgate, 2000).

20 Oldrich Bures, "EU Counter-terrorism Policy: A Paper Tiger?" *Terrorism and Political Violence* 18, no. 1 (2006): 58–60.

21 Peter Andreas and Ethan Nadelmann, *Policing the Globe: Criminalization and Crime Control in International Relations* (New York: Oxford University Press, 2006), 101–2.

22 Doron Zimmermann, "The European Union and Post-9/11 Counter-terrorism: A Reappraisal," *Studies in Conflict and Terrorism* 29, no. 2 (2006): 125.

23 Bures, "EU Counter-terrorism Policy," 59–60, citing Anastassia Tsoukala, "Democracy against Security: The Debates about Counter-terrorism in the European Parliament, September 2001–June 2003," *Alternatives* 29, no. 4 (2004): 29.

24 The strategy is available at http://register.consilium.eu.int/pdf/en/05/st14/st14469-re04.en05.pdf. For discussion, see Annegret Bendiek, "EU Counter-terrorism Strategy: Steps Towards a Coherent Policy Network," SWP Research Paper no. 12 (Berlin: German Institute for International and Security Affairs, 2006).

25 *Implementation of the Strategy and Action Plan to Combat Terrorism (June–November 2008)*, Council of the European Union document 15912/08 (19 November 2008).

26 Bures, "EU Counter-terrorism Policy," 65–66.

27 Monica den Boer, Claudia Hillebrand and Andreas Nölke, "Legitimacy under Pressure: The European Web of Counter-terrorism Networks," *Journal of Common Market Studies* 46, no. 1 (2008), 101–24; Oldrich Bures, "Europol's Fledgling Counter-terrorism Role," *Terrorism and Political Violence* 20, no. 4 (2008): 498–517.

28 Zimmermann, "The European Union and Post-9/11 Counter-terrorism," 134.

29 On the controversy surrounding the sharing of passenger name record (PNR) data between the US and the EU, see Rey Koslowki, "Possible steps towards an international regime for mobility and security," *Global Migration Perspectives*, no. 8 (Geneva, Switzerland: Global Commission on International Migration, 2004).

30 Bruce Hoffman, "Is Europe Soft on Terrorism?" *Foreign Policy*, no. 115 (1999): 62–76; Rohan Gunaratna, "The Post-Madrid Face of al Qaeda," *The Washington Quarterly* 27, no. 3 (2004): 91–100.

31 Wyn Rees and Richard J. Aldrich "Contending Cultures of Counter-terrorism: Transatlantic Divergence or Convergence?" *International Affairs* 81, no. 5 (2005): 905–23; Wyn Rees, *Transatlantic Counter-terrorism Cooperation: The New Imperative* (London: Routledge, 2006).

32 Zimmermann doubts whether the EU is the right vehicle for combating terrorism ("The European Union and Post-9/11 Counter-terrorism"). Writing

from the US perspective, Nora Bensahel suggests that the EU is a better partner for terrorist financing and law enforcement cooperation than for military and intelligence cooperation, which is best pursued bilaterally (*The Counterterror Coalitions: Cooperation with Europe, NATO and the European Union* (Santa Monica, Calif.: RAND, 2003)).

33 The European Commission's terrorism site provides links to current work on violent radicalization (under "Prevent") and external relations (under "International dimension"): http://ec.europa.eu/justice_home/fsj/terrorism/fsj_terrorism_intro_en.htm

34 Rosand et al., *The UN Global Counter-terrorism Strategy and Regional and Subregional Bodies*, 13–15.

35 This and other relevant OSCE documents are available at www.osce.org/atu/

36 For a recent summary, see Raphael Perl, "Countering Terrorism: the OSCE as a Regional Model," International Terrorism Conference, Royal United Services Institute, London, 2 October 2008, available at www.osce.org/atu

37 OSCE/Office for Democratic Institutions and Human Rights, *Countering Terrorism, Protecting Human Rights: A Manual* (2007), available at www.osce.org/publications/odihr/2007/11/28294_980_en.pdf

38 Rosand et al., *The UN Global Counter-terrorism Strategy and Regional and Subregional Bodies*, 14–15.

39 Ibrahim J. Wani, "The African Union Role in Global Counter-terrorism," in *African Counter-terrorism Cooperation: Assessing Regional and Subregional Initiatives*, ed. Andre Le Sage (Washington, D.C.: Potomac Books, 2007), 39–56; Martin Ewi and Kwesi Aning, "Assessing the Role of the African Union in Preventing and Combating Terrorism in Africa," *African Security Review* 15, no. 3 (2006): 32–46.

40 Wani, "The African Union Role in Global Counter-terrorism," 47–49.

41 Wani, "The African Union Role in Global Counter-terrorism," 49–50.

42 Wani, "The African Union Role in Global Counter-terrorism," 51.

43 Wani, "The African Union Role in Global Counter-terrorism," 52.

44 IGAD's members are Djibouti, Ethiopia, Eritrea, Kenya, Somalia, Sudan and Uganda. See Monica Juma, "The Role of the Inter-governmental Authority on Development in Preventing and Combating Terrorism," in *African Counter-terrorism Cooperation*, ed. Andre Le Sage, 57–76.

45 See http://icpat.org/index.php/home-mainmenu-1

46 Eric Rosand, Alistair Millar, and Jason Ipe, *Implementing the UN Global Counter-terrorism Strategy in East Africa* (Washington, D.C. and New York: Center on Global Counter-Terrorism Cooperation, 2008), 22–27; Rosand et al., *The UN Global Counter-terrorism Strategy and Regional and Subregional Bodies*, 10–12. ISS's website is www.issafrica.org/

47 This passage draws on the more detailed analysis by Rosand et al., *Implementing the UN Global Counter-terrorism Strategy in East Africa*.

48 The EAC membership comprises Burundi, Kenya, Rwanda, Tanzania and Uganda. For further discussion, see Wafula Okumu, "Counter-terrorism Measures in the East African Community," in *African Counter-terrorism Cooperation*, ed. Andre Le Sage, 77–98; and Rosand et al., *Implementing the UN Global Counter-terrorism Strategy in East Africa*, 26–27.

49 The SADC membership comprises Angola, Botswana, the Democratic Republic of Congo, Lesotho, Madagascar, Malawi, Mauritius, Mozambique, Seychelles, South Africa, Swaziland, Tanzania, Zambia, and Zimbabwe.

For further discussion, see Julius E. Nyang'oro, "Terrorism Threats and Responses in the Southern African Development Community Region," in *African Counter-terrorism Cooperation*, ed. Andre Le Sage, 99–111; and Michael Rifer, "SADC and Terrorism: Where is the Regional Strategy?" *African Security Review* 14, no. 1 (2005): 107–16.

50 Rosand et al., *The UN Global Counter-terrorism Strategy and Regional and Subregional Bodies*, 12; Eboe Hutchful, "Economic Community of West African States Counter-terrorism Efforts," in *African Counter-terrorism Cooperation*, ed. Andre Le Sage, 113–26.

51 Rosand et al., *Implementing the UN Global Counter-terrorism Strategy in East Africa*, 24.

52 Sean McFate, "US Africa Command: A New Strategic Paradigm?" *Military Review* 88, no.1 (2008): 10–21; Greg Mills and Jeffrey Herbst, "Africa, Terrorism and AFRICOM," *RUSI Journal* 152, no. 2 (2007): 40–45.

53 Toby Archer and Tihomir Popovic, *The Trans-Saharan Counter-terrorism Initiative: The US War on Terrorism in Northwest Africa* (Helsinki, Finland: Finnish Institute for International Affairs, 2007); Jessica R. Piombo, "Terrorism and US Counter-terrorism Programs in Africa: An Overview," *Strategic Insights* VI, no. 1 (2007): 5. Of course, these efforts are often supported by bilateral assistance, including the 2002 Combined Joint Task Force–Horn of Africa and the 2003 East African Counter-terrorism Initiative.

54 The six members are Bahrain, Kuwait, Oman, Qatar, Saudi Arabia, and the United Arab Emirates. The GCC's website is www.gccsg.org/eng/index.php

55 Most recently, see the statement from the 19th GCC-EU Joint Council and Ministerial Meeting, Muscat, 29 April 2009, available at www.gccsg.org/eng/index.php?action=Sec-Show&ID=299&W2SID=31955

56 For example, see "Gulf Cooperation Council Forum on Terrorism Concludes Discussions in Riyadh," BBC Monitoring Worldwide (Lexis-Nexis), 31 March 2009.

57 Other members are Afghanistan, Bangladesh, Bhutan, Maldives, Nepal, and Sri Lanka.

58 Smruti S. Pattanaik, "Making Sense of Regional Cooperation: SAARC at Twenty," *Strategic Analysis* 30, no. 1 (2006): 139–60; Rohan Perera, "Suppression of Terrorism—Regional Approach to Meet the Challenges," *Sri Lanka Journal of International Law* 16, no. 1 (2004): 19–26.

59 According to Pattanaik, Pakistan introduced the distinction between terrorism and struggles of national liberation into the negotiations: "Making Sense of Regional Cooperation," 148–50.

60 Rosand et al., *The UN Global Counter-terrorism Strategy and Regional and Subregional Bodies*, 19.

61 "SAARC Ministerial Declaration on Cooperation in Combating Terrorism," Thirty-first Session of the Council of Ministers, Colombo, Sri Lanka, 28 February 2009. Available at www.saarc-sec.org

62 BIMSTEC comprises Bangladesh, Bhutan, India, Myanmar, Nepal, Sri Lanka and Thailand. See www.bimstec.org/

63 Rosand et al., *The UN Global Counter-terrorism Strategy and Regional and Subregional Bodies*, 19; "BIMSTEC Summit Decides to Hold Anti-Terror Meet," *India News Online* (17 November 2008).

64 The members of SCO are China, Kazakhstan, Kyrgyzstan, Russia, Tajikistan, and Uzbekistan. Observer states are India, Iran, Mongolia, and Pakistan.

For background, see www.sectsco.org/EN/index.asp and Alyson J. K. Bailes and Pál Dunay, "The Shanghai Cooperation Organization as a Regional Security Institution," in *The Shanghai Cooperation Organization* (SIPRI Policy Paper no. 17), ed. Alyson J. K. Bailes, Pál Dunay, Pan Guang, and Mikhail Troitskiy (Stockholm, Sweden: Stockholm Peace Research Institute, 2007), 1–29.

65 Bailes and Dunay, "The Shanghai Cooperation Organization," 6. The RATS website is www.ecrats.com/en/. See also Rosand et al., *The UN Global Counter-terrorism Strategy and Regional and Subregional Bodies*, 13.

66 "Joint Communique of Meeting of the Council of the Heads of the Member States of the Shanghai Cooperation Organization," 15–16 June 2009, Yekaterinburg, Russia.

67 "Ban Voices Appreciation for Partnership with Eurasia Against Global Terrorism," UN News Centre, 16 June 2009.

68 A detailed discussion of counter-terrorism cooperation in the Asia-Pacific Region is provided by the Center on Global Counter-Terrorism Coopera- tion, *Implementing the United Nations General Assembly's Global Counter- terrorism Strategy in the Asia-Pacific* (New York and Washington, D.C.: Center for Global Counter-terrorism Cooperation, 2007).

69 ASEAN's members are Brunei, Cambodia, Indonesia, Laos, Malaysia, Myanmar, the Philippines, Singapore, Thailand and Vietnam. For a more detailed discussion, see: Ralf Emmers, "Comprehensive Security and Resi- lience: ASEAN's Approach to Terrorism and Sea Piracy," Working Paper, S. Rajaratnam School of International Studies, Singapore, 10 July 2007; Center on Global Counter-Terrorism Cooperation, *Implementing the United Nations General Assembly's Global Counter-terrorism Strategy in the Asia- Pacific*, 7–10; Jonathan T. Chow, "ASEAN Counter-terrorism Cooperation since 9/11," *Asia Survey* 45, no. 2 (2005), 302–21.

70 A list of ASEAN declarations is at www.aseansec.org/4964.htm

71 The convention is available at www.aseansec.org/19250.htm. The term "conditions conducive" reflects the UN Global Counter-terrorism Strategy.

72 Center on Global Counter-Terrorism Cooperation, *Implementing the United Nations General Assembly's Global Counter-terrorism Strategy in the Asia- Pacific*, 7.

73 Emmers, "Comprehensive Security and Resilience."

74 Daljit Singh, "ASEAN Strategy Works in Keeping Terrorism at Bay," *The Straits Times* (Singapore), 4 August 2008.

75 The ARF comprises 27 members: Australia, Bangladesh, Brunei, Cambo- dia, Canada, China, European Union, India, Indonesia, Japan, Democratic People's Republic of Korea, Republic of Korea, Laos, Malaysia, Myanmar, Mongolia, New Zealand, Pakistan, Papua New Guinea, Philippines, Rus- sian Federation, Singapore, Sri Lanka, Thailand, Timor Leste, USA, and Vietnam.

76 Center on Global Counter-Terrorism Cooperation, *Implementing the United Nations General Assembly's Global Counter-terrorism Strategy in the Asia- Pacific*, 11–13; see also the ARF website, www.aseanregionalforum.org

77 Co-Chairs' Summary Report, "Sixth ASEAN Regional Forum Inter-Sessional Meeting on Counter-Terrorism and Transnational Crime," Semarang, Indo- nesia, 21–22 February 2008. See also Center on Global Counter-Terrorism Cooperation, *Implementing the United Nations General Assembly's Global*

Counter-terrorism Strategy in the Asia-Pacific, 11–13, and Tanya Ogilvie-White, "Non-proliferation and Counterterrorism Cooperation in Southeast Asia: Meeting Global Obligations through Regional Security Architectures?" *Contemporary Southeast Asia* 28, no. 1 (2006): 1–26.

78 Rosand et al., *The UN Global Counter-terrorism Strategy and Regional and Subregional Bodies*, 18–20.

79 See www.apec.org

80 Cameron Stewart, "Ministers Highlight Threats to Economies," *The Australian*, 7 September 2007.

81 Ogilvie-White, "Non-proliferation and Counterterrorism Cooperation in Southeast Asia," 12–15; Center on Global Counter-terrorism Cooperation, *Implementing the United Nations General Assembly's Global Counter-terrorism Strategy in the Asia-Pacific*, 6–7.

82 Center on Global Counter-terrorism Cooperation, *Implementing the United Nations General Assembly's Global Counter-terrorism Strategy in the Asia-Pacific*, 6.

83 APEC's counter-terrorism actions are summarized at www.apec.org/apec/apec_groups/som_committee_on_economic/som_special_task_groups/counter_terrorism.html

84 Sixteenth APEC Economic Leaders' Meeting, "A New Commitment to Asia-Pacific Development," Lima, Peru, 22–23 November 2008; "APEC Focus Shifts Back to Trade (Terrorism, Corruption Take Back Seat to Global Financial Crisis)," *Business World* (Manila), 25 November 2008.

85 Andreas and Nadelmann, *Policing the Globe*, 169–74.

86 See www.ileabangkok.com/index.html

87 See www.searcct.gov.my

88 Dato' Hussin Nayan (Director, SEARCCT), "Regional Capacity Building Against Terrorism," National Convention on Nuclear and Radioactive Material Safety, Security and Safeguards, Putrajaya, Malaysia, 10 December 2007. Available at www.aelb.gov.my/events/nc2007dok/pdf/S3/Topic6.pdf

89 See www.jclec.com; "Australia-Indonesia Training Centre Focuses on Transnational Crime," *Jakarta Post*, 15 January 2008.

90 Mick Keelty, "Counter-terrorism and Capacity-Building," *Australian Journal of Forensic Sciences* 39, no. 1 (2007): 3–9.

91 For example, see "Subregional Ministerial Conference on Counter-terrorism: Co-chair's Statement," Jakarta, Indonesia, 5–6 March 2007. Available at www.dfat.gov.au/globalissues/terrorism/Co_Chairs_Statement.htm

92 The members of the PIF are Australia, Cook Islands, Federated States of Micronesia, Fiji, Kiribati, Nauru, New Zealand, Niue, Palau, Papua New Guinea, Republic of Marshall Islands, Samoa, Solomon Islands, Tonga, Tuvalu, and Vanuatu: see www.forumsec.org.fj/index.cfm

93 Beth K. Greener-Barcham and Manuhuia Barcham, "Terrorism in the South Pacific? Thinking Critically about Approaches to Security in the Region," *Australian Journal of International Affairs* 60, no. 1 (2006): 67–82; Neil Boister, "New Directions for Regional Cooperation in the Suppression of Transnational Crime in the South Pacific," *Journal of South Pacific Law* 9, no. 2 (2005), online.

94 "Nasonini Declaration on Regional Security," Thirty-third Pacific Islands Forum, Suva, Fiji, 15–17 August 2002. Available at www.forumsec.org.fj/_resources/article/files/Nasonini%20Declaration%20on%20Regional%20Security.pdf

95 Dell Higgie (New Zealand Ambassador for Counter-Terrorism), "Terrorism and Counter-Terrorism: Their Place on Pacific Island Security Agendas," Asia-Pacific Centre for Security Studies Conference, Honolulu, July 2005.

96 Center on Global Counter-terrorism Cooperation, *Implementing the United Nations General Assembly's Global Counter-terrorism Strategy in the Asia-Pacific*, 65–66.

97 Speech by PIF Secretary-General, Greg Urwin, to the Pacific Regional Terrorism, Transnational Crime and Border Security Seminar, Suva, Fiji, 27 January 2006.

98 The members of the Arab League are Egypt, Iraq, Jordan, Lebanon, Saudi Arabia, Syria, Yemen, Libya, Sudan, Morocco, Tunisia, Kuwait, Algeria, UAE, Bahrain, Qatar, Oman, Mauritania, Somalia, Palestine, Djibouti, and Comoros. The text of the convention is available at www.unhcr.org/refworld/publisher,LAS,3de5e4984,0.html

99 Rosand et al., *The UN Global Counter-terrorism Strategy and Regional and Subregional Bodies*; *Index of International, Regional and Subregional Organizations*, 45–48.

100 *Measures to Eliminate International Terrorism*, Report of the Secretary-General, General Assembly document A/63/173 (25 July 2008), paras. 122–24.

101 The OIC has 56 members. They are listed at www.oicun.org/categories/Mission/Members/. The text of the convention is available here www.oicun.org/articles/55/1/OIC-Convention-on-Combating-International-Terrorism/1.html

102 Rosand et al., *The UN Global Counter-terrorism Strategy and Regional and Subregional Bodies*, 15–16.

103 *Measures to Eliminate International Terrorism*, Report of the Secretary-General, General Assembly document A/62/160 (27 July 2007), paras. 115–16.

104 NAM's list of members is available here: www.namegypt.org/en/About-Name/MembersObserversAndGuests/Pages/default.aspx. Past statements from NAM's major meetings are available here: www.nam.gov.za/

105 *Final Document*, Ministerial Meeting of the Non-Aligned Movement Coordinating Bureau, Havana, Cuba (21–30 April 2009), paras. 164–65. Available at www.namegypt.org/en/RelevantDocuments/Pages/default.aspx

106 Information on the membership and mission of the Commonwealth—as well as the News Archive, which I have drawn on, below—is available at www.thecommonwealth.org

107 "Commonwealth Committee on Terrorism: Chairman's Statement," *Commonwealth News Archive*, 29 January 2002.

108 For example, see: "Combating Money Laundering and Financing of Terrorism," *Commonwealth News Archive*, 12 May 2005; "Anti-Terrorism Training in Africa," *Commonwealth News Archive*, 23 September 2004; "Strengthening Efforts to Combat Terrorism," *Commonwealth News Archive*, 18 March 2004.

109 "Caribbean Police Undergo Counter-terrorism Training," *Commonwealth News Archive*, 2 April 2008; "Caribbean Receives Counter-terrorism Training," *Commonwealth News Archive*, 4 November 2008.

110 "Tackling Violence and Extremism Through Education," *Commonwealth News Archive*, 3 April 2009; "We Need a World Court of Human Rights'—UN Expert Tells Commonwealth," *Commonwealth News Archive*, 3 June 2009.

111 By contrast, the Collective Security Treaty Organization (comprising Armenia, Belarus, Kazakhstan, Kyrgyzstan, Russia, Tajikistan, and Uzbekistan), has set rather a different course in its approach to counter-terrorism, for example, by endorsing the UN Global Counter-terrorism Strategy. See Rosand et al., *The UN Global Counter-terrorism Strategy and Regional and Subregional Bodies*, 12–13.

112 Note the citations provided by Renée de Nevers, "NATO's International Security Role in the Terrorist Era," *International Security* 31, no. 4 (2007), notes 2–5.

113 Lord Robertson (NATO Secretary-General), "Tackling Terror: NATO's New Mission," Speech to the American Enterprise Institute, Washington, D.C., 20 June 2002. Available at www.nato.int

114 After the admission of Albania and Croatia in 2009, NATO now has 28 members (see www.nato.int/cps/en/natolive/nato_countries.htm). The issue of whom to admit has been a point of controversy on occasions. In 2008, European members resisted the US attempts to include Georgia and Ukraine, viewing it as a provocation to Russia.

115 de Nevers, "NATO's International Security Role," 37.

116 This passage draws on NATO's terrorism website (www.nato.int/cps/en/natolive/topics_48801.htm), as well as de Nevers, "NATO's International Security Role."

117 NATO/ISAF, "International Security Assistance Force and Afghan National Army Strength and Laydown," 30 April 2009. Available at www.nato.int/ISAF/docu/epub/pdf/isaf_placemat.pdf

118 de Nevers, "NATO's International Security Role," 48–55.

119 For example, see Robert Marquand, "Obama, the Pragmatist, Wins NATO Kudos but Few Troops for Afghan Mission," *Christian Science Monitor*, 5 April 2009, 6.

120 The NATO website on Operation Active Endeavor is www.nato.int/cps/en/SID-ACC3B6F5-0E8BB53B/natolive/topics_7932.htm. See also de Nevers, "NATO's International Security Role," 41–42.

121 Of course, some NATO members have contributed more broadly to the "coalition of the willing" in Iraq: de Nevers, "NATO's International Security Role."

122 de Nevers, "NATO's International Security Role," 63–66.

123 Daniel Byman, "Remaking Alliances for the War on Terrorism," *The Journal of Strategic Studies* 29, no. 5 (2006): 799. See also Nora Bensahel, *The Counterterror Coalitions*.

124 Eric Rosand, "The G8's Counter-terrorism Action Group," Policy brief, Center on Global Counter-terrorism Cooperation, May 2009; Andre Belelieu, "The G8 and International Terrorism: The Evolution of Terrorism at the Summits and Prospects for the 2004 Sea Island Summit," Speech to the G8 Research Group, 5 March 2004; Andre Belelieu, "The G8 and Terrorism: What Role Can the G8 Play in the 21st Century?" *G8 Governance*, no. 8 (June 2002), available at www.g8.utoronto.ca/governance/belelieu2002-gov8.pdf

125 This paragraph draws on Belelieu, "The G8 and Terrorism."

126 Belelieu, "The G8 and Terrorism," 19.

127 Belelieu, "The G8 and Terrorism," 26.

128 The summit and ministerial documents cited in this passage are archived at www.canadainternational.gc.ca/g8/index.aspx?lang=eng

129 "G8 Cooperation against Terrorism (Backgrounder)," G8 Kananaskis Summit, 26 June 2002.
130 "Cooperative G8 Action on Transport Security," G8 Kananaskis Summit, 26 June 2002.
131 "Building International Political Will and Capacity to Combat Terrorism," G8 Evian Summit, 2 June 2003.
132 Foreign Affairs and International Trade, Canada, "Counter-terrorism Action Group (CTAG)" (20 August 2008). Available at www.international. gc.ca/crime/ctag-gact.aspx?lang=eng
133 "Enhance Transport Security and Control of Man-Portable Air Defense Systems (MANPADS)—a G8 Action Plan," G8 Evian Summit, 2 June 2003.
134 "Global Partnership against the Spread of Weapons and Materials of Mass Destruction—a G8 Action Plan," G8 Evian Summit, 2 June 2003.
135 "G8 Secure and Facilitated International Travel Initiative (SAFTI)," G8 Sea Island Summit, 9 June 2004.
136 "G8 Statement on Counter-terrorism," G8 Gleneagles Summit, 8 July 2005.
137 Rosand, "The G8's Counter-terrorism Action Group."
138 "Report to G8 Summit Leaders from the G8 Experts on International Terrorism and Transnational Crime," G8 Hokkaido Tokyo Summit, 7–9 July 2008; "Report on G8 Support to the United Nations' Counter-Terrorism Efforts," G8 Heiligendamm Summit, 8 June 2007; "G8 Statement on Strengthening the UN's Counter-terrorism Program," G8 St. Petersburg Summit, 16 July 2006.
139 Rosand, "The G8's Counter-terrorism Action Group."
140 Kal Raustiala and David G. Victor, "The Regime Complex for Plant Genetic Resources," *International Organization* 58, no. 2 (2004): 277–309. See also Karen J. Alter and Sophie Meunier, "The Politics of International Regime Complexity," *Perspectives on Politics* 7, no. 1 (2009): 13–24, and the other essays in the forum that Alter and Meunier introduce.
141 On migration control, see Koslowski, "Possible Steps" and IOM, *International Terrorism and Migration* (Geneva, Switzerland: International Organization for Migration, 2003). On non-proliferation, see Peter van Ham and Olivia Bosch, eds., *Global Non-Proliferation and Counter-Terrorism: The Impact of Resolution* 1540 (Washington, D.C.: Brookings Institution Press, 2007) and note the recent emergence of the Global Initiative to Combat Nuclear Terrorism (www.state.gov/t/isn/c18406.htm).
142 Mathieu Deflem, *Policing World Society: Historical Foundations of International Police Cooperation* (New York: Oxford University Press, 2002), 228–31.
143 For a brief overview of Interpol's response to terrorism, see Interpol, "Terrorism," Fact sheet COM/FS/2009-06/PST-01. Available at www. interpol.int/Public/ICPO/FactSheets/PST01.pdf
144 Mathieu Deflem, "Global Rule of Law or Global Rule of Law Enforcement? International Police Cooperation and Counter-terrorism," *Annals of the American Academy of Political and Social Science* 603, no. 1 (2006): 249.
145 Rosand et al., *Implementing the UN Global Counter-terrorism Strategy in East Africa*, 25–26. The members of EAPCCO are Burundi, Djibouti, Eritrea, Ethiopia, Kenya, Rwanda, the Seychelles, Somalia, Sudan, Tanzania, and Uganda.

146 "Aseanapol Headquarters to Be Set Up in Malaysia: Report," Agence France-Presse, 14 May 2009.
147 Bures, "Europol's Fledgling Counter-terrorism Role"; Mathieu Deflem, "Europol and the Policing of International Terrorism: Counter-terrorism in Global Perspective," *Justice Quarterly* 23, no. 3 (2006): 336–59.
148 "The Post-9/11 NYPD: Where Are We Now?" Address by Commissioner Raymond Kelly (New York City Police Department) to the Council on Foreign Relations, New York, 22 April 2009. Available at www.cfr.org/ publication/19198/post911_nypd.html
149 For example, on Indonesian-Australian collaboration in the wake of the first Bali bombing, see Greg Barton, *Indonesia's Struggle: Jemaah Islamiyah and the Soul of Islam* (Sydney: University of New South Wales Press, 2004).
150 On the role of intelligence in counter-terrorism policy (albeit from a US perspective), see: Paul Pillar, "Intelligence," in *Attacking Terrorism: Elements of a Grand Strategy*, ed. Audrey Kurth Cronin and James M. Ludes (Washington, D.C.: Georgetown University Press), 115–39; Paul Pillar, *Terrorism and US Foreign Policy* (Washington, D.C.: Brookings Institution Press, 2003), 110–23.
151 Jennifer E. Sims, "Foreign Intelligence Liaison: Devils, Deals and Details," *International Journal of Intelligence and Counter-intelligence* 19, no. 2 (2006): 202.
152 Chris Clough, "*Quid Pro Quo*: The Challenges of International Strategic Intelligence Cooperation," *International Journal of Intelligence and Counter-intelligence* 17, no. 4 (2004): 608.
153 Clough, "*Quid Pro Quo*"; Eric Schmitt and Mark Mazetti, "US Relies More on Aid of Allies in Terror Cases," *New York Times*, 24 May 2009; Sims, "Foreign Intelligence Liaison"; Derek S. Reveron, "Old Allies, New Friends: Intelligence-Sharing in the War on Terror," *Orbis* 50, no. 3 (2006): 453–68; Richard J. Aldrich, "Dangerous Liaisons: Post-September 11 Intelligence Alliances," *Harvard International Review* (Fall 2002): 50–54.
154 Richard J. Aldrich, "Global Intelligence Cooperation versus Accountability: New Facets to an Old Problem," *Intelligence and National Security* 24, no. 1 (2009): 26–56.
155 These are described in greater depth by Stéphane Lefebvre, "The Difficulties and Dilemmas of International Intelligence Cooperation," *International Journal of Intelligence and Counter-intelligence* 16, no. 4 (2003): 527–42; and Sir Stephen Lander, "International Intelligence Cooperation: An Inside Perspective," *Cambridge Review of International Affairs* 17, no. 3 (2004): 481–93.
156 Lefebvre, "The Difficulties and Dilemmas of International Intelligence Cooperation," 533–34.
157 These are available at www.un.org/sc/ctc/resources.html
158 Lander, "International Intelligence Cooperation," 484.
159 Aldrich, "Dangerous Liaisons," 54.
160 Thomas J. Biersteker, Sue E. Eckert, and Peter Romaniuk, "International Initiatives to Combat the Financing of Terrorism," in *Countering the Financing of Terrorism*, ed. Thomas J. Biersteker and Sue E. Eckert (New York: Routledge, 2008), 234–59; Kathryn L. Gardner, "Terrorism Defanged: The Financial Action Taskforce and International Efforts to Capture

Terrorist Finances," in *Uniting Against Terror,* ed. David Cortright and George A. Lopez (Cambridge, Mass.: MIT Press), 157–86.

161 William C. Gilmore, *Dirty Money: The Evolution of Money Laundering Counter Measures* (3rd ed.), (Strasbourg, France: Council of Europe Press, 2004).

162 The FATF today comprises 32 states (Argentina, Australia, Austria, Belgium, Brazil, Canada, China, Denmark, Finland, France, Germany, Greece, Hong Kong (China), Iceland, Ireland, Italy, Japan, the Netherlands, Luxembourg, Mexico, New Zealand, Norway, Portugal, Russian Federation, Singapore, South Africa, Spain, Sweden, Switzerland, Turkey, United Kingdom, United States) and two regional bodies (the European Commission and Gulf Cooperation Council). See www.fatf-gafi.org

163 Daniel W. Drezner, *All Politics is Global: Explaining International Regulatory Regimes* (Princeton, N.J.: Princeton University Press, 2007), 142–48.

164 Eric Helleiner, "The Politics of Global Financial Reregulation: Lessons From the Fight Against Money Laundering." Working Paper no. 15, CEPA Working Paper Series III (New York: Center for Economic Policy Analysis, New School for Social Research, 2000); Eric Helleiner, "State Power and the Regulation of Illicit Activity in Global Finance," in *The Illicit Global Economy and State Power,* ed. H. R. Friman and P. Andreas (Lanham, Md.: Rowman and Littlefield, 1999), 53–90; Beth A. Simmons, "The International Politics of Harmonization: The Case of Capital Market Regulation," *International Organization* 55, no. 3 (2001): 589–620.

165 On the external relations of the FATF, see Gilmore, *Dirty Money,* 141–52.

166 FATF, *Annual Report 2000–01* (Paris: FATF).

167 FATF, *Annual Report 2000–01.*

168 Michael Levi, "Money Laundering and Its Regulation," *Annals of the American Academy of Political and Social Sciences* 582 (2002): 181–94; Nigel Morris-Cotterill, "Money Laundering," *Foreign Policy* 124 (May/June 2001): 16–22.

169 Drezner, *All Politics is Global,* 142–45; Simmons, "The International Politics of Harmonization"; Helleiner, "The Politics of Global Financial Reregulation."

170 Clunan argues that the United States has "succeeded in globalizing the anti-money laundering framework and recasting it as a regime to combat terrorist financing": Anne L. Clunan, "US and International Responses to Terrorist Financing," *Strategic Insights* 4, no. 1 (2005): 4.

171 FATF, *Annual Report 2001–02* (Paris: FATF).

172 The SRs are available at www.fatf-gafi.org

173 The UNODC-hosted website of the International Money Laundering Information Network provides links to all of the FSRB websites: https://www.imolin.org. See also Biersteker et al., "International Initiatives to Suppress Terrorist Financing."

174 Paul Vlaanderen, "The Essential Role of FATF-Style Regional Bodies (FSRBs) in the Fight Against Money Laundering and Terrorist Financing," Opening remarks by FATF president Paul Vlaanderen at the 12th APG Annual Meeting, Brisbane, Australia, 7 July 2009.

175 Joint Forum (of the Basel Committee on Banking Supervision, the International Organization of Securities Commissions, and the International Association of Insurance Supervisors), "Initiatives by the BCBS, IAIS and

IOSCO to Combat Money Laundering and the Financing of Terrorism," IOSCO Public Document no. 146, June 2003.

176 Offshore Group of Banking Supervisors, "OGBS welcomes Eight Special Recommendations on Terrorist Financing," Press release, 14 November 2001; Offshore Group of Banking Supervisors, "OGBS Welcomes Revised FATF Recommendations," Press release, July 2003.

177 Wolfsberg Group, "Wolfsberg Statement on the Suppression of the Financing of Terrorism," January 2002.

178 "Blacklist of 'Dirty Money' Havens Put on Temporary Hold," *Financial Times*, 26 September 2002.

179 Vlaanderen, "The Essential Role of FATF-Style Regional Bodies."

180 Note the essays in Biersteker and Eckert, eds., *Countering the Financing of Terrorism*. For an interesting perspective from the private sector, see World Bank/IMF/UNODC, *Final Report*, CTITF Working Group on Tackling the Financing of Terrorism, January 2009, available at www.un.org/terrorism/pdfs/wg5-financing.pdf. More generally, there is a growing literature on terrorist financing, see *Terrorist Financing Bibliography*, Targeting Terrorist Finances Project, Watson Institute for International Studies. Available at www.watsoninstitute.org/ttf/TTF_Bibliography.pdf

181 Hartmut G. Hesse and Nicolaos L. Charalambous, "New Security Measures for the International Shipping Community," Information paper, Maritime Safety Division, International Maritime Organization (2004); IMO, "IMO 2004: Focus on Maritime Security," Background paper, World Maritime Day 2004 (2004); Hartmut G. Hesse, "Maritime Security in a Multilateral Context: IMO Activities to Enhance Maritime Security," *International Journal of Marine and Coastal Law* 18, no. 3 (2003): 327–40.

182 "Review of Measures and Procedures to Prevent Acts of Terrorism Which Threaten the Security of Passengers and Crews and the Safety of Ships," IMO document A.224 (22), November 2001.

183 MTSA 2002 §70116(b)(1) and (4).

184 Summarized in "Prevention and Suppression of Acts of Terrorism Against Shipping," IMO Doc. MSC 75/17/1, 25 February 2002 (Note by the Secretariat).

185 "Prevention and Suppression of Acts of Terrorism Against Shipping," IMO Doc. MSC 75/17/12, 12 April 2002 (Submitted by Belgium, Finland, France, Germany, Ireland, Italy, Portugal, Spain, and Sweden).

186 For a detailed discussion of the substantive provisions of the Code, see Hesse and Charalambous, "New Security Measures"; IMO, "IMO 2004: Focus on Maritime Security"; and Hesse, "Maritime Security in a Multilateral Context."

187 Janet Porter and Justin Stares, "Ports At Risk of Missing ISPS Code Deadline," *Lloyd's List*, 11 March 2004.

188 "Maritime Security on Agenda as USCG Visits IMO," IMO Briefing 12/2005, 17 February 2005; "Security Compliance Shows Continued Improvement," IMO Press briefing 28/2004, 6 August 2004.

189 For updates on the code, and information on related IMO activities, see the "Maritime Security" page of the IMO website: www.imo.org/Safety/mainframe.asp?topic_id=551

190 For an overview of CSI, see www.cbp.gov/xp/cgov/trade/cargo_security/csi/

191 "Cooperative G8 Action on Transport Security," G8 Kananaskis Summit, 26 June 2002.

192 R. G. Edmonson, "Taking Shape: WCO Fleshes Out Plan to Balance Security and Trade Facilitation," *Journal of Commerce*, 28 February 2005; "WCO Endorses Framework Annexes for Security, Facilitation" *Journal of Commerce Online*, 29 April 2005.

193 The framework is available at www.wcoomd.org/files/1.%20Public% 20files/PDFandDocuments/Home_Tender/SAFE/SAFE_Framework_EN_ 2007.pdf

194 Courtney Tower, "WCO Trade Regime Faces Hurdles," *Journal of Commerce Online*, 13 May 2005.

195 For updates, see www.wcoomd.org/home_wco_topics_epoverviewboxes_tools _and_instruments_epsafeframework.htm

196 On the Seafarers' ID Convention, see ILO, "Strengthening Security on the High Seas and in World Ports: ILO Convention on Seafarers' ID Gains New Momentum," ILO Public Information and Communications Unit, 25 January 2008. Note that the United States, despite playing a leadership role on other aspects of maritime security, is not a signatory to the Seafarers' ID Convention, in part because the ILO use of biometrics imposes a lesser standard than that required in ICAO-approved biometric passports. On the development of the ICAO standard, see the website of the Machine Readable Travel Document Technical Advisory Group (http:// www2.icao.int/en/mrtd/Pages/default.aspx)

197 Andrew C. Winner, "The Proliferation Security Initiative: The New Face of Interdiction," *The Washington Quarterly* 28, no. 2 (2005): 129–43; Stephen G. Rademaker, "The Proliferation Security Initiative (PSI): A Record of Success." Testimony before the House International Relations Committee, Subcommittee on International Terrorism and Nonproliferation. Washington, D.C. (9 June 2005).

198 Available at www.state.gov/t/isn/c10390.htm

199 Statement of Interdiction Principles, para. 4(c).

200 Rademaker, "The Proliferation Security Initiative."

201 Mark J. Valencia, *The Proliferation Security Initiative: Making Waves in Asia*, Adelphi Paper no. 376, International Institute for Strategic Studies (New York: Routledge, 2005), 8, ch. 3.

202 Winner, "The Proliferation Security Initiative." See also Michael Byers, "Policing the High Seas: The Proliferation Security Initiative," *American Journal of International Law* 98, no. 3 (2004): 526–45.

203 Rademaker, "The Proliferation Security Initiative."

204 "Gleneagles Statement on Non-Proliferation," G8 Gleneagles Summit, 8 July 2005.

205 *In Larger Freedom: Towards Development, Security and Human Rights for All*, Report of the Secretary-General, General Assembly doc. A/59/200 (21 March 2005), para.100.

206 Mark J. Valencia, "The Proliferation Security Initiative: A Glass Half-full," *Arms Control Today* 37, no. 5 (2007): 17–21; Mark J. Valencia, "Is the PSI Really the Cornerstone of a New International Norm?" *Naval War College Review* 59, no. 4 (2006): 123–30.

207 M. B. Nitikin, *Proliferation Security Initiative (PSI)*, Congressional Research Service, RL34327. Washington, D.C. (16 January 2008), 10.

208 Contrast Joel Doolin ("The Proliferation Security Initiative: Cornerstone of a New International Norm," *Naval War College Review* 59, no. 2

(2006): 29–57) with Valencia, "The Proliferation Security Initiative," and Valencia, "Is the PSI … ?" See also Gabriel H. Oosthuizen and Elizabeth Wilmshurst, "Terrorism and Weapons of Mass Destruction: United Nations Security Council Resolution 1540," Chatham House, Briefing paper 04/01 (2004).

209 The security of the Malacca Straits is itself an interesting example of multilateral action in response to emerging threats such as piracy and terrorism. For background, see: Mohd Nizam Basiron, "Steady as She Goes: Cooperation in the Straits of Malacca and Singapore Enters a New Era," Commentary, Maritime Institute of Malaysia (2007); Joshua H. Ho, "The Security of Sealanes in Southeast Asia," *Asian Survey* 46, no. 4 (2006): 558–74; Joshua H. Ho and Catherine Zara Raymand, eds., *The Best of Times, The Worst of Times: Maritime Security in the Asia-Pacific* (Singapore: World Scientific, 2005); Lt. John F. Bradford, "Southeast Asian Maritime Security in the Age of Terror: Threats, Opportunity and Charting the Course Forward," Working Paper no. 75, Institute for Defence and Strategic Studies, Singapore (April 2005); Lt. John F. Bradford, "The Growing Prospects for Maritime Security Cooperation in Southeast Asia," *Naval War College Review* 58, no. 3 (2005): 63–86. For a recent update, note the presentations given at the Sixth Maritime Institute of Malaysia Conference on the Straits of Malacca: Charting the Future, Kuala Lumpur, 23–24 June 2009 (www.mima.gov.my).

210 Eric Rosand and Sebastian von Einsiedel, "9/11, the War on Terror, and the Evolution of Multilateral Institutions," in *Cooperating for Peace and Security: Evolving Institutions and Arrangements in a Context of Changing US Security Policy*, ed. Bruce D. Jones, Shepard Forman, and Richard Gowan (New York: Cambridge University Press, forthcoming).

211 Robert Keohane, *After Hegemony* (Princeton, N.J.: Princeton University Press, 1984).

Select bibliography

Books

Olivia Bosch and Peter van Ham, eds., *Global Non-Proliferation and Counter-terrorism: The Impact of UNSCR 1540* (Washington, D.C.: Brookings Institution Press, 2005).

Jane Boulden and Thomas G. Weiss, eds., *Terrorism and the UN: Before and After September 11* (Bloomington: Indiana University Press, 2004).

David Cortright and George A. Lopez, eds., *Uniting Against Terror: Coopera-tive Nonmilitary Responses to the Global Terrorist Threat* (Cambridge, Mass.: MIT Press, 2007).

Martha Crenshaw, *Terrorism and International Cooperation*, Occasional Paper no. 11, Institute for East-West Studies (New York: Westview Press, 1989).

Audrey Kurth Cronin and James M. Ludes, eds., *Attacking Terrorism: Elements of a Grand Strategy* (Washington, D.C.: Georgetown University Press, 2004).

Lawrence Freedman, C. Hill, A. Roberts, R. J. Vincent, P. Wilkinson, and P. Windsor, eds., *Terrorism and International Order* (London: Routledge and Kegan Paul, 1985).

Rosalyn Higgins and Maurice Flory, eds., *Terrorism and International Law* (London: Routledge, 1997).

Richard Bach Jensen, *The International Campaign Against Anarchist Terrorism, 1880–1914* (forthcoming).

Alistair Millar and Eric Rosand, *Allied against Terrorism: What's Needed to Strengthen the Worldwide Commitment* (New York: Century Foundation, 2006).

Giuseppe Nesi, ed., *International Cooperation in Counter-terrorism: The United Nations and Regional Organizations in the Fight Against Terrorism* (Aldershot, UK: Ashgate, 2006).

Paul R. Pillar, *Terrorism and US Foreign Policy* (Washington, D.C.: Brookings Institution Press, 2003).

Victor V. Ramraj, Michael Hor, and Kent Roach, eds., *Global Antiterrorism Law and Policy* (New York: Cambridge University Press, 2005).

Wyn Rees, *Transatlantic Counter-terrorism Cooperation: The New Imperative* (New York: Routledge, 2006).

Ben Saul, *Defining Terrorism in International Law* (New York: Oxford University Press, 2006).

Alex P. Schmid, ed., *Countering Terrorism through International Cooperation*, proceedings of the international conference on "Countering Terrorism through Enhanced International Cooperation," Courmayeur, Mont Blanc, Italy, 22–24 September 2000.

Websites

Center on Global Counter-Terrorism Cooperation: www.globalct.org
UN Action to Counter Terrorism: www.un.org/terrorism

Index